新航道
NEW CHANNEL

9分达

雅思口语真题还原及解析

2012年-2011年雅思口语高频考题

◎ 深度剖析高频考题，以不变应万变
◎ 系统总结应试方法，以少胜多、以一敌百
◎ 全面解读考官心理，解决非技术性难题

2012.8
Describe a wild animal

2012.7
Describe your ideal housing

2012.7
Describe a historical building

2012.4

2012.7
Describe an occasion when others celebrated for you

2012.7
Describe a small business you want to do in the future

2012.6
Describe an exciting experience

2012.7
Describe your ideal job

2012.5

2012.5

温馨提示：本书收录的真题均为高频考题和最新真题，请细心准备！

Are you ...
Currently, I am living in a two-bedroom apartment wi... parents. It is near the CBD (central business district) area of our city. My neighbourhood is fairly convenient and my apartment is only steps to almost every kind of facilities, including public transportation, shopping places, schools, medical services and sports ...

最新真题

中国出版集团
中译出版社

图书在版编目（CIP）数据

9分达人雅思口语真题还原及解析 / 于磊编著. —
北京：中国对外翻译出版有限公司，2012，9
ISBN 978-7-5001-2914-1

Ⅰ. ①9… Ⅱ. ①于… Ⅲ. ①IELTS—口语—题解
Ⅳ. ①H319.9-44

中国版本图书馆CIP数据核字（2012）第223842号

出版发行 / 中译出版社
地　　址 / 北京市西城区车公庄大街甲4号物华大厦六层
电　　话 /（010）68338545　68353673　68359101
读者热线 /（010）68353673
邮　　编 / 100044
传　　真 /（010）68357870
电子邮箱 / book@ctpc.com.cn
网　　址 / http：// www.ctpc.com.cn

策划编辑 / 吴良柱　吴　蓉
责任编辑 / 吴良柱　唐峰雁

印　　刷 / 北京合众伟业印刷有限公司
经　　销 / 新华书店

规　　格 / 787×1092毫米　1/16
印　　张 / 18.5
字　　数 / 530千字
版　　次 / 2012年9月第1版
印　　次 / 2016年1月第11次

ISBN 978-7-5001-2914-1　　　　定价：42.00元

前言

2007 年 2 月 9 号，Simon 在生日的那天开始了悉尼四年的留学和工作生涯。那时候的 Simon 和大家一样，充满了对未来的期盼、对前途的迷茫、对未知的恐惧、对祖国大陆的思念和对外面世界的好奇。那时候的 Simon，连餐巾纸都不知道用英文怎么说。当别人问我“What's your DOB?”的时候，我无言以对（后来才知道 DOB 是 date of birth 的意思）。工作时，当别人问我“Do you have a glue(胶水)?”时，我的回答竟然是“Er…is it a kind of drink?”到了国外了，我才知道他们讲“你好”不用“How do you do?”，而是说“How's everything going?”表达感谢时不光能说“Thanks!”，还能说“Ta!”、“Cheers!”等。每天听到的是“No worries! Mate!”或“Good day! Mate!”等。

2007 年至 2008 年，Simon 有一段时间要同时就读于两所大学甚至三所大学，并且还要奔走于不同的地方工作。这样做不光是为了生存，更多是要把自己当做一块海绵，拼命地吸取生活中所有的“正能量”。每天出门前，我都要告诉自己：Open your mind; open your heart; to share, to learn and today, I will make some differences!

2009 年，澳大利亚移民局要求所有申请移民的海外学生的雅思成绩要达到 4 个 7 分的标准。在此前后，Simon 重新审视了这个对海外学生来说无比艰苦却又无法避免的挑战，同时也静下心来，潜心研究雅思考试。当时，Simon 实现了从 6 分（2006 年第一次考雅思）到 8 分（2008 年第二次考试）的飞跃。Simon 在实现自己人生目标的同时，发现自己的准备方法和学习技巧其实有着很强的可复制性，并且可以让更多人因此获益。

2010 年，Simon 回国后加盟了新航道，至今一直从事雅思口语、听力和词汇的教学研究。在这期间，Simon 接触了大量的学生，并得知许多人都对英语口语的学习感到无奈和无助。这是因为英语口语表达习惯的养成需要系统的、科学的训练和长期的积累，是现今浮躁的环境所不能造就的。所以，一直以来，Simon 都想为我的学生做两件事情：

第一：写一本薄薄的涵盖听、说 、读、写四个方面的单词书。

第二：将我的方法系统地总结出来，从而让更多的人能够从中受益，最终实现自己对高分的期冀。

本书，旨不在“teaching”，而在“sharing”。读者不光要学到知识点，更多是要学会一种思维方式，即考官所代表的西方人的思维方式。本书所有的讲解都会从读者的角度出发，为大家的口语备考甚至今后的学习生活带来新的视角和灵感。

“Work hard！ Be Kind！ And something Amazing will happen!”

于磊（Simon）

2012 年 9 月于北京

本书所收录题目及对应考试日期一览

Work and Study

Media and Culture

People and Wildlife

Travel and Transportation

Describe a place you want to visit in the future.	参考 P179	(2012.8)
Describe a vehicle you want to buy.	详见 P183	(2011.12)
Describe your favourite mode of transportation.		(2012.8)
Describe a person who you want to travel with.	详见 P182	(2011.6)
Describe some travelling you have done.		(2011.10)
Describe something expensive you want to buy.		(2012.8)

Shopping and Lifestyle

Describe your favourite shop/place for shopping.	参考 P194	(2011.10)
Describe something expensive you want to buy if you have the money.		(2012.8)
Describe a product you want to buy from a foreign country.	详见 P193	(2012.3)
Describe an electronic product.	详见 P190	(2012.4)
Describe a piece of furniture.		(2011.9)
Describe a vehicle you want to buy.		(2012.1)
Describe your favourite way of communicating with your friends.		(2012.5)
Describe your favourite website.		(2011.5)
Describe your favourite (modern) building.		(2011.9)
Describe a gift you received from others.		(2012.8)
Describe a gift you gave to others.		(2012.8)
Describe something you lost.		(2012.3)
Describe your favourite clothing style.	详见 P196	(2011.12)
Describe a piece of clothing for a special occasion.		(2012.6)
Describe your favourite restaurant.	详见 P197	(2012.1)
Describe your favourite foreign food.	详见 P199	(2011.3)
Describe a special meal you want to have with others.		(2011.12)
Describe an occasion when others celebrated for you.		(2012.5)
Describe something you made by yourself.		(2011.4)
Describe a new law that can make our life better.		(2011.6)

Fitness and Environment

Describe a person who has a healthy lifestyle.	参考 P207	(2012.3)
Describe a positive change you want to make in your life.	参考 P207	(2011.5)
Describe your favourite outdoor activity.	参考 P208	(2012.6)
Describe something good for your health.		(2012.1)
Describe something you do to keep healthy.		(2011.6)
Describe something you can do to protect our environment.	参考 P210	(2011.12)
Describe a kind of noise.	参考 P210	(2011.5)

Housing and Places

Describe your ideal housing.	详见 P215	(2012.7)
Describe your favourite room.		(2012.1)

Describe the place you lived during your childhood.		(2011.8)
Describe a peaceful place.		(2011.5)
Describe a place near a lot of water.		(2011.5)
Describe something expensive you want to buy if you have the money.		(2012.8)
Describe a beautiful park/garden.	详见 P218	(2012.4)
Describe a historical building.	详见 P220	(2012.7)
Describe a modern building.	详见 P222	(2012.7)
Describe an open-air place you can relax yourself.		(2012.5)
Describe a leisure centre.		(2011.7)
Describe a place open to the public.		(2011.1)
Describe a place you have often visited.		(2011.5)
Describe a street.		(2011.11)

Memories and Experiences

Describe an exciting experience.	详见 P241	(2012.6)
Describe something that made you laugh.		(2012.6)
Describe a piece of clothes or jewellery you wore in a special occasion.		(2012.5)
Describe an occasion when you needed to be polite.		(2012.8)
Describe a historical event.		(2012.8)
Describe a sport event.		(2012.5)
Describe a bad weather you have experienced.		(2011.10)
Describe a trip that was longer than your expectation.		(2011.5)
Describe an occasion when you were late.		(2011.1)
Describe a wedding.	参考 P238	(2012.8)
Describe a family event.		(2011.11)
Describe your favourite photo.		(2012.7)
Describe an interesting life you had before in your family.		(2012.5)
Describe an occasion when others celebrated for you.	详见 P237	(2012.7)
Describe a special birthday celebration.		(2012.5)
Describe a kind of noise.		(2011.5)
Describe an occasion when you got a bit angry.	详见 P236	(2011.11)
Describe something you lost.		(2011.10)
Describe a gift from others.		(2012.8)
Describe an occasion when you listened to a foreign music.		(2011.12)
Describe your favourite time of day.		(2012.7)
Describe an occasion when others helped you.		(2012.7)
Describe support you received from others.		(2012.6)
Describe something old you kept in your family.		(2011.8)
Describe your favourite toy in your childhood.		(2012.8)(2012.4)
Describe a conversation over the telephone.	详见 P234	(2011.9)
Describe a letter you have received.	详见 P232	(2012.1)
Describe an occasion when you received money as a gift.		(2012.4)
Describe the most difficult time in your life.	详见 P240	(2012.6)
Describe a piece of advice from others.		(2011.12)

Describe a group activity you joined with others.		(2011.3)
Describe a club or group you joined before.		(2012.5)
Describe a sport or match you took part in before.		(2012.7)
Describe your favourite weather.		(2012.6)
Describe a journey you took in your childhood.		(2012.3)
Describe a book you liked to read in your childhood.		(2011.10)
Describe a character in a childhood story.	详见 P243	(2011.9)
Describe a game you liked to play in your childhood.	参考 P243	(2012.4)
Describe a happy childhood event.		(2011.10)

目录 Contents

第四章

Part Two 分秒必争

卡片题大解析

第五章

Part Three 哲学思想的辨证与统一

Part Three 问题归类

Part Three蕴含的社会动态Societal Trends

第六章

雅思口语题库总结

第一节 Work and Study

第二节 Media and Culture

第三节 People and Wildlife

第一章

如何在考官的心目中建立起积极的形象

请考生试想以下 10 种情况

1

一个炎热的下午，考官已经在你之前面试了 10 个学生，经受了各种发音的考验和折磨，你是第 11 个进入 test room 的考生。请问：你认为考官想看到你怎样的表现？你想给考官留下什么样的印象？

2

考官在面试的过程中，觉得你的成绩介于 5.5 分和 6 分之间，给你 5.5 也行，给你 6 分也行，他应该根据什么来判断呢？

3

考官已经对诸如以下的回答感到崩溃：

What is the most popular sport in your country?	Ping Pong.
What is your favourite animal?	Panda.
What is your favourite festival?	Spring Festival.
What is your favourite movie?	Harry Potter.
What is your favourite flower?	Rose.
Why do you like taking subway?	Because it is convenient.

4

考官在竭尽全力地试图理解考生的观点，但是考生动辄就拿出具有中国特色的词汇：

我有关系：I have a good relationship with somebody.
人人网：I often talk with my friends on Renren.
喜鹊：My favourite bird is Xi Que.
扭秧歌：In China, people like to dance Yangge.
世上只有妈妈好：The song I would like to talk about is "My Mum Is the Best in the World."
这时候考官是不是眉头紧锁呢？

5

考官给出一个话题：Describe what you did last weekend.

考生答案：Well, it was a great day, I went to a really great restaurant, I had a great lunch with my girlfriend, the environment was so great, they had great background music and food. From where we sat, we could have a great lake view and after that, we went to see a movie nearby, it was so great...

考官是不是有点 hold 不住了呢？

6

在两个人聊天的十几分钟里，考生从不转换语调，也不会强调句子中的某个重要单词，整个句子都是一个调调。考官在想：这是在背书吗？

7

考官问了一个问题：What's your ideal job?

考生答案：Well, you know, I am still a student, so I don't have a job.

考官在想：你有听到“ideal”吗？

8

考官问：Do you like music?

考生答案：...en...I like pop music, because it is...um...very...popular, and I also like rock, because it is...also welcomed by...um...young people, sometimes, I also listen to some...um...hip hop.

考官是不是有点想调静音模式的冲动呢？

9

考官在听一个考生充满感情地抒发自己喜欢火车的原因：Well, I like train very much, last summer vacation, I took the train to Yunnan Province, when the train was coming out from tunnel (隧道), wow, the sunshine was shining upon my body and shining upon my soul, I felt that my whole spirit and mind had been uplifted and raised, I felt so good, it seemed that I was reborn (涅槃重生了). So, I like train so much!

考官是不是有点不淡定了呢？ Why？因为答案貌似压根跟火车没有关系！

10

考官在听一个女生讲她的男朋友：Well, I want to talk about my boyfriend, she is very nice to me, and we often go travelling to different places, he often told me some jokes and if there is any problem, she could take care of me.

考官在纠结：Is your boyfriend a boy or a girl?

而以上 10 种情况恰恰诠释了雅思口语考试的四项评分标准

- Fluency and Coherence
- Lexical Resource
- Grammatical Range and Accuracy
- Pronunciation

在这四项中，没有一项跟回答内容有关，也就是说考官考察的是你的英文水平，对你的答案和内容并不做限定，你可以对问及的事物表示喜欢或者反感，但前提是你一定要能够自圆其说。

They don't care what you are going to talk about, the only thing that matters is the way to support your main ideas. So, you can show your preference, but you need to make sense.

对于一个 6 分以下的考生，考官往往会给出以下评论

• Fluency and Coherence

Too many pauses and hesitation	太多停顿和犹豫
Lack of support and logic	缺乏支持和逻辑
Lack of specifics and examples	缺乏细节和实例
Too abstract and general	过于抽象和笼统

• Lexical Resource

Limited range of vocabulary	词汇有限
Lack of connectives	缺少连接词
Lack of flexibility and variety on different topics	对不同话题的表达缺乏灵活性和多样性
Rare attempts on paraphrase	很少尝试改述

● Grammatical Range and Accuracy

Too many basic errors	太多基本的语法错误
Lack of self-correction	缺乏自我纠正
Lack of complex structures	缺乏复杂句式
Apparent dependence on prepared utterances	明显依赖于准备好的段子

● Pronunciation

Lack of variation and tones	缺乏变化和声调
Lack of clarity	发音不清楚
Lack of vowels	缺少元音
Mispronunciation	错误发音

大多数考生都会在以上的评论中找到各自的弱项，而这也恰恰是考生需要提高和改进的地方，考官看得很清楚，听得也很清楚，他们可以在很短的时间内判断出以下几个方面：

- 考生平时使用英文的频率
- 考生用英文描述不同话题的能力
- 考生是否使用准备好的段子应付考官

所以，雅思口语考试是中国学生很难准备和走捷径的考试。它需要考生能够静下心来从最基本的做起，不要去想所谓的技巧或者方法。英语口语其实很简单，就是用下面的这个公式来表达自己的观点：

合适的句型

名词或者动名词（观点）——>形容词或动词短语（理由）

考官问：What is your most favourite music?

名词：Well, personally, my most favourite music is classical music

句型：simply because

形容词和动词短语：it is really powerful and besides, it could purify my heart and boost my personal cultivation(古典乐很有力量，另外，它可以净化我的心灵并提高我的个人修养).

考官问：Do you prefer eating at home or eating at restaurants?

动名词：Well, mostly, I prefer eating at restaurants

句型：mainly because compared with eating at home,

形容词：it is more time-saving and more labour-saving(跟在家吃比，在餐厅吃更省时间更省事).

此时，我们要问问自己：

我们积累的单词够多够全面吗？

我们积累的句型能够表达出我们的意图吗？

我们背诵的形容词和动词短语能够给出足够的论据吗？

如果答案是NO的话，Simon希望和各位考生一起来重新审视我们的雅思口语，重新定义我们的学习方式。

同时，我们也一起来思考这样一个问题：

如何才能在考官的心目中建立起一个积极的形象呢？（先卖个关子，详解见第三章）

英语口语的学习分为三个步骤

模仿　改造　创造

一直以来，传统的雅思参考书和雅思培训都在解决前两个步骤：

告诉你说些什么或者背些什么	What to say and what to memorize
如何遣词造句	How to make sentences
雅思口语题库	What questions interviewers will ask you
考官怎么评分	How interviewers score your performance
平时怎么学习英语	How to study English

但是第三个步骤——创造，却是最难以把握和涉及的领域。Why？因为世界上没有两片完全相同的树叶，也没有两个生活经历和背景完全相同的人，不存在一种能够解决所有人的问题的唯一方法，也不存在所有的人都遵循的一种回答问题的思路和逻辑。

※所以，在这本书里，Simon 想要告诉你的是：

- How Westerners think
  （西方人的主流价值观）
- How to produce your own train of thoughts with appropriate expressions
  （怎样用原汁原味的单词、词组和句型储备，来创造出不同的组合与结构，以表达自己的思路和观点）
- How to develop the following ways of thinking:
  - independent thinking （独立性思考）
  - critical thinking （批判性思考）
  - creative thinking （创造性思考）
  - analytical thinking （分析性思考）
  - reversal thinking （逆向思考）
  - visual thinking （形象化思考）
- How to behave with etiquette in a formal occasion
  （怎么样在正式场合表现出合适的一面）
- How to survive in this New Media Era
  （如何在新媒体时代学好英语）

※所以，在这本书里，Simon 要讲述的是：

- 联想法总结题库——帮助更集中地准备所有话题
- 归纳八大核心场景——任何雅思口语话题都可以归到以下八种场景之一

✓ Work and Study
✓ Media and Culture
✓ People and Wildlife
✓ Travel and Transportation
✓ Shopping and Lifestyle
✓ Fitness and Environment
✓ Housing and Places
✓ Memories and Experiences

- 三位一体装备——native speakers 每天都在使用的单词、词组和句型
- 手把手答案解析——每一步都有思考的方向和途径
- 雅思实战战略板——每一个潜在的问题，Simon 都想到了一种有效的处理方法
- 迷你 MBA 课堂——Simon 希望跟你一起分享在国外攻读 Finance, Accounting, Law 和 Management 时所学到的知识

最终，我们不光是学到雅思口语知识，更多的是学会适应国外的课堂教学和社会环境；不单是通过一项考试，更多的是为自己以后的学习、工作和人生创造一个更好的机会，因为雅思口语和海外生存是密不可分的。

大部分的书籍之所以不能够改变我们，是因为我们读得太急，没有花时间停下来领悟和思考。Simon 一直是慢生活的提倡者，因为慢节奏的生活会让人学会欣赏更多沿途的风景。对于这本书，Simon 真诚地希望大家不是匆匆翻阅，而要领悟其中所传递的信息。Simon 也鼓励大家在能引起共鸣的地方做标记，并在旁边写下自己的感想，从而使这本书最终能随时为你所用，在今后的备考或者留学的过程中都能够常备你的左右。

最后，一句话与大家共勉：

Simplicity is the ultimate sophistication.
至繁归于至简

第二章

所有你需要积累的

句首给力副词

在句首使用恰当的副词可以体现讲英文的腔调和态度，并且可以为自己争取到 2 秒钟冷静思考的时间

➤ Do you prefer A or B?
回答：Well, personally... 个人而言……

➤ What are you doing now?
回答：Well, currently... 目前来讲……

➤ What does the movie talk about?（可以是描述一个事件或者个体）
回答：Well, basically... 基本上来说……

➤ What do you think of...?（当被问及观点和理由时，可给出更多细节）
回答：Well, precisely/specifically... 具体来说……

➤ What's your plan when you...?（对未来的一种假设和美好想象）
回答：Well, hopefully/wishfully/probably... 希望最好是……

➤ How often/When do you do...?（当被问及频率或者时间的时候）
回答：Well, normally/generally/mostly speaking... 通常来讲……

➤ Do you like...?（要道出心中的真实想法、委婉地表达 NO 或者表示不确定的时候）
回答：Well, actually/honestly/frankly speaking... 坦白讲，事实上……

➤ Is...important?（当想要表达非常肯定的观点的时候）
回答：Well, absolutely/definitely/certainly/undoubtedly/surely/obviously/apparently yes... 绝对地，毫无疑问地，明显地……

基本句型

句子逻辑关系

（例句全部来自 Part Two）

考生的回答中，大部分的语法错误其实有两大来源：

1. 大脑习惯了用中文的思维方式来表达，从而忽略了语法。因为中文中没有单复数之分，也没有动词过去式等概念，所以在思考下一句说什么和避免犯语法错误的纠结之中，考生往往会漏洞百出。
2. 中式英语 (Chinglish)。英文造句其实很简单：首先，时间空间提前或者置后 (in my leisure time/at such a place)，然后找准主语、谓语动词和宾语，或者主语、系动词和表语，其余的统统放到后面去（包括通过什么方式、用什么工具、在什么样的条件下，即 through, with, by, under)。比如说：

业余时间我喜欢在网络上听英文广播 (FM 88.7 和 FM 91.5)，因为我认为这是目前来讲在中国我能找到的最好的提高我的英文水平的方式。

这个句子很长，但是再复杂的句子也是由主谓宾和主系表构成的，所以我们来分解一下：

- 时间提前
  In my spare time,
- 找到主谓宾，其他的放后面
  I like to listen to English radio program on the internet
- 条件和限定放在后面，加上连接词
  because this is the best way I can find to improve my English in China up to now.

First thing first，梳理好主次信息，造句就不再那么痛苦。以下是英语句子的基本逻辑关系，我们一起来做练习：

并列关系

Keywords

and; as well as; apart from A, it also has B, C and D

举例

我喜欢打篮球和游泳。

I have a fancy for playing basketball as well as swimming.

Apart from/Besides playing basketball, I am also quite into swimming.

牛刀小试（练习）

我喜欢吃日本料理和韩国料理。（不用 I like...）

苹果店除了卖电子产品之外(electronic products)，还卖软件(software)和配件(accessories)。

除了流行音乐，我还喜欢摇滚和嘻哈乐。

（答案见 P19）

因果关系

Keywords

because; simply because; mainly because; since; given that; as; this is due to the fact that...

举例

我喜欢看美剧，主要是因为它可以提高我的英文口语水平。

I am really into watching American TV sitcom simply because/mainly because/since I consider that it is beneficial for boosting my spoken English level.

I enjoy watching American TV series; this is due to the fact that my oral English level could be improved.

牛刀小试（练习）

我选择在游泳池游泳是因为那比在大海里面游泳更安全。

我喜欢吃涮涮锅 (mini hot pot)，主要是因为一顿饭大概 (roughly) 只花我 30 块钱。

我认为看美剧和好莱坞的电影能够提高我的英文水平，因为我需要不停地 (constantly/continuously) 学习新的单词和句子。

（答案见 P19）

递进关系

Keywords

especially; among…, I love…in particular

举例

在所有我中意的音乐中，我最喜欢乡村音乐。

I am a big fan of a variety of types of music, especially the country music.

Among all my favourite types of music, I adore country music in particular.

牛刀小试（练习）

我超级想去不同的国家旅行，特别是美国和欧洲。(I am dying to do…)

业余时间我喜欢看不同类型的电影，比如说侦探片、纪录片，我最爱看的是科幻片。

户外运动可以让我放松自己，特别是我最近在准备雅思考试，极度需要减压和休息。

（答案见 P19）

转折关系

Keywords

but; yet; while; whereas; however; on the other hand

举例

这部电影很搞笑，但是结尾有点悲剧。

The movie is pretty hilarious, yet a little bit sad in the end.

The movie is funny, however, the ending is quite tragic.

牛刀小试（练习）

我被国外的大学录取了，但是专业不是我想去的那个。(...is not what I want/wish)

在中国，你可以做的很时尚的事情有很多，但是吃鱼翅汤绝不应该是其中的一种。

旅游业可以促进当地经济的发展，但是过度依赖于它会导致对生态环境的破坏。

(答案见 P19)

让步关系

Keywords

even though; even if; although

举例

尽管一开始所有的人都不看好她，但是最后她还是赢了总决赛。

Although everybody was against her at the very beginning, she won the final competition.

She won the final round, even though/even if no one was bullish on her performance at first.

牛刀小试（练习）

尽管我拿驾照 5 年多了，但是我很少在街上开车。

尽管我不打算在这个店里面买任何东西，但是这些店员还是很好客 (hospitable)。

我特别喜欢跳舞，尽管我的身体协调性 (body coordination) 很差。

(答案见 P20)

对比关系

Keywords

unlike A, (sth of) B tends to be; A is…, while B is more likely to be…; compared with A, B is less likely to be…; A is…, while B is…

举例

跟小城市相比，大城市的生活节奏往往比较快。

Unlike small cities, the life pace in big cities tends to be faster.

The life pace is slower in small cities, while it is more likely to be faster in big cities.

Compared with big cities, the life pace in small cities is less likely to be faster.

牛刀小试（练习）

跟大城市相比，小城市的生活成本一般来说比较低。

跟外国电影相比，中国电影的主题 (theme) 往往比较单一和沉闷 (monotonous and humdrum)。

年轻人喜欢听一些动感 (dynamic) 音乐，然而老年人更倾向于听一些令人放松的音乐。

（答案见 P20）

总分收结构

举例不止一个，元素需要罗列。

Are there any famous places in your hometown?

What kind of special dish do they serve in this restaurant?

What kinds of activities will people do in such a place?

What kind of sports do you like to do in your spare time?

举例

总 I like to do heaps of sports in my spare time(把考官的疑问句变成陈述句，加上一个表示“许多”的词，这样做是为了举例子时不用另起一句）

代替 many 的词组有：a wide range of/a variety of/loads of/all sorts of/heaps of

分 （罗列名词）	including/such as/like playing basketball, swimming, camping, jogging
收	and so on/you name it/I can go on and on/something like that/some stuff like that

牛刀小试（练习）

北京有很多世界文化遗产，比如长城、故宫、天坛、颐和园等等。
在这个地方，人们会做不同的户外运动，比如钓鱼、划船、野餐等等。
我感兴趣的事情有很多，例如旅游、唱K、逛街等等。
（答案见P20）

参考答案

1. 并列关系
   - I am a big fan of Japanese cuisine as well as Korean cuisine.
   - At Apple Store(将状语提前，例如 In China,... / In my spare time,...), apart from selling electronic products, they also provide software and accessories.
   - Besides pop music, I am also fond of rock and hip hop.
2. 因果关系
   - I choose to swim in the swimming pool, simply because it is much safer than swimming in the ocean.
   - I love mini hot pot, mainly because it only costs me roughly 30 yuan per meal.
   - I consider that watching American TV series and Hollywood movies could enhance my English level, this is due to the fact that I need to learn new words and sentences constantly and continuously.
3. 递进关系
   - I am dying to travel to different countries, especially the States and Europe.
   - In my spare time, I like to watch all types of movies, including detective, documentary, and I love sci-fi in particular.
   - Outdoor activities provide me a great chance of relaxation, this is especially necessary given that I have been exhausted in preparing my IELTS exam.
4. 转折关系
   - I am admitted to a foreign university, but the major is not what I wanted.
   - In china, there are countless fashionable things you can do, however, eating shark-fin soup should not be one of them.
   - The tourism industry could promote local economic development, yet it might lead to ecology tragedy if they rely too much on it.

5. 让步关系

➢ Although I have obtained a driver's license for more than 5 years, I rarely drive on the street.

➢ Even though I am not going to buy anything in this store, these staffs are still pretty hospitable.

➢ I am fascinated with dancing, even if my body coordination is poor.

6. 对比关系

➢ Compared with big cities, the living cost in small cities tends to be lower.

➢ Unlike foreign movies, the theme of Chinese movies is more likely to be monotonous and humdrum.

➢ Youngsters prefer listening to some dynamic music, whereas the elderly tend to enjoy more relaxing ones.

7. 总分收结构

➢ In Beijing, there are a number of world cultural heritages, including the Great Wall, the Forbidden City, the Temple of Heaven, the Summer Palace and so on.

➢ At this place, people would take part in a variety of outdoor activities, such as fishing, boating, picnicking and something like that.

➢ I am interested in a wide range of hobbies, like travelling, singing karaoke, going window-shopping and some stuff like that.

雅思口语最高频替换句型

我喜欢

口语化

I like/enjoy/love/prefer/adore doing /to do sth
I am a big fan of...
I have a crush on...
I am quite/really into...
sth/doing sth is really my favourite thing to do(强调置首)

基本化

I am fond of...
I am in favor of...
I fancy/have a fancy for...
I am keen on...

进阶

I am partial towards...
...is really my weakness

偏爱

I like A better than B
I have a preference for...
I prefer A to B
I'd rather do sth

我想，我认为

普通的个人想法

In terms of..., I think that...
When it comes to..., I just consider that...
Speaking of..., I feel/find that...
Regarding to..., my point is that...
It occurs to me that...

强烈的个人看法

Personally, it seems to me that...
From my perspective, I strongly believe that...
It is my belief that...

更加精确地表达个人意见

To put it simply...
Well, obviously/apparently...
As far as I am concerned/To my knowledge...

我能做某事

由于…我能干什么

Through something, I could...
Thanks to..., I am able to...
I am capable of doing sth

…能让我干什么

sth enables me to...
sth empowers me to...

我计划做某事

我打算

I am planning to/I plan to...
I have decided to...
I am thinking of doing sth
I intend to...

不打算

I don't intend to...
It is not my intention to...

应该（需要）做某事 / 不应该（需要）做某事

我需要

I should/ought to/have to…
I am supposed to/expected to…
I need to…

不需要

I don't need to/have to…
I am not obliged to…

我希望做某事

I hope/wish that…
I am hoping that…
Hopefully, I would/could…
I expect that…
How I wish I could…
As long as I could…, I would…

雅思口语中的多样句型

主动句

My father took the photo.

被动句

The photo was taken by my father.

强调句

It was my father who took this photo.

虚拟语气

Whenever my father was free from his work, he would take photos by walking around.
How I wish I could be there to celebrate your birthday.

倒装句

Only in this way can we solve the problem.
Seldom do I go to school by bus.
Rarely have I seen such a stunning ocean view at Hainan Island.
By no means would I travel without my friends' company.
Not only did my teacher give me suggestions on how to study English, but he also offered me direct help.

从句——叙述一个事物的背景

Well, the restaurant I want to share with you is called Golden Jaguar, which is a kind of buffet restaurant/cafeteria specialising in a wide range of cuisines from all over the world.

雅思口语最好用的小词和词组

break

break out 爆发
break up 分手
give a break 休息
break through 突破
break down 分解
break in 闯进
prison break 越狱
give me a break 别烦我

carry

carry out 执行
carry on 继续
carry forward 推进
carry in 携带

catch

catch up with 赶上……
catch up on 和……叙旧
catch on 理解

come

come across 碰到，遇到
come along with 和……一起来
come and go 来来去去
come true 变成现实

drop

drop in/by 顺便拜访
drop out 辍学
drop off 减少
a drop of water 一滴水

fit

fit for 适合
fit in 适应
keep fit 保持健康

get

get over 克服
get used to 习惯于
get rid of 摆脱
get along well with 和……相处得好
get away 离开，逃脱

give

give up 放弃
give birth to 生(孩子)
give away 泄露，分发
give oneself to 专心致力于
give in 屈服，让步

go

go through 经历
go on 继续
go against 反对
go ahead 前进
go after 追逐
go bananas 发疯

hang

hang around 闲荡　hang in there 坚持，加油　hang on 等一下
hang out 出去玩　hangover 宿醉　hang up 挂电话，搁置
get the hang of 获得……的窍门

keep

keep on 继续　keep up 保持　keep up with 和……保持同步
keep in mind 记住　keep in touch 保持联络　keep to oneself 不与别人交往

kick

kick back 休息　kick off 开始做　kick out 开除

look

look after 照顾　look down on 瞧不起　look into 调查
look up 查阅　look forward to 期待　look out 当心

off

ease off 缓和　off and on 断断续续的　off my back 别烦我
off my school/work 放学 / 下班　one day off 一天休息

pass

pass away 过世　pass on 传递　pass by 经过　pass the buck 推卸责任

pay

pay back 偿还　pay off 还清，回报　pay as you go 现买现付

pick

pick up 拾起　pick over 拣选　pick off 摘下

pull/push

pull over 路边停车　push oneself 鞭策自己　push forward 推进　push-up 俯卧撑

put

put aside 搁置　put away 收起来　put down 写下　put right 改正
put up with 容忍，忍受

reach

reach out a helping hand 伸出援手　reach an agreement 达成协议　out of reach 够不着

run

run into 碰见　run out of 耗尽　run through 浏览　run away 逃跑
in the long/short run 从长 / 短期来看

set

set back 使受挫折　set off 出发　set up 建立

spare

spare time 空闲时间　spare no effort to 不遗余力地　spare part 备用零件

stay

stay in 呆在家里　stay up 熬夜　stay calm 保持冷静　stay with 和……一起

stick

stick to/by 遵守　stick with 和……一起　stick around 在附近徘徊

take

take off 起飞，脱下
take over 接收，接管
take up 拿起，开始从事
take in 吸收，理解

try

try on 试穿，实验　try out 尝试

turn

turn down 拒绝　turn in 上交　turn into 变成　turn on/off 开 / 关
turn out to be 结果是　by turns 轮流　turn upside down 颠倒
turn the situation 扭转局面

up

ups and downs of life 人生的起起伏伏
up against 面临，遭到
team up 联手合作
still up in the air 悬而未决
speed up 加速
pair up 配对

流行语 Catchphrases

- a little bit refreshing 小清新
- anxious 忐忑的
- box news 花边新闻
- come out of the closet 出柜
- disclose/disclosure 吐槽
- flashy cars and luxury brands 炫车和奢侈品
- fraudulent/cheating 坑爹的
- group buying 团购
- hipster/trendsetter 潮人
- homebody 宅男宅女
- iFans 果粉
- made-for-the-web film 微电影
- meaningful/insightful 有内涵的
- new rich/new money/nouveau riche 暴发户
- post -80s/post -90s 80 后 90 后
- scalper 黄牛党
- streaking 裸奔
- supportive 给力
- time-travel TV series 穿越剧
- ultrabook 超级本
- adorable 萌的
- awkward and embarrassing 囧的
- chillax 淡定
- copycat/knockoffs/counterfeits 山寨货
- drifters 北漂
- flaunt wealth 炫富
- gold digger 拜金女
- LOHAS (Lifestyles of Health and Sustainability) 乐活族
- hogwash oil 地沟油
- homeboy 发小
- Isn't it? 有木有
- mafia 杀人游戏
- netizen 网民
- plastic operation 整容手术
- rumors and gossips 绯闻八卦
- shocked 被雷到了
- street chic/street snap 街头时尚 / 街拍
- the most dazzling ethnic sensation 最炫民族风
- tragic 悲催的
- vulnerable and fragile 伤不起

以 y 结尾的实用小词

- brainy 聪明的
- dusty 落满灰尘的
- rainy 多雨的
- stormy 暴风雨的
- cheesy 劣质的
- clumsy 笨拙的
- creamy 奶油的
- crispy 脆的
- dizzy 晕眩的
- drifty 漂流的，不固定的
- fatty 多脂肪的
- floppy 松软的，邋遢的
- greedy 贪婪的
- homey 舒适的，像家一样的
- juicy 多汁的
- messy 凌乱的
- nasty 肮脏的
- nerdy 书呆子式的
- picky 挑剔的
- pushy 有进取心的
- rosy 红润的
- spicy 辣的
- silly 傻的
- girly 像少女的
- smelly 臭的
- speedy 迅速的
- sticky 粘的
- tasty/yummy 好吃的
- witty 机智的，幽默的
- chilly 寒冷的
- foggy 多雾的
- snowy 多雪的
- windy 风大的
- chunky 矮胖的
- comfy 舒适的
- creepy/scary 吓人的，恐怖的
- curvy 弯曲的
- dodgy/foxy/crafty 狡猾的
- drowsy 昏昏欲睡的
- flashy 华而不实的
- fussy 难取悦的
- handy 便携的
- icy 冰冷的，结满冰的
- leafy 郁郁葱葱的
- moody 喜怒无常的
- needy 贫困的
- oily/greasy 油腻的
- pricy 昂贵的
- risky 有风险的
- salty 咸的
- shiny 有光泽的，闪耀的
- sissy 娘娘腔的
- skinny/boney 瘦的
- spacy 宽大的，广大的
- steady 稳定的
- stuffy 闷热的
- tricky 棘手的
- wordy 唠叨的

英文经典背诵

Work and Study

1. 态度就是一切。
Attitude is everything.
2. 细节决定成败。
Detail is the key to success.
3. 我相信这个行业以后会非常有前途。
I believe that this sector will be especially promising and highly demanded in the near future.
4. 毕业后，我打算接手我们的家族生意。
After graduation, I plan to take over the family business.
5. 我相信行行出状元。
I always hold the belief that every profession has its own master.
6. 这次实习的经历让我学会了脚踏实地做事情。
This internship experience made me realise that I need to have a down-to-earth attitude towards work.
7. 这个工作最大的好处就在于我可以和各种各样的人接触。
The best part of this job is that I could interact and socialise with different types of people.

Media and Culture

8. 我从这个电影学到了真爱是不会因为时光的荏苒和生命的终结而改变的。
I learnt from this movie that genuine love is everlasting regardless of the passage of time and termination of life.
9. 以其人之道还治其人之身。
We should let him have a dose of his own medicine.
10. 约翰尼·德普的表演给我留下了深刻的印象。
Jonny Depp's performance has been deeply rooted in my mind.
11. 从看到他的第一眼，我就被他所深深的吸引了。
I was deeply mesmerised by him at first sight.

12. 他的歌声太有穿透力了，仿佛穿过了我的身体。
His voice is so penetrating; it seems like getting into my skin.
13. 我想说的是：能听到这样的歌声，我三生有幸。
I just want to say that it is really a privilege and honour to listen to such a beautiful song.
14. 选秀节目中，我们可以见证平凡的人也有不平凡的才能。
On talent show, we can witness that ordinary people could possess extraordinary talents.
15. 招聘节目可以让我们为未来的职场做好准备。
By watching job-hunting show we can get ourselves well prepared for future career.
16. 这则广告可以提高人们保护环境的意识。
This ad could raise people's awareness of preserving our environment.

People

17. 天才就是 1% 的灵感加上 99% 的努力。
Genius is 1% inspiration and 99% perspiration.
18. 他总是第一个到教室，最后一个离开。
He is always the first to come and last to leave.
19. 我坚持，我成功。
I should persist until I succeed.
20. 一个有智慧的人总是能够三言两语把一个复杂的事情说清楚。
A wise man could always explain something difficult and complicated in an easy and simple way.
21. 乔布斯的设计理念是：至繁归于至简。
Steve Jobs always believe that simplicity is the ultimate sophistication.
22. 他很聪明，总是能够在最短的时间内获得学习的窍门。
He is brainy, and he is always able to master the hang of study in the shortest time.
23. 他经历了良心的拷问，最终选择了忏悔。
He was torn by his conscience, and eventually he repented.
24. 我们对很多问题的看法都是一致的。
We are on the same wavelength about a number of issues.
25. 他是我的精神导师，每当我遇到困难，他都是我第一个想要寻求帮助的人。
He is my spiritual mentor, for whenever I come across difficulties, he will be the first person I turn to for help.
26. 他是我一直想成为的那种人。
He is the kind of man I have always wanted to be.
27. 他是一个天生的戏骨。
He was born to be an actor.
28. 迈克尔·杰克逊的太空步是最令人惊叹的舞蹈之一。
Michael Jackson's Moon Walk is one of the most breathtaking dance moves.

29. 比尔·盖茨和他的盖茨梅琳达基金会不遗余力地帮助非洲儿童。
Bill Gates, along with the Bill & Melinda Gates Foundation spares no effort in helping the needy children in Africa.

Travel and Transportation

30. 旅行可以为我以后在国外的独立生活铺就道路。
Travelling could pave the way for me to live abroad independently in the coming years.
31. 在旅途中，你看到的越多，你的生命就会越丰富。
During the trip, the more you see of this world, the richer your life will be.
32. 旅行给我们提供了一个远离喧嚣的机会。
Travelling provides us a great opportunity to escape the crowds.
33. 旅行重新激起了我对生活的兴趣。
Travelling has rekindled my interest in life.
34. 我们应该尽可能地去使用公共交通，减少开私家车。
We should use public transportation as much as possible instead of driving private cars.
35. 北京的地铁网络四通八达。
The subway network has been greatly linked, and you can get anywhere you want in Beijing.
36. 如果所有的人都乘坐公共交通的话，道路会通畅很多。
If all commuters take public transportation, I believe that the traffic will be much smoother.
37. 为了响应低碳生活的号召，我决定买辆自行车作为我的代步工具。
In order to answer the call of living a low-carbon lifestyle, I have decided to buy a bicycle as my means of transportation.

Shopping and Lifestyle

38. 点一点鼠标，购物就像点击声听起来那样简单。
With the click of a mouse, shopping is as easy as it sounds.
39. 电子商务正在改变人们的购物习惯。
The advancement of B2C industry has been converting the consumer's way of shopping.
40. 这个购物场所为顾客提供了一站式的购物体验。
This shopping place provides customers with one-stop shopping experience.
41. 他们承诺七天包退换，七天之内，有任何不满意都可以退货或者是调换。
They guarantee that you can exchange or refund anything you buy in this shop within 7 days without any fuss.

42. 有些人因为入不敷出而陷入财政危机。
Some fell into debt crisis since they spent beyond earnings.
43. 这个餐厅提供了以顾客为导向的服务。
The restaurant provides customer-oriented service.
44. 寿司被认为是世界上最健康的食物。
Sushi is regarded as the healthiest food in the world.
45. 这家餐厅的招牌菜是牛排。
Steak is their signature dish.

Health and Fitness

46. 今天的人们普遍过着一种久坐不动的生活方式，我们需要多到户外去活动活动。
Today's people tend to live a sedentary lifestyle, and we do need to stretch out and do aerobics outdoors.
47. 我曾经沉溺于电脑游戏，但是现在我想拥有一个更加积极、健康的人生。
I used to be addicted to computer games, yet now I am thinking of having a more positive and healthy life.
48. 缺乏运动会导致一系列的慢性疾病。
A lack of exercise will lead to a series of chronic diseases.
49. 我喜欢游泳是因为这个运动的强度不大。
I am partial towards swimming because it is less intense.

Places

50. 每当来到这个公园，我都会回忆起我无忧无虑的童年。
Whenever I come to this park, it would remind me of my carefree childhood.
51. 这个安静的公园简直就是沙漠中的一片绿洲。
This peaceful park is like an oasis in the middle of the desert.
52. 只要我没有了创作思路，我就会在这个地方随便逛逛，找找灵感。
As long as I come across a bottleneck, I'd like to bum around this place seeking for inspiration.
53. 在这拥挤的城市拥有一片绿地简直是一种奢望。
In such a crowded city, having a green field is almost a luxury.
54. 为了引起参观者的兴趣并给人们留下深刻的印象，这个博物馆设计了一些体验式环节。
In order to attract the interest of visitors and leave a deep impression, the museum designed some hands-on experiments.
55. 这个地方距离地铁和购物中心只有几步之遥。
It only takes a few steps to get to the subway and the shopping center.

Experiences and Memories

56. 照片可以锁住记忆、将瞬间凝固。
Photos could lock up memories and freeze the moment.
57. 作为表弟，我在他们的婚礼上表达了我最衷心的祝福。
As their cousin, I expressed my wholehearted blessing and best wishes to them at their wedding.
58. 夫妻双方无论是顺境还是逆境都应该相亲相爱。
The couple should love and cherish each other for better or for worse.
59. 我们对他们这种推三阻四的态度彻底无语了。
We were completely speechless towards their buck-passing attitude.
60. 鉴于这是我的第一次电话面试，我当时超级紧张。
Given that it was my first telephone interview, I was extremely off my mood.
61. 我是多么想回到以前，重新来过。
How I wish I could go back to the past and start everything over again.

第三章

Part One
考官想听什么

关于雅思口语，你必须知道的事儿

评分标准解读

首先，我们先回答在第一章里面提出的问题：如何在考官的心目中建立起积极的形象？
在此，我们根据各项评分标准给考生提供如下作业守则：

• Fluency and Coherence

讲话要有逻辑：

1. 给出观点 2. 拿出简单的，直接相关的理由 3. 举例子

讲话的内容：

考官问的很多问题都会涉及到你的生活经历和中国的文化，所以，最好不要讲大部分中国考生都会想到的内容。尽量做一个文化的使者，你需要给考官讲有特色的东西，或者给考官讲述一个你自己独有的经历。比如在描述动物时，除了讨论熊猫，你还可以讲述你在云南旅游时看到的大象表演；你可以述说几年前你看过的一本名为《狼图腾》的书，里面有对狼的描述等等。比如在描述餐厅时，除了说它好吃不贵，更重要的是那是你和男朋友或者女朋友相识的地方。比如在描述一部电影时，除了谈论《狮子王》，你还可以描述《哈姆雷特》。比如在描述一个你想去的地方时，除了美国和欧洲，你可以说你很想去日本，因为你是一个动漫迷。在谈论自己喜欢和熟悉的领域时，你的描述可以更加形象和生动。也即是说，你可以在答案中设计一两个亮点。当你在讲一个故事的时候，请把握对戏剧三要素的运用：人物（故事背景）、冲突（故事高潮）、语言（故事观点）

比如考官问你一个话题：Describe an occasion you got a little bit angry.

Last month, I failed my IELTS, I was greatly depressed and frustrated. My girlfriend asked me out for dinner, and afterwards, I was told that the dinner was a celebration—a celebration for my failure. (背景) At the very beginning, I was so confused and angry, yet when she told me the reason behind it, I was totally encouraged and touched.(冲突和矛盾) My girlfriend told me that I should be thankful for this failure, simply because in my past two decades, I have been taking every good thing in my life for granted, and I didn't know that I need to work hard to get things that I want, and this frustration was a lesson for me to be down-to-earth to chase after my dream, and that's why it was so impressive. (给出想表达的观点)

口语考试像是在推销自己，把自己的东西卖出去。你要告诉考官：我的英文是可以的，我有这个能力。你要想尽一切办法让考官接受这个想法，让他给予你肯定。（缺乏气场的考生请参考北京秀水街或电视购物的推销员）

• Lexical Resource

Simon 在这本书的目录后面给出了所有你需要的元素，请大家注意：

1. 避免使用你太过熟悉的词，比如说 I like, I think, beautiful, delicious 等。
2. 形容词尽量按对记，按对使用，以增加说英文的韵律。
   It is so tasty and yummy.
   He is pretty considerate and thoughtful.
3. 能用被动的不用主动；能用虚拟语气的不用一般现在时；能用倒装的不用正常顺序；能用从句的尽量不用简单句；能用给力副词和时间、地点状语的尽量加上。
4. 把流行语加入到自己的英文中，把你真实的生活内容讲述给考官听。
5. 能用词组的地方尽量不要用高级词汇或者自己读着不顺口的形容词或动词，这样才能使表达更加的原汁原味，比如说 I could fit in the local life very smoothly 就比 I could adapt to the local life very smoothly 更地道。
6. 末尾加 y 的小词在形容日常生活时更顺手：
   handy——convenient　　comfy and cosy——comfortable
   pricy —— expensive　　wordy——talkative
7. 使用连接词，学会讲故事。

• Grammatical Range and Accuracy

1. 搞清楚最基本的语法：主谓宾；主系表；从句；词性；时态等。
2. 培养自我纠错能力：讲到 I go to Hainan Island last summer holiday 时，要感到特别特别的别扭。
3. 把自己说的英语录下来，自己给自己挑毛病，或者让水平较高的同伴记下自己语句中错误的个数，或者用视觉法刺激自己，讲一个过去发生的事情，然后在墙上写下大大的“did, was, were, –ed”来提醒自己。
4. 多记正确的句型和句子，尽量避免“自造英文”。

● Pronunciation

1. 通过听听力练习发音，剑桥雅思听力是最好的材料。
2. 背单词时找到相应的音频材料，可以跟读，把握好重音。
3. 不用纠结于美式发音还是英式发音，重点是要 speak more clearly and loudly。
4. 每天养成跟读对话的习惯，我们生来并不是会讲英文，必须要先听 foreigner 是怎么说的，才能够由模仿变成创造。

Simon 在这里推荐《英语情景口语 100 主题》(by Mark Griffiths and Carol Rueckert；中国广播电视出版社)

5. 说话要像唱歌一样讲究声调和韵律。考生在考试中要尽量：

✓ 使用重音和适当的停顿来体现语句中的重要信息

Excuse me sir, do you want to pay by cash (升调) or credit card(降调)?

所谓的重音就是在主要信息出来前停顿一下，然后再着重念出，读次要信息时声调应保持平稳。

✓ 语速不要过快或过慢

一句话当中尽量不要出现过多停顿，要分清主语、谓语和宾语，成分较多的主语也应当作为一个整体来念。

例如：A talent show called Britain Got Talents(将主语当成一个词，中途不要停顿) is my favourite.

✓ 掌握一个单词的地道读法

每个单词都有重音部分，读单词的秘诀如下：

1. 读慢一点。
2. 在重音的地方发力，用气息摩擦音节，在非重音的地方声调尽量要平。
3. 每个词中都有一个元音，这个元音一定要发得饱满一点，让元音“飘”一会。

比如说：

e'conomy ex'perience teamwork s'pirit uni'versity congratu'lation

United S'tates 'literature a'mazing unbe'lievable conver'sation

考官希望从你身上看到的

1. 自信——你可是花了钱去的 (you are meant to be impressive)

不要把和考官的面试当成一种强势和弱势的对峙，考官期望看到一个自信、乐观、乐于分享的面试者坐在他的对面，考官希望你能够最大限度地用英文表达出你自己的故事和经历，考官还希望你能够用自己的答案给他留下深刻的印象。

2. 节奏——跟考官唱“同一首歌”(sing the same song with the interviewer)

考生回答问题时，第一句话都应该把考官的疑问句变成陈述句，以此进行转述，然后给出自己的立场：

考官问：Should public transportation be free?
回答：Well, honestly, I don't think that public transportation should be free of charge, simply because...

考官问：Do you prefer living in big cities or living in small cities?
回答：Well, personally, I prefer living in big cities, this is due to the fact that...

3. 态度——表现出对问题的兴趣 (be proactive)

考官很难对一个无精打采的人产生很大的兴趣。不论是喜欢还不喜欢，考生都要表现出鲜明的态度，通过提高音调来体现积极的一面。

4. 西式的思维方式——换位思考 (specific and detailed)

考官的思维方式其实很简单，那就是要看得见，摸得着，比如说：
Subway is pretty convenient.
Subway is less costly/less congested/more punctual/more frequent/faster.
第二个句子明显要更具体和详细，考官一下子会有一个直观的理解。作为生活背景和意识形态都有很大差别的两国人来说，难免会出现一些理解上的偏差。考生应该多为考官考虑，当我们在描述一个东西时，我们要问自己：他们知道我在讲什么吗？原则就是讲地球人都能够明白的事情。我们要把以上的各点作为准备雅思的标准，每一次练习都来看看距离目标还有多远。从本章起，我们来重新认识雅思口语，开启新的思维模式。

雅思口语怎么考

Part One (Questions and Answers)：总共 4-5 分钟，考官会问你三个不同的话题（一问一答的形式，话题覆盖衣食住行、吃喝玩乐），每个话题下面会有四个小问题，所以一共是 12 个问题，每个问题可以分配到 30 秒左右的时间。按照平常的语速，每个问题考生大概需要回答 4 到 5 句话。所以，Part One 的每个问题用时 30 秒钟，讲 4-5 句话。

Part Two (Monologue)：话题环节，考生拿到一张卡片，首先用一分钟做笔记，然后讲 1-2 分钟的独白。

Part Three (Discussion)：根据第二部分的话题进行一个深入的讨论，时间 4-5 分钟。

模拟考试视频地址：http://v.youku.com/v_show/id_XMzI3NjkzMjI0.html

这个过程中，考官可能的心理活动是：

- ✓ 希望考生能够熟悉整个流程
- ✓ 我会严格按照时间来面试，希望考生尽快讲到重点
- ✓ 希望考生不要用准备好的答案来应付我，而是能够跟我分享考生自己的故事
- ✓ 一下午已经面试了 10 个学生，疲劳是不可避免的
- ✓ 发音时，声音尽量大一点、清楚一点
- ✓ 你好，我也好

Part One 全扫描

Part One 最高频问题（考官必问）

- ✓ Your study or work 学习或者工作
- ✓ Your hometown 你从哪里来
- ✓ Your hobbies and interests 兴趣和爱好

必问问题 1：Your study or work

真题还原

Are you a student or a worker?
Why did you choose your major?
Is your major/job popular in China these days?
How do you like your major/job?
Is there anything you dislike about your major/work?

迷你管理课堂 SWOT 分析法

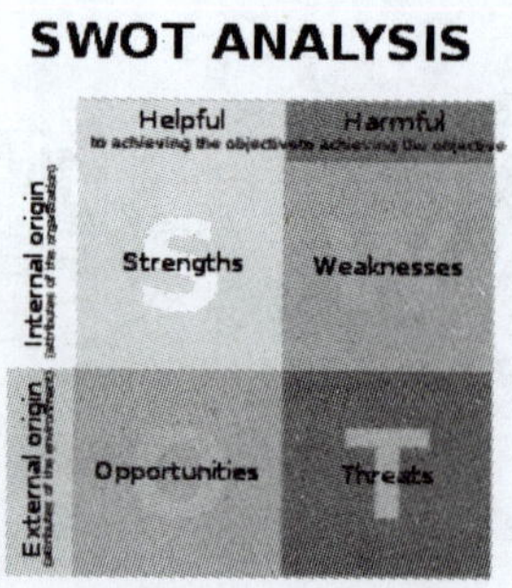

Strengths: 选择这个专业（学校、留学国家）的优势
Weaknesses：选择这个专业（学校、留学国家）的劣势
Opportunities：这个专业以后的就业机会
Threats：选择这个专业所存在的风险
考官的问题也遵循 SWOT 的角度，例如：
What kind of language can you speak?
What are the benefits of speaking a foreign language?
What is the most difficult part of learning another language?
What is the most efficient way of learning another language?
所以我们在平时的备考中，也要经常锻炼自己全面思维的能力。

学生类 SWOT

你的专业

首先，在考官问你有关专业的问题时，最重要的是别让考官重复询问细节。因此，我们的回答要涵盖所有的基本要素，包括学校、专业、年级甚至学科的方向。下面给出三个示范性回答：

高中生

Currently，I am a year 12 student studying at XXX High. I haven't decided my major yet, but I am really into business studies.

大学生

Currently, I am a senior student at Renmin University, majoring in computer science and technology（系）and specialising in programming(专业).

毕业新鲜人或者自由职业者

Well, I am a fresh graduate from XXX University, and currently, I am studying full time on IELTS at a training school, and preparing to further my studies at XXX this coming July.

选择这个专业的优势和机会

句型：
I chose it simply because…
The reason why I picked up XXX is that…
The incentive (starting point) was that I found XXX was quite…

理由一：梦想
I am really into…, and I am always a believer that I was born for XXX, and my dream is to be

a XXX one day.

理由二：大趋势

It is well acknowledged that XXX is a big trend/megatrend (大趋势), so I believe that an increasing number of people will devote themselves into this area (我相信越来越多的人会投身到这个领域中来).

理由三：有前途的（同时回答这个专业在你们国家是否流行）

Personally, I strongly believe that the sector of... (这一行) will be promising (有前途的)/highly demanded (需求量很大的)/a sunrise industry (朝阳产业).

进一步支持

And after my graduation, there will be a guarantee for my future job hunting, which means I could get a well-paid job.

理由四：听父母的话

Honestly, it was not my choice, since I was told to...

理由五：家族产业

The biggest reason is that my father is a successful businessman, and I plan to follow his footsteps after graduation.

如果不喜欢自己的专业或者考虑换专业，我们可以这样回答：

Actually, I am considering transferring my major from A to B, since I think that...

1. I am not good at...and the study of...is really not my cup of tea.
2. ...is the one that I really could not get over/is fairly demanding for me to overcome.
3. On the other hand, I am more talented/gifted in...

工作类 SWOT

Strength

Generally, the best thing about my job is ..., simply/mainly because...

喜欢自己的工作的理由：

- ✓ Boost my people skills 培养与人沟通的能力
  I enjoy interacting/communicating/mingle with different types of clients.
- ✓ Expand my social network 积累人脉
  I could establish a sound relationship in this area.
- ✓ Meet my requirements 满足我的需要
  - *Financial security* 经济保障
  - *Promotion opportunity* 晋升机会
  - *Self-improvement* 自我提高
  - *Work competence* 工作能力

马斯洛金字塔需求层次理论

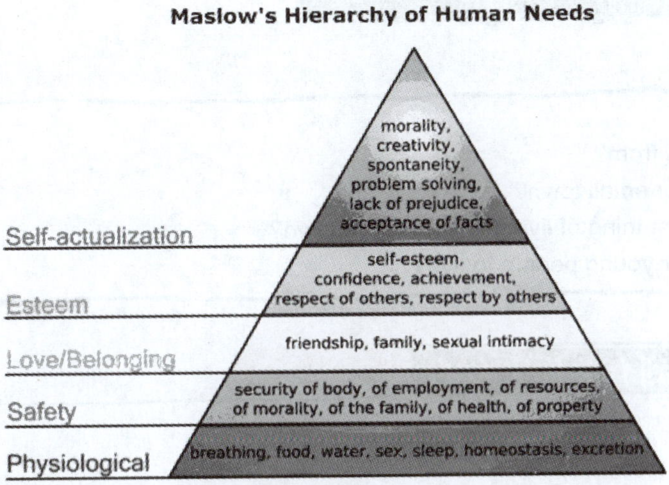

第一层：生理需求	Basic and daily necessities
第二层：安全需求	Sense of safety and security
第三层：社会需求	Love and sense of belonging
第四层：尊重需求	Self-esteem and respect from others
第五层：自我实现需求	Sense of fulfillment or self-actualisation

一个理想的工作，一个你热爱的工作，至少要符合其中几层甚至全部，可以以此为出发点阐述自己对工作的看法。

Weakness

Honestly, the worst I have to say about my job is ..., since...

不喜欢自己的工作的理由或工作中的困难：

- ✓ 我更想和人打交道。
  I am a little bored about sitting in front of a computer screen all day long, and I am longing for a job that involves dealing with people.
- ✓ 我在工作中遇到了一些瓶颈，想通过留学来提升我的职业竞争力。
  Frankly speaking, I am currently experiencing some bottlenecks at work, and I want to actively look for some breakthrough, so I chose to improve my competence through studying abroad.
- ✓ 我想从目前朝九晚五的轨迹中逃离出来，过一种不同的生活。
  I hunger for escaping from my daily life routine and live a different life.

必问问题 2：Your hometown

真题还原

Where are you from?
Is it a big city or small town?
What is the best thing of living in your hometown?
Is it suitable for young people to live?

考官期待听到有关你家乡的

地理位置

My hometown is located in the eastern/western/southern/northern/central part of China.
我的家乡在中国东 / 西 / 南 / 北 / 中部。

最大特征

My hometown features seafood and stunning ocean view.
我家乡最大的特色是海鲜和美丽的海景。
My hometown is the birth/origin place for XXX.
我的家乡是 XXX 的故乡。
My hometown has the worldwide reputation for XXX.
我的家乡以 XXX 而闻名天下。

城市大小

My hometown is a...

- ✓ metropolitan with millions of dwellers（百万人的大都市）.
- ✓ medium city with well-developed facilities（设施发达便利的中等城市）.
- ✓ small city with beautiful natural landscape（有着迷人自然风光的小城市）.
- ✓ collection of villages with rich natural resources（自然资源丰富的小镇）.

家乡特色

The biggest feature of my city is...
The most unique characteristic of my hometown is...
When it comes to my hometown, ...will be the first thing that comes into people's mind.

家乡历史

There are many time-honoured cultural relics in my hometown, such as XXX temple（寺庙）/

XXX historical site（遗址）/XXX national park（国家公园）/XXX Chinese pagoda（古塔）/XXX ancient battlefield（古战场）...

The history of...could be dated/traced back to...

我们家乡……的历史可以追溯到……

My hometown used to be the capital city of XXX dynasty

我们家乡曾经是……朝古都。

家乡评价（是否适合年青人居住）

适　合：Definitely yes, my hometown is a perfect place for young people to live in, simply because...

不适合：No, I don't think so, since my hometown...

Facility 设施

适　合：The facilities are well-developed, including gyms, schools, hospitals, public transportation and even leisure facilities.

不适合：The facilities are less-developed and the resources are a bit limited.

Selection 选择

适　合：Young people have all sorts of choices in my city, they can go shopping, enjoy fantastic delicacies, watch movies and so on.

不适合：The life content in my hometown is a bit monotonous, young people have few entertainment options.

Opportunity 机会

适　合：Opportunities in my city are various, from education to job hunting, from making friends to watching a show, you name it.

不适合：Young people could hardly find a well-paid job in my hometown.

Life pace 生活节奏

适　合：My hometown is less competitive and stressful than big cities, so young people could live a comfy and cosy life in such an environment.

不适合：The living cost is a little bit higher than in small places, and people seldom have time to stop and enjoy what they are supposed to have.

Air quality 空气质量

适　合：My hometown is pretty peaceful and tranquil, it is the perfect place for young people to grow up in.

不适合：The air pollution is increasingly serious and there are traffic congestions everywhere, and I guess young people ought to live in a less crowded place.

思维拓展

以上论点同样适合回答以下问题：

Do you prefer living in a big city or small city and why?

What are the differences between big cities and small towns?

必问问题 3：Your hobbies and interests

真题还原

What do you like to do in your spare time?

How would you spend your holidays or weekends?

What is your favourite way of relaxation?

除了上面三道题目外，其他所有跟个人爱好有关的问题，包括 travelling, dancing, reading, sports, music, movies, TV program, collection 等都可以用以下的答题结构进行解答。

回答结构

In my spare time, I'd like to...

✓ catch up on gossip with my best friends 和好朋友叙旧聊天
✓ see a movie with my BF/GF 和男 / 女朋友去看电影
✓ go window-shopping with my bestie 和闺蜜去逛街
✓ play video games (WII/PS3/XBOX) 打电视游戏
✓ go travelling around the country/world 环游全国 / 世界
✓ sing karaoke with my classmates/colleagues 和同学 / 同事一起唱 K
✓ play mahjong/cards/board games/mafia with my buddies 和哥们一起打麻将 / 牌 / 桌游 / 杀人游戏
✓ play some sports, like hiking/jogging/swimming/yoga/badminton 运动，如远足 / 慢跑 / 游泳 / 瑜伽 / 羽毛球
✓ go on a picnic/barbecue with my family members 和家人一起去野餐 / 烧烤
✓ walk my dog or play Frisbee with my dog 遛狗或者和狗狗玩飞盘

simply because it could/I could..

✓ 休息：relax myself/wind down/unwind/kick back/lay back/take a load off/ease my mind

进一步解释：Since I am a full time student, I need to learn how to refresh and recharge myself.

✓ 减压：release my pressure/put down my burden/ease my stress
进一步解释：Apparently, I have been pretty stressful about my IELTS examination and my future, so I need a way out.

✓ 保持健康：keep fit/keep in good shape/keep good figure/work out my body/build my body/lose weight/live a well-balanced life
进一步解释：Since I used to be a nerdy man, you know, sitting in front of the computer all day long, I'd better live a healthier life by doing some sports.

✓ 维持情感纽带：boost family concord/maintain bonds with friends and family members
进一步解释：You know, I am about to study overseas, and I probably would be away from them for quite a while, so I'd like to cherish every possible chance to socialise with them.

Part One 终极分类

在 Part One 中，考官的问题可以分为两大类，分别是：

- 宽泛的问题、拉家常型
- 具体的问题、观点型

宽泛的问题

所谓**宽泛的问题**，就是考官需要你就一个话题展开回答，最常见的问题形式是 Do you like…?

常见问题

Do you like music?
Do you like watching TV programs?
Do you like travelling?
Do you like swimming?
Do you like shopping?
Do you like collecting things?
Do you use computers?
Can you drive a car?
Do you like watching movies?
Do you like dancing?
Do you like doing sports?
Do you like reading?
Do you like drawing?
Do you use mobile phone?
Do you have a driver's license?

解决方案

A+W 法

A—直接回答考官的问题

W—What（类型） **Where**（地点） **When**（时间） **Who**（人物） **Why**（原因）

音乐

Do you like music?

A—肯定：Definitely yes, everyone enjoys music, and I am no exception! I love...

否定：Well, honestly speaking, music is really not my cup of tea, simply because...（给出直接原因）

What—pop, techno（电音音乐）, hip-hop, rock, meditation（冥想乐）and especially light music.(罗列名词)

Where—Normally speaking, I would like to listen to music with my earphones when I take a ride on public transportation.（给出一个具体的场景）

When—As long as I couldn't go to sleep, I'd like to listen to some light music to calm myself down.（给出一个条件：As long as I..., I would...)

Who—My most favourite singers include Adele, James Blunt, Avril Lavigne, and so forth.（喜欢的歌手）

Why—I am fond of music mainly because it can cheer me up greatly when I feel down/low/blue/bored/tired/depressed.（心情不好的时候让我高兴起来）

Besides, I also believe that music is an indispensable part of culture and tradition, through which I could have a better understanding of different cultures around the world, including cowboy culture, African-American street culture, the three main religions and so on.（有助于理解不同的文化）

音乐的核心价值

- ✓ Purify my heart with melodious rhythms (light/gospel/meditation)
- ✓ Produce great chemical reaction in my mind (pop)
- ✓ Wake me up when I feel drowsy in the morning (rock/punk)
- ✓ Blow my mind with strong beats and rhythms (hip-hop/R&B/rap)
- ✓ Promote my personal cultivation (classical/musical/opera/symphony/orchestra)
- ✓ Be versatile（多才多艺）and can play musical instruments, like piano, violin, guitar, cello, Jazz drum, flute, saxophone and so on

电影

Do you like watching movies?

A—Speaking of movies, yes, I am a big fan of all types of movies, such as...

What—comedy, action, romance, sci-fi, manga, vampire, zombie, animation...

Where—Normally speaking, I enjoy watching movies at cinemas, for it has a better atmosphere with better sound/visual/audio effect.

When & Who—As long as I am available during weekends, I would like to see a movie with my bestie/GF/BF.

Why—I love watching movies simply because I could/it could...

✓ 放松
cheer myself up/amuse myself/relax myself/release my pressure (comedy)

✓ 不同的体验
escape from my daily life, and experience something that could hardly happen in real life (vampire+romance—Twilight)

✓ 视觉冲击
have a blast and blow my mind (action—Mission Impossible 4)

✓ 激发想象力
boost my imagination and cause a visual impact (sci-fi—Avatar, Inception)

✓ 孩童般的乐趣
maintain my child's interest and find simplicity (animation—Kung Fu Panda)

✓ 增加我对人生的感悟
provoke thought towards humanity and life (ethical—Shawshank Redemption,The Pursuit of Happiness)

✓ 扩展视野
broaden my horizon and enrich my knowledge (documentary—Inside Job)

跳舞

Do you like dancing?

A—肯定：Yes, I am partial towards dancing.

否定：No, frankly speaking, I could hardly find an opportunity to learn how to dance from anyone nearby.

Where & When—As long as I am off work/school, I would dance in a dance studio/gym/square/dancing school.

Why—I love dancing mainly because dancing is a way of...

✓ 休闲、健身和社交
relaxation / keeping fit/escaping from daily life routines/interaction and socialisation (ballroom dance)

✓ 展现个性
showing off individuality (street dance/popping/locking)

✓ 接触新的文化
learning an exotic culture (salsa/belly dance/Latin)

旅游

Do you like travelling?

A—Undoubtedly yes, travelling is my most favourite.

When & Who—As long as I am free from study, I would like to travel to different places with my friends or family members.

Where—We would make trips to big cities like Hong Kong, ancient towns like Lijiang in Yunnan province and so on.

Why—Through travelling, I could…

✓ 不同的体验
meet different people/ try different food/ experience another culture

✓ 寻找新鲜感
have a sense of freshness and newness

✓ 远离熟悉的生活轨迹
escape from daily life routines

✓ 为以后到国外读书做准备
get myself well prepared for the future overseas life

✓ 我的梦想
achieve my life-long dream of taking a round-the-world tour

运动

Do you like doing sports?

A—Absolutely yes, I am greatly fascinated by all sorts of sports, including…

What—badminton, billiards, jogging, hiking, cycling, skiing, skating, swimming…

Who & Where—Occasionally, I would play B-ball with my classmates/roommates on the basketball court/in the stadium.

Why—I find sports could be beneficial in a variety of ways, for example, through playing sports, I could…

✓ 放松
relax myself/release the pressure/release study burdens/ease tiredness

✓ 锻炼身体
keep fit/keep in good shape/lose weight/build my body/work out my body

✓ 团队合作
strengthen teamwork spirit and improve cooperation skills

✓ 社交
socialise/interact with my peers

✓ 培养竞争意识
learn the concept of winning and losing/maintain a sense of competition

阅读

Do you like reading?

A—Yes, I love reading.

What—I normally read novels, newspapers, magazines, textbooks and so on.

Where & When— As long as I am in the subway, reading is what I would do to kill time and sometimes, I would read books/magazines or listen to audio books on my iPhone/iPad/Kindle.

Why— Reading, essentially, is a part of my daily life, since reading could…

✓ 扩展视野
broaden my horizon

✓ 丰富知识
enrich my knowledge

✓ 和世界保持同步
help me keep up with the latest news and information

✓ 锻炼思维方式
cultivate my way of thinking (independent/critical/creative/analytical)

✓ 找到灵感
enlighten my mind/set a fire in my mind

✓ 增添乐趣
add a bit of fun to my life

购物

Do you like shopping?

A—Oh, when it comes to shopping, I have to say that I am really a shopaholic.

When & Where—In my spare time, I would like to go shopping at a mall, a convenience store, a grocery store, a supermarket, a department store or go shopping online.

What—Mostly, I would shop for daily necessities, like cosmetics, skincare products, fashion stuff, snacks, clothes, sneakers…

Why—I love shopping for a variety of reasons, for example, I could…

✓ 放松
relax myself/release my pressure

✓ 日常需要
meet my requirements on a daily basis

✓ 有一种满足感
get a sense of satisfaction and fulfillment

✓ 爱美之心
buy myself a brand new dress/try on different clothes

✓ 好友相伴
have an opportunity to catch up with besties

- ✓ 追赶潮流
  catch up with the latest trend and fashion
- ✓ 数码达人
  facilitate my daily life with new technologies

绘画

Do you like drawing/painting?

A—Yes, I used to learn how to draw/paint when I was young.

What—I've learnt how to draw portrait, sketch, watercolor, comics, traditional Chinese painting and oil painting.

When & Where—When I was around 10 years old, I attended a tutorial session about...

Why—I believe that drawing/painting is 100% vital in some ways, because it could/I could...

- ✓ 审美观
  improve my artistic/aesthetic standards
- ✓ 培养兴趣
  cultivate my interests in life and nature
- ✓ 提高手和眼的协调能力
  improve hand-eye coordination.
- ✓ 提升美感
  heighten people's sense of beauty
- ✓ 未来职业之路
  be a future career choice
- ✓ 闲情逸致
  be a pastime/way of entertainment.
- ✓ 文化传承
  represent a kind of culture

收藏

Do you like collecting things?

A— Without a doubt, I have always considered collecting as my hobby.

What—I have a fancy for a wide selection of collections, such as stamps, DVDs, dolls, toys, coins, artworks, antiques...

When & Where—Ever since I was in my primary school, I have been encouraged to pursue my own interests, so I tried almost every possible way to collect...

Why—Collecting could be advantageous in many ways, it could...

- ✓ 学习知识
  help me acquire the knowledge of the world (stamps/coins/paper note)
- ✓ 扩展视野

broaden my horizon/widen my outlook

✓ 个人情节

express personal sentiment/attachment (vampire/zombie DVDs)

I am a fancier/die-hard fan/hobbyist of certain themes.

✓ 收到的礼物

show my fondness for gifts from friends or family members (dolls/4WD cars/teddy bears)

✓ 投资回报

be a way of earning high ROR (rate of return)/making profit (Maotai)

拉家常型问题中，还有一类涉及你对周围生活的看法

How would you like to improve your current accommodation?
Is there any bird that has a special meaning in your country?
What's your favourite flower and why?
Who gave you your name and what is the meaning of your Chinese name?
What do you think of noise?

牛刀小试（练习）

Are you living in an apartment or a house?

Currently, I am living in a two-bedroom apartment with my parents. It is near the CBD (central business district) area of our city. My neighbourhood is fairly convenient and my apartment is only steps to almost every kind of facilities, including public transportation, shopping places, schools, medical services and sports center.

具体的问题

所谓**具体的问题**，就是考官给出问题让你做选择，你要回答是还是不是，然后给出理由。对于具体类型的问题，考官考察的角度是：

A. 是否给出了明确的观点	(standpoint)
B. 是否进行了直接的解释	(explanation)
C. 是否能够用自己的生活经历给出一定的支持	(concrete examples)
D. 是否能够从反证角度给予阐述	(disproof)
E. 是否能够想到问题的另一面	(contrary aspect)

针对考官的每一个考察点，我们也能相应地组织和发展自己的思路：

"高分公式"

A. 起——用考官的话直接回答问题，给出自己的立场或者观点（跟考官步调一致）

B. 承——用 KISS (keep it simple and straightforward) 原则给出一个核心关键词（形容词或动词短语）进行解释

keywords: simply because/mainly because/since...

C. 接——用自己或者身边的例子给考官一个"看得见、摸得着"的体验

keywords: by this I mean/take me for example/for instance....

D. 反——从反证的角度做出假设

keywords: Without..., I couldn't/How could I.../If I chose..., I would..., so...is much better...

E. 转——考虑到事物的另一面，从而给出更全面、客观的评价

keywords: However, I do realise that.../On the other hand, I have to say that...

F. 合——告诉考官：我讲完了，这就是我的立场

keywords: So, generally, that's why I believe...

真题剖析

例 1: Is your family important to you?

完整版：

起 Definitely yes, my family means everything to me,

承 simply because they gave me life, raised me up and have supported almost every decision that I have ever made.

接 For example, I am about to study overseas and my family would give me sufficient financial support, so I wouldn't need to worry about my living expenses and tuition.

反 Without my family, I don't believe I could survive for more than three days.（反证、夸张、虚拟语气等都是考官给分的重点）

合 So without any doubt, my family is the most important thing in my life.

实用版：

起、承、接、反、转、合就好像六张牌。第一张，回答问题、给出立场牌为必打，其他的可以根据具体问题和答题习惯选择性出牌。考试时考生可以按不同顺序搭配使用，形成不同的效果，但是要注意逻辑关系，比如说举例子要放在解释之后。搭配方式多种多样，大家只要记好关键词和逻辑顺序，完全可以自由组合。

真题剖析

例 2: Is computer important to you?

直接反证：

起 Yes, computer is extremely necessary in my daily life, just like eating and sleeping.

反 Without a computer, I wouldn't be able to get access to my online social networks, like Weibo/Renren/QQ/email, and then I would lose connection with most of my friends and classmates. Without computers, it would be inconvenient for me to finish my assignment, prepare my class presentation and do research online. Without computers, my life would be boring and monotonous, simply because I am used to amusing myself by listening to music, watching movies, playing computer games on computers every day.

考生甚至可以反问考官：

Can you imagine life without your computer?

Can you imagine birds flying without wings?

Can you imagine people living without air and water?

So...

So, you tell me how important computer is!!

真题剖析

例 3: Do you prefer eating at home or eating at restaurants?

起 Normally speaking, I am keener on eating at restaurants,

承 simply because I can try a wider range/selection of food at restaurants.

接 For example, I can enjoy Japanese food, like sushi, sashimi and udon noodle.

反 But if I eat at home, I probably could only have Chinese food, since my mum has no idea of how to cook Japanese food.

转 However, I do know that food safety is becoming increasingly alarming these days in China. So, somehow eating at home will be more hygienic and guaranteed.

技术分析：

回答问题的最难点在于如何以最快的速度找准思路，并且还要清晰明了。其实思路很明显，那就是提到这个问题时，大多数人都会想到的观点。比如说：

在家吃——money-saving/hygienic/better family atmosphere/sharing moment/homemade...

在外吃——time-saving/labour-saving/wider range of selection/more appropriate for business banquet

真题剖析

例 4: Do you prefer swimming in the ocean or in a swimming pool?

起 Personally speaking, I would rather swim in a swimming pool than swim in the ocean,

承 simply because swimming in a pool is much safer than swimming in the ocean.

接和反 For example, If I swim in the ocean, I would face great danger, say, coming across a shark.

合 So I'd rather swim in a peaceful swimming pool.

真题剖析

例 5: Do you like watching movies at home or in the cinema?

起 Mostly, I have a fancy for watching movies at home,

承 mainly because it is money-saving, and besides, I could rewind and pause at any time.

转 But I do know that watching movies in cinemas could offer us better atmosphere and better audio-visual effects.

合 So it depends on the situation. For some highly recommendable blockbusters, I would choose to watch the movie in a cinema.

在电影院看的其他理由：

- The thrill of watching movies on a bigger screen 荧幕更大，更加震撼
- Atmosphere is more exciting 更加紧张刺激
- More deeply involved in the movie 更加投入
- Only place to watch a premiere 可以看到首映

在家看的其他理由：

- More cosy/homey/comfy 更舒服
- Switch it off or switch channels when you feel uninterested 不感兴趣可以关掉或者换台
- Share opinions and discuss with friends while watching 边看边聊

考场模拟

Do you prefer to be a driver or a passenger?
Do you prefer to write a letter or an email?
Do you prefer to make a phone call or send a text message?
Do you prefer watching sports on TV or online?
Is it necessary to protect animals?
Is learning a foreign language important to you?

总结

回答具体的问题要遵循总分总的结构，以承接考官的话为开始，然后从不同的角度去证明你的观点，最后得出结论，告诉考官你讲完了。

Part One 和 Part Three 问题的区别在于，前者更多是问考生个人的情况，后者更多是问有关考生的国家、周围的人、社会等等。前者简单，后者更复杂。我们所学习的起、承、接、反、转、合是回答问题的角度和思路，可以自由组合使用。

在 Part One 中，尽量给出一个解释，并附上实例相佐。如果反证更能说明问题，就尽量虚拟一个场景，说明问题所在。

在 Part Three 中，除了以上要求，还应该多从正反两个角度去说明，因为 Part Three 的主题就是冲突、对比、好坏处和一分为二的论述。

Part One 考场还原演练

旅游类 Travel

01 Do you like travelling?

A—Yes, I guess everyone enjoys travelling and I am no exception.

When & Who—Normally speaking, in my spare time, I would travel to different places with my parents or my best friends.

Where—I have travelled to many places, including coastal cities like Hainan Island, minority gathering areas like Xinjiang and Inner Mongolia. I also went to Hong Kong last summer vacation.

Why—I like travelling since it definitely brings me heaps of benefits.

观点 1：Firstly, my horizon can be greatly broadened, as I can meet different people from different places, try different food and even learn different languages and cultures.

观点 2：Besides, I always regard travelling as a perfect chance for me to get away from my daily life routines. You know, life gets monotonous if you stay in one place all year long, and through travelling, my life can be revitalised.

旅游的核心价值

- Broaden horizon 扩展视野
- Unwind/relax/release pressure 放松减压
- Escape from daily life routines 远离日常生活轨迹
- Boost family/friend bonding 增进情感
- Experience new customs/visit brand new sceneries 增长见识
- Meet personal needs, like shopping/attending a meeting/visiting friends or relatives 购物 / 出差 / 探亲

02 Do you prefer to travel alone or with others?

起 Well, normally I prefer travelling with others,

承 simply because I could share many things, such as accommodation, transportation and even laughter with my mates during the trip.

反 If I travel alone, I guess I will be lonely and I may even be helpless when there is a trouble.

转 However, occasionally travelling alone can be more flexible and free, and I won't need to synchronise with other people.

合 So, it depends on my mood, but mostly, I prefer travelling in a group.

公共交通类 Transportation

03 What is your favourite mode of transportation?

There are a variety of transportation choices in my city, including…, and my most commonly used one is…

分述交通工具类单词装备

- commuter 通勤者
- metro/subway/tube 地铁
- tram 有轨电车
- Bus Rapid Transit(BRT) 快速公交
- ferry 轮渡
- monorail 单轨电车
- shuttle bus 穿梭巴士
- express train 动车
- private jet 私人飞机
- commute 通勤
- cruise/passenger liner 邮轮
- light rail 轻轨
- double-deck bus 双层巴士
- cable car 缆车
- minibus 中巴
- long-haul coach 长途巴士
- high-speed rail 高铁
- yacht 游艇

地铁的好处 (especially during peak hours)

- More punctual than bus 更准时
- Faster than other modes of transportation 更快速
- Less likely to be congested 不堵车
- Less expensive than taking a taxi 更省钱
- More frequent, train arrives every 30 seconds during rush hours 更频繁
- More handy subway station location and well developed network, linking the whole city together 更便捷发达

04 What kind of transportation would you choose when taking a long-distance trip?

起	Personally, I would choose airplane as my priority for a long-distance trip.
承	Apparently, airplane is the fastest way of transportation and I don't need to waste my time on the trip.
接和反	For example, I am planning to study overseas, if I use other forms of transportation instead of airplane, say, ship, it will be ridiculous, since it might take me several months to get there.
合	So, it seems like airplane is the only choice left for me to reach my destination.

驾驶和驾照类 Driving

05 Do you have a driver's license?

Yes, I got my driver's license when I was 20 years old, and currently, I am thinking of buying a car as long as my work is set.

06 Do you prefer to be a driver or a passenger?

起	Normally speaking, I prefer to be a passenger,
承	mainly because it is more labour-saving and time-saving, I don't need to focus on the traffic situation and I can spend the spare time doing something else, like playing games on my phone.
接和反	For example, if I am the driver, I may lose my way or get stuck in a traffic jam, which would be really annoying.
转	Yet, I do agree that driving sometimes can bring me lots of joy and freedom, for example, I can take a self-drive tour to the grassland near our town.
合	But given that I spend most of my time in town, I'd rather to be a passenger.

假期类 Holiday/Weekend

07 How often do you have holidays?

Well, normally speaking, since I am still a college student, there are two periods when I can have long holidays, which are the summer vacation and winter vacation.

08 What will you do during holidays?

During holidays, I would like to go travelling, just as many other young people...
Besides, I would also try to find a part-time job or an intern job. Since I am about to hunt for a job in the coming year, it is pretty necessary to enrich work experience.

09 Is it important to have holidays?

起	Yes, absolutely yes, having holidays is really necessary,
承	mainly because holiday gives us a chance to rest and we can do whatever we want to.
接	For example, we can learn new skills, travel to different places or spend time with parents, and after the holiday, we will be revitalised and refreshed for study or work.
反	Without holidays, I guess we will probably be exhausted and have no time for adjustment.
合	So that's why everyone loves holidays!

Part One 核心观点大总结

从以上的总结中我们可以发现，当考官问我们为什么喜欢音乐、体育、旅游等问题时，我们都可以回答放松 (relax myself)、减压 (release my pressure)、保持健康 (keep fit)、开阔视野 (broaden my horizon)、保护环境 (protect the environment)，节约能源 (conserve the natural resources) 等等。这是因为：

- ✓ 作为学生和年轻人，大部分的生活元素及经历都是类似和有限的，包括学习、工作、休闲和娱乐。我们在回答考官的问题时，都可以从以下四大领域中找到我们所需要的理由。
- ✓ 作为西方人生活的主流价值观，以下这些观点更容易被考官所理解和接受。

因此请各位考生务必熟记，并且能够重组和创新，最终为自己所用，在考试中脱口而出、对答如流。

效率 Efficiency

现在，不论是社交网络 (social network) 的流行（包括国外的 Facebook、Twitter、YouTube 和国内的人人网、微博、优酷等），还是各种团购 (group purchase)、全球代购 (global purchase agent)、新能源汽车 (new energy vehicles)、太阳能产业 (solar industry)、环保产业 (environmental protection industry)，甚至是快递行业 (Logistics) 的兴盛，都是为了让人们的生活更加方便和快捷。现如今，人们更多是关注如何提高生活品味和生活质量，追求更好的物质和服务享受。以下列举了五个有关节省的词汇：**time-saving, money-saving, labour-saving, fuel-saving, energy-saving**

可以用于回答诸如以下的问题：

Do you prefer eating at home or at restaurants?

Do you prefer making a phone call or sending a text message?

Do you prefer to be a driver or a passenger?

环境 Environment

以下列举四个有关环保的描述：
environmental protection is such a big/mega trend these days（环保是今天一个大的趋势），**eco-friendly, low-carbon lifestyle, zero-emission**
可以回答诸如以下的问题：
Should all people take public transportation?
Yes, if all people take public transportation, there will be less fuel consumption and less gas emission, and the air pollution can be eased.

Do you read newspapers?
Yes, but I mostly read e-newspaper on the website instead of paper form, because it can help save the natural resources and e-newspaper is totally free of charge. I can read news on my mobile phone anytime anywhere.

新科技 Technology

New technology has dramatically changed our life, including reading, entertainment, lifestyle, social communication and ideology.
问答模式如下：
How has…changed recently?
Well, we used to...in a traditional and conventional way（传统的）
But now, people are more likely to…（新技术下的生活方式，首先联想到互联网）
比如说：
How has the way of reading changed?
Well, people used to read in a traditional way, like reading books or newspapers in paper form. But now, people tend to read in a variety of ways, including reading through the internet, reading on a mobile phone or even listening to an audio book.

个人的

(physical fitness/mental wellness/ personal attachment/interpersonal communication)

身体健康

keep fit　**build my body**　**work out my body**　**keep a good shape/figure**
enhance body coordination/balance ability　**increase my body flexibility**
（回答运动类问题）

心理调节

relax myself　**release my pressure**　**ease my mind**　**wind down**
maintain a well-balanced life　**cheer myself up when I feel tired/low/blue**
（回答爱好类问题）

个人情节

personal attachment/sentiment　**I am partial towards...**　**I am in the mood for...**
喜欢某个爱好，就是个人情节使然
回答个人选择类问题，比如：

Which colour would you choose when you plan to repaint your bedroom?
Well, when it comes to pick a favourite colour to paint my bedroom, I'd like to choose sky blue, simply because I have a strong sentiment for oceans, and sky blue could remind me of that sensation.

What is your favourite type of movie?
Well, speaking of my favourite type of movie, I will say I am quite into hero movies, simply because I have a strong attachment towards heroes. You see, everyone wants to have super-power and be able to help others.

人际关系

boost friendship **foster cooperation and coordination** **cultivate team spirit**

通过……可以促进和……的感情，比如：

Why do you like to play basketball?

Well, apart from easing my mind, playing basketball could also help cultivate my team spirit and get myself well prepared for future career life.

个人发展

读书、出国、旅游、探险、看电影等均可以：

- ✓ broaden my horizon
- ✓ widen my outlook
- ✓ enrich my knowledge of...
- ✓ extend my own limits
- ✓ get myself well prepared for future's career life

Part One 最常考题库

以下是 Part One 最常考题库，所有的话题都分为宽泛的问题和具体的问题（或记叙型问题和议论型问题）。大家在练习时要：

- ✓ 判断问题类型
- ✓ 对于每个问题都形成固定思路和回答策略，比如：
  What—罗列名词或者动名词（总分结构）
  When/How often—给出一个条件，注意时态（描述过去的事物时要用过去式）
  Who—不同人的身份
  Where—地点名词
  Why—找到核心价值和理由，给予逻辑支持，给出实例和反证
- ✓ 熟悉每个话题的核心词汇
- ✓ 注意回答问题时所用的时态
- ✓ 大量使用我们以上总结的核心观点
- ✓ 每个问题说 4-5 句话

Accommodation

常问问题

What is your favourite room?
How would you like to change your room?
Who do you live with now?
How is your accommodation like?

相关词汇

dormitory 宿舍
mansion 大厦
courtyard dwellings 四合院
two-bedroom apartment 两居室
flat-roof house/bungalow 平房
courtyard house 庭院式住宅

villa 别墅
balcony 阳台
gym 健身房
homey 如家的
lawn 草坪
pool 游泳池
park view 园林景观
urban 市区的
duplex 复式楼
cellar 酒窖
spacious 宽敞的
tidy and neat 干净整洁
children's slide 儿童滑梯
pond 池子
river view 河景
suburb 郊区的
cloak room 衣帽间
home theatre 家庭影院
cosy 舒适的
sun room 阳光房
fountain 喷泉
ocean view 海景
waterfront house 滨海房
coastal 海边的
vibrant landscaped community 生机勃勃的园林社区

Bird

常问问题

What is your favourite bird?
How do people in your country treat birds?
Should we protect birds?
Is there any special meaning of birds in your country?

相关词汇

parrot 鹦鹉
sparrow 麻雀
hummer 蜂鸟
eagle 鹰
dove/pigeon 鸽子
magpie 喜鹊
seagull 海鸥
woodpecker 啄木鸟
owl 猫头鹰
crow/raven 乌鸦

不同的鸟所代表的含义

Phoenix 凤凰
✓ mythical bird 神鸟
✓ symbol of the empress in olden days 古代皇后的象征
✓ high position and prosperity 代表地位和繁荣
Magpie 喜鹊
✓ auspicious sign 祥瑞
✓ lucky bird 幸运鸟
✓ meeting on the Magpie Bridge stands for matchmaking 鹊桥相见代表了相亲
Crow/Raven 乌鸦
✓ smart and can use strategies to get food and water 聪明，可以想方设法获取食物和水

✓ pure black feather 纯黑色羽毛
✓ favoured by Goth 哥特人的最爱

Seagull 海鸥
✓ adorably pure white feather 可爱的纯白羽毛
✓ special attachment/sentiment for ocean/sea 海鸥让我想到大海

Pigeon/Dove 鸽子
✓ traditional symbol for peace and innocence 和平的象征
✓ can be trained as carrier pigeon 可以训练成信鸽传递信息
✓ can be raised as domestic pets 可以成为家养宠物

Parrot 鹦鹉
✓ can mimic/imitate human speech 模仿人说话
✓ intimate companion of people 人们的亲密伴侣
✓ colourful feather 色彩缤纷的羽毛

Car and Driving

常问问题

Do you have a car in your family?
Are you able to drive?
How's the traffic situation in your city?
Do you prefer to be a drive or a passenger?

相关词汇

well-rounded protection 全方位保护
compact vehicle 紧凑型车
4x4/four-wheel drive 四轮驱动
well-appointed vehicle 装备齐全的车辆
sports utility vehicle(SUV) 运动型多功能车
off-road ability 越野功能

sedan 轿车	hatchback 掀背车	caravan 房车
trailer 拖车	racing car 赛车	roadster 跑车
convertible 敞篷车	pickup car 皮卡车	driver's license 驾照
parking lot 停车场	parking space 停车位	speed limit 限速
over-speed 超速	pedestrian 行人	headlight 大灯
trunk 后备箱	dashboard 仪表盘	steering wheel 方向盘
bumper 保险杠	license plate 车牌	horn 喇叭
gear lever 排挡杆	air bag 气囊	reverse parking 倒车
make a U-turn 掉头	slippery 滑的	bumpy 颠簸的

break down 抛锚
gas pump 气泵
premium gasoline 高级汽油
traffic congestion 交通堵塞
flat tire 爆胎
fill it up 加满
unleaded petrol 无铅汽油
peak hour 高峰期
gas station 加油站
regular gasoline 普通汽油
maintenance service 维修业务
off-peak hour 非高峰期

Childhood Activities

常问问题

Did you travel to many places in your childhood?
What is your favourite game in your childhood?
What is your favourite book in your childhood?

相关词汇

military model 军事模型
teddy bear 泰迪熊
swing 秋千
bumper cars 碰碰车
rubber band 橡皮筋
snow fight 打雪仗
rock-paper-scissors 石头剪刀布
building blocks(Lego) 积木
tumbler 不倒翁
slide 滑梯
hula hoop 呼拉圈
shuttlecock 毽子
make a snowman 堆雪人
Barbie doll 芭比娃娃
catapult 弹弓
kite 风筝
sand bag 沙包
hide-and-seek 捉迷藏

Colour

常问问题

What is your favourite colour?
What colour would you like to paint your bedroom?
What colour do you dislike?
Is colour very important to you when you are buying something?
Do you prefer light or dark colours?

重点解析

Colour is the reflection of one's inclination and psychological hint/personality.
不同的颜色代表不同的心理暗示：
The colour of…represents/stands for/symbolises…

- white—pureness/holiness and calm 白色代表纯洁与宁静
- black—low key/profile and conservation 黑色代表低调和保守
- blue—maturity and inspiration 蓝色代表成熟和灵感
- green—security and peace 绿色代表安全与和平
- red—passion and creativity, confidence and courage 红色代表激情和创造力，象征自信和勇气
- yellow—romance and safety 黄色代表浪漫和安全
- violet—elegance and grace 紫色代表优雅

Computer

常问问题

Do you use computers?
How often do you use your computer?
What kind of activities involves using computers?
How important is your computer to you?
What kind of computer skills do you have?

相关词汇

laptop 笔记本电脑
smart phone 智能电话
desktop 台式机
projector 投影仪
all-in-one machine 一体机
ultrabook 超级本
ram 内存
processor 处理器
hard disk 硬盘
screen and case 屏幕和机箱
mouse and keyboard 鼠标和键盘
USB flash disk/USB drive/USB stick U 盘
stereo speaker 立体声音响

Collection

常问问题

Did you collect anything when you were a child?
Do you still collect?
What do Chinese often collect?
What would you want to collect if you have enough money?

相关词汇

stamp 邮票
sneaker 球鞋
insect 昆虫
antique, calligraphy and painting 古董字画
postcard 明信片
DVD collection 电影收藏
toy 玩具
paper money and coins 钱币

Dance

常问问题

Do you like dancing?
Where could people learn how to dance?
Why do some people like dancing?
What is the most popular dance in your country?

相关词汇

ballroom dance 交际舞
street dance(robot/popping/locking/breaking) 街舞
pole dancing 钢管舞
waltz 华尔兹舞
yangge 秧歌
Latin dance 拉丁舞
aerobics dance 健美操
square dance 方块舞
belly dance 肚皮舞
salsa 萨尔萨舞
folk dance 民族舞

Email

常问问题

How often do you send an email?
Who do you often write to?
Do you prefer sending an email or writing a letter?
Who do you normally write an email or letter to?

Flower

常问问题

Do you like flowers?
What is your most favourite flower?
Why do some people like flowers?
Is there any special meaning of some flowers?

相关词汇

peony 牡丹
lily 百合
cactus 仙人掌
violet 紫罗兰
fragrant 芬芳的
sunflower 向日葵
daisy 雏菊
lavender 薰衣草
jasmine 茉莉花
fragrance/aroma 香味
carnation 康乃馨
tulip 郁金香
vanilla 香草
orchid 兰花
blossom 花团锦族

不同的花所代表的含义

Peony 牡丹

- ✓ one of the most well-known flowers in China—national flower 国花
- ✓ beautiful and fragrant 美丽芬芳
- ✓ symbol of elegance, wealth and prosperity 代表荣华富贵
- ✓ auspicious 吉祥的
- ✓ one of the most common elements in traditional Chinese paintings 中国传统绘画中最常见元素之一

Sunflower 向日葵

- ✓ always positive and optimistic, facing towards the sun 积极乐观的象征，向着太阳
- ✓ full blossom of sunflower field is gorgeous and spectacular 美丽壮观的向日葵园
- ✓ sunflower seed is a kind of snack in China 向日葵籽可作为零食
- ✓ sunflower cooking oil 葵花烹调油
- ✓ an element used in Plants vs Zombies 植物大战僵尸中的元素

其他

- ✓ Rose means romance and is a Valentine's Day gift. 玫瑰代表浪漫，是情人节的礼物。
- ✓ Lily represents pureness and is used when visiting patients. 百合代表纯洁，可用来探望病人。
- ✓ Tulip is favoured for its rich fragrance and bright colour. 郁金香因浓郁的芳香和鲜艳的颜色而备受青睐
- ✓ Carnation is the symbol of Mother's Day. 康乃馨是母亲节的象征。
- ✓ Violet/Vanilla/Lavender is my favourite flavour of ice cream/hand cream/body lotion... 我最喜欢紫罗兰 / 香草 / 薰衣草味的冰淇淋 / 护手霜 / 润肤露……

Food

常问问题

What is the staple food in China?
Do you prefer eating at home or at restaurants?
What kinds of food are considered healthy?
Are you good at cooking?
Who taught you how to cook?

相关词汇

蔬菜

lettuce 生菜
onion 洋葱
spinach 菠菜
Chinese cabbage 大白菜
celery 芹菜
eggplant 茄子
cucumber 黄瓜
olive 橄榄

食物

congee 粥
cookies/biscuit 饼干
preserved egg 皮蛋
soy milk 豆奶
instant noodle 方便面
spring roll 春卷
appetiser 开胃菜
soybean milk 豆浆
sausage 香肠
shark fin 鱼翅
egg tart 蛋挞
yoghurt 酸奶

lolly 棒棒糖
steamed bun 馒头
steamed stuffed bun 包子
sweet dumpling 元宵
rice dumpling 粽子
wonton 云吞
yum cha 广式饮茶
dim sum 点心
preserved vegetables 酱腌菜

肯德基 / 麦当劳

Big Mac 巨无霸
French fries 炸薯条
Cheese Burger 芝士堡
Family Big Box 全家桶
Nugget 上校鸡块
Chicken Drumsticks 小鸡腿
Mashed Potatoes 土豆泥
Sprite 雪碧
ice-cream cone 甜筒
set meal/combo 套餐
sundae 圣代
milk shake 奶昔
pudding 布丁
ketchup 番茄酱
beverage 饮料
straw 吸管

外国餐

spaghetti 意大利面
pasta 通心粉
lasagna 千层面
steak 牛排
sushi(roll) 寿司（卷）
sashimi 生鱼片
sake 清酒
sushi train 回转寿司
tempura 天妇罗
udon 乌冬面
miso soup 味增汤
teriyaki 照烧
bibimbap 石锅拌饭
kimchi 泡菜
cold noodle 冷面
fried rice cake 炒年糕
barbecue 烧烤
curry 咖喱
Pat Thai 泰式炒米粉
Tom Yam Kung 冬阴功汤
kebab 土耳其烤肉

营养类

nutrition 营养
nutritious 营养的
healthcare products 保健品
organic 有机类
carbohydrate 碳水化合物
vitamin 维生素
protein 蛋白质
fiber 纤维
energy 能量
fat 脂肪
calorie 卡路里
antioxidant 抗氧化剂
calcium 钙
Low GI 低血糖
oily 油的
greasy 油腻的
MSG(monosodium glutamate) 味精
hogwash oil/second-hand cooking oil 地沟油

Handicraft

常问问题

Have you made any handicraft?
Where can you learn how to make handicrafts?
What kind of handicrafts do people usually make by themselves?
Is making handicraft important for children?

相关词汇

Chinese knot 中国结
sculpture 雕塑
traditional Chinese painting 国画
ice carving 冰雕
paper-cutting 剪纸
kite 风筝
flower arrangement 插花
pottery 陶艺
cross-stitch 十字绣
plasticine 橡皮泥

Holiday

常问问题

How often do you have holidays?
When do Chinese normally have holidays?
What will you do during holidays?
Is holiday important?

相关词汇

Spring Festival 春节
April Fools' Day 愚人节
Halloween 万圣夜
Lantern Festival 元宵节
Dragon Boat Festival 端午节
Thanksgiving Day 感恩节
Valentine's Day 情人节
Mid-Autumn Festival 中秋节
Christmas 圣诞节

Hometown

常问问题

Where are you from?
Is there anything famous in your hometown?
Is your hometown a big city or a small town?
Is it suitable for young people to live?

相关词汇

world-renowned 闻名世界的
Industrial 工业的
time-honoured 历史悠久的
minority gathering area 少数民族聚集区
World Cultural Heritage 世界文化遗产
mountainous 多山的
tourist attractions 旅游景点
multicultural 多元文化的
coastal 海滨的
distinctive 有特色的
transport junction 交通枢纽
quiet/peaceful/serene/tranquil 安静的

Indoor Activities

常问问题

How much time will you spend on indoor activities per day?
What kinds of indoor activities do you like to do?
Do you prefer indoor activities or outdoor activities?
Why do some people like doing outdoor activities?

Mobile Phone

常问问题

Do you often use your mobile phone?
What do you do on your mobile phone?
What are the disadvantages of using mobile phones?
Do you like sending messages?

Movie

常问问题

Do you like watching movies?
How often do you watch movies?
Do you prefer watching movies at home or in a cinema?
Do you prefer watching Chinese movies or foreign movies?

相关词汇

TV sitcom 情景喜剧
swordsman movie 武侠电影
manga movie 漫画改编电影
animation 动画片
suspense movie 悬疑片
fantasy 魔幻
ethical 伦理的
special/sound/visual effect 特殊 / 声 / 视觉效果
leading role 主角
dubbed movie 配音电影
lifelike 逼真的
thought-provoking 发人深省的
twisting 曲折的
spoof 恶搞
TV drama/series 电视剧
martial arts movie 武术电影
documentary 纪录片
anime 日本动漫
horror movie 恐怖片
vampire 吸血鬼
storyline/plot 情节
supporting role 配角
subtitle 字幕
touching/moving 感人的
devastating 灾难性的
meaningful 有意义的
soap opera 肥皂剧
sci-fi film 科幻片
affectional film 爱情片
thriller 惊悚片
witchcraft 魔法
zombie 僵尸
soundtrack 原声大碟
acting/performance skill 演技
costume 服装
sequel 续集
terrifying 骇人的
intriguing 引起好奇心的
hilarious 欢闹的

Music

常问问题

Do you like listening to music?
How often do you listen to music?
Is music important?
Have you ever learned to play a musical instrument?

相关词汇

hip-pop /rap 说唱乐
techno 电子音乐
symphony 交响乐
soul 灵魂乐
meditation music 冥想乐
lyrics 歌词
beat 拍子
tune 调子
album 唱片
blues 布鲁斯
post-rock 后摇
orchestral music 管弦乐
remix 混录版
gospel 赞美诗歌
chorus 合唱
tempo/rhythm 节奏
gig 演唱会
indigenous opera 地方戏曲
heavy metal 重金属
punk 朋克
musical 音乐剧
campus song 校园歌曲
choir 唱诗班
solo 独唱
concert 音乐会

Name

常问问题

Is there any special meaning of your name?
How do you like your name?
Who gave you your name?
Is there any tradition to give a child a name?

Noise

常问问题

What are the common noises in your living area?
What are the consequences of these noises?
What do you think of these noises?
How would you deal with these noises?

相关词汇

traffic noise(horn and engine) 交通噪音
construction-site noise 建筑工地噪音
neighbourhood noise(quarrel/bark/party/laughing/music/renovation) 邻里噪音
snoring/snore 打鼾
teeth grinding 磨牙
sleep talking 说梦话
airport noise 机场噪音
bird's chirping 鸟叫
broadcasting noise 广播噪音

Shopping

常问问题

Do you like shopping?
How often do you go shopping?
Do you prefer shopping in a large department store or in a small shop?
Do you prefer shopping online shopping or at real stores?

相关词汇

购物饮食

shopping mall/centre 购物中心
commercial complex 商场
department store 百货商店
convenience store 便利店
grocery store 杂货店
outlets 品牌折扣店
online shopping 网上购物
group purchase 团购
purchasing agent 代购人
stall 小摊
auction 拍卖
flea market 跳蚤市场
boutique 精品店
counterfeit/copycat/knockoff 山寨货
name brand 名牌
luxury goods 奢侈品
fruit market 水果市场
food court 美食街
buffet 自助餐
snack bar 小吃店
bakery 面包店
cafeteria/eatery/canteen 餐厅
cafe 咖啡厅
take-away 打包
feast 盛宴

衣服

leisurewear 休闲服
sportswear 运动服
T-shirt T恤
leggings 紧身裤
down jacket 羽绒服
hoodie 风帽衣
cardigan 开衫
pullover 套头衫
V-neck 鸡心领
skinny jeans 紧身牛仔裤
shorts 短裤
pyjamas 睡衣
sneaker 运动鞋
slipper 拖鞋
sandal 凉鞋
flip-flop 人字拖
jersey 球衫
belt 皮带
scarf 围巾
glove 手套
bow tie 领结

wedding dress/wedding gown 婚纱

tuxedo 无尾礼服

家具

bunk bed 高低床
swivel chair 转椅
bookcase 书柜
folding guest bed 折叠床
closet/wardrobe 衣柜
nightstand 床头柜
wine cabinet 酒柜
sofa bed 沙发床
shoe rack 鞋架
dresser 化妆台
drop-leaf table 折叠桌
IKEA 宜家
ready-to-assemble furniture 自行组装的家具

Sports

常问问题

Do you like playing sports?
Where do you often play sports?
What is the most popular sport in your country?
Is playing sports important?

相关词汇

track and field 田径
skydiving 跳伞运动
billiards 台球
jogging 慢跑
rock climbing 攀岩
boxing 拳击
karate 空手道
ice hockey 冰球
tournament 锦标赛
Tour de France 环法自行车赛
referee 裁判员
backstroke 仰泳
butterfly 蝶泳
badminton 羽毛球
rugby 英式橄榄球
paintball 彩弹球
hiking 远足
cycling 骑自行车
kick boxing 踢腿拳击
skiing 滑雪
curling 冰壶
elimination series 淘汰赛
stadium 体育场
cheerleader 啦啦队长
freestyle 自由泳
snorkelling/scuba-diving 潜水
kicking shuttlecock 踢毽子
gateball/croquet 门球
camping 露营
marathon 马拉松
taekwondo 跆拳道
skating 溜冰
triathlon 铁人三项
trophy 奖品
gymnasium 健身房
breaststroke 蛙泳
dog-paddle 狗刨式游泳

Study and Work

常问问题

What's your major/job?
How do you like your major/job?
What is the best thing about your major/work?
Is your major/job popular in China these days?

相关词汇

工作

freelancer 自由职业者
civil servant 公务员
journalist 记者
entrepreneur 企业家
project manager 项目经理
fashion designer 时装设计师
human resource specialist 人力专员
pharmaceutical representative 医药代表
tour guide 导游
accountant 会计
architect 建筑师
secretary 秘书
salesman 推销员
consultant/counsellor 顾问
self-employed 个体经营的
engineer 工程师
programmer 程序员
psychologist 心理学家
mechanic 技工
cashier 收银员
joint venture 合资企业

学习

freshman 大一
junior 大三
Bachelor of Arts 文学学士
affiliated school 附属学校
comprehensive university 综合性大学
Linguistics 语言学
Hospitality Management 酒店管理
Landscape Engineering 园林工程
International Trade 国际贸易
Veterinary Studies 兽医学
Cross-cultural Studies 跨文化研究
Nursing 护理学
Clinical Medicine 临床医学
part time job 兼职工作
sophomore 大二
senior 大四
Bachelor of Science 理学学士
normal university 师范大学
Accounting 会计学
Business Administration 工商管理
Logistics 物流
Finance 金融学
Pharmaceutics 药剂学
Journalism 新闻学
Public Relations 公共关系
Telecommunication Studies 通信研究
full time job 全职工作
job application 工作申请

promotion 晋升
specialist 专业人士
specialise in…field/sector/area 专注于……领域

Travelling

常问问题

Do you like travelling?
How often do you travel?
Where do you like to travel?
Why do you like travelling?

相关词汇

tour group 旅行团
tourist 游客
tourism 旅游业
tour agency 旅行社
youth hostel 青年旅店
bunk bed 上下铺
self-service 自助式服务
inbound 入境
outbound 出境
airfare 飞机票价
window seat 靠窗座位
aisle seat 靠过道座位
low-cost airline 廉价航空
long-haul coach 长途巴士
itinerary 旅游路线
indigenous 本土的
exotic 异国风情的
tropical 热带的
peninsular 半岛的
natural scenery 自然景观
cultural landscape 人文景观
well-known mountains and rivers 名山大川
round world tour 环球旅行
idyllic 田园的
theme park 主题公园
shopping mecca 购物圣地
duty-free 免税的
palm tree 棕榈树
bathing beach 海滨浴场
suntan 晒黑
sunbath 日光浴
must-have items 必备物品
must-do activities 必做活动
must-see destination 不可错过的景点

TV Program

常问问题

What is the most popular TV program in your country?
Why do people like watching TV?
What is your favourite TV program?
How often do you watch TV programs?

相关词汇

TV host 节目主持人
guest 嘉宾
variety show 综艺节目
talent show 选秀节目
quiz show 智力竞答节目
reality show 真人秀
blind dating show 相亲节目
CCTV Gala 春晚
stand-up comedy show 脱口秀
job-hunting show 求职节目
hilarious 搞笑的
interactive 互动性强的
insightful 有深度的
instructive 有指导意义的
relaxing 放松的
intense and exciting 紧张激烈的

Weather

常问问题

What is your favourite weather?
What is the weather like in your hometown?
Have you ever experienced any bad weather?
What kind of weather do you dislike?

相关词汇

stuffy 闷热的
scorching 炎热的
freezing and chilly 寒冷的
snowy 多雪的
moist and humid 潮湿的
breeze 微风
pleasant and delightful 愉快的
cosy 舒适的
tropical 热带的
subtropical 亚热带的
four distinct seasons 四季分明

Weekend/Outdoor Activities

常问问题

What will you normally do during weekends?
What is the most popular outdoor activity in your city?
Is relaxation important?

相关词汇

mahjong 麻将
hula hoop 呼拉圈
Chinese checker 中国跳棋
blind date 相亲
mafia 杀人游戏
backpacker 背包客
clubbing 泡吧
dog walking 遛狗
sing karaoke 唱 K
window-shopping 逛街
tea ceremony 茶道
extreme sport 极限运动
nail painting 美甲
picnic 野餐
rubber band jumping 跳皮筋
Chinese chess 中国象棋
video game 电子游戏
board game 桌游
yoga 瑜伽
graffiti 涂鸦

第四章

Part Two 分秒必争

在 Part One 结束之后，考官会对考生说：
OK, thank you for the Part One, now let's go to Part Two. During the Part Two section, you will have a cue card question(然后考官会把一张过了塑的卡片或者试题本的一页传给考生).In this section, you will have one minute to prepare your answer, you can have this pencil and a piece of paper(考官把一支笔和一页白纸递给考生), after one minute, you can start talking for one to two minutes.
注：在 2010 年以前，考官说的都是 2 minutes，2011 年开始考官的用词改为 1 to 2 minutes。也就是说，考生哪怕只讲了 1 分 30 秒，考官也可能会因为失去耐心而对考生说：Ok, time's up, I have to stop you and now let's go to Part Three.

卡片题大解析

传统意义上讲，雅思的卡片题分为四种类型，即人物、物品、事件、地点。而 Simon 为了方便大家准备和归纳，把卡片题重新分成了以下八种类型：

Work and Study 工作和学习

favourite subject　ideal job　small business　workplace
a job you wanted to do when you were little

Media and Culture 媒体和文化

book　movie　advertisement　TV program
magazine　newspaper　website　foreign culture
a new law that can make our life better
some changes that happened in your hometown

People and Wildlife 人物和野生动物

an old person　a small child　a famous person　a good student
a good friend　a neighbour　a wild animal
a person in the news you want to meet

Travel and Transportation 旅游和交通

travel destination　favourite mode of transportation

Shopping and Lifestyle 购物和生活方式

shop　electronic device　restaurant　foreign food

something you want to buy from a foreign country

Fitness and Environment 健康和环境

positive change　　healthy lifestyle　　outdoor activity　　favourite sport

Housing and Places 房屋和地点

ideal housing　　park　　garden　　a place near water
a street

Memories and Experiences 回忆和经历

photo/family photo　　something you lost　　wedding
a conversation　　a letter you received　　a special family event
an occasion you got angry　　an occasion you were late
a occasion you heard a foreign music　　a trip that was longer than expectation
a bad weather you experienced(during a travel)

下面是一道 Part Two 的例题：

Describe a person in the news you want to meet.

You should say: who the person is
how you knew this person
what you will say to him/her when you have a chance to meet him/her
and explain why you want to meet this person.

我们通过此例题来得出卡片题的一些特点：

- ✓ 所有的卡片题都是要求考生：Describe something
- ✓ 每一张卡片题中共有四个子问题，前三问都是“记叙文”，最后一问是“议论文”。在第一问中，考官想
  听到考生讲述对象的名字或背景，例如：
  People——Who
  Object——What
  Event——When
  Place——Where
- ✓ 第二和第三问的问题类型：What, Where, Who, When, How often, How much
- ✓ 最后一问只有一种问法，那就是：Why

如果这道题是关于 Wedding，那么它的四问应该是：

You should say: when that was
who the new couple was
what people did
and explain why you want to talk about this wedding.

第一步

当考官说“Now you can start talking for one to two minutes.”的时候，考生需要给出一个带有正式口吻的独白。考官中途不会插话，直到独白结束。我们可以用以下这个模板套话给出问题的背景：

Well, the...*(话题的关键词)*...I want to share with you is called...*(讲述对象的名字)*...,
后面引导出一个从句：
- ✓ ***which is a kind of...*(性质)*, specialising in...*(细节)**
- ✓ ***which is one of the most...*(最高级)*in China these days.*(因为最……，才想讲这个)**
- ✓ ***which/who is...*(基本属性或者最大特征——基本信息)**
- ✓ **回答第一问**

下面给出六个例子：

Describe your favourite restaurant.

模板套话：Well, the restaurant I want to talk about is called Pizza Hut, which is a western style restaurant, specialising in pizza and spaghetti. It is one of the most popular and famous restaurants in China these days.

Describe your favourite shop.

模版套话：Well, my most favourite shop is called Amazon, which is a kind of B2C website, specialising in selling books.

Describe a famous person.

模板套话：Well, the famous person I want to talk with you about is Michael Jackson, who used to be a world-renowned singer, dancer, performer, entertainer and the “King of Pop”.

Describe a leader.

模板套话：Well, the leader I want to talk with you about is Steve Jobs, who is the founder of the Apple company and a world-renowned entrepreneur.

Describe a small child.

模板套话：Well, the small child I want to talk about is called Rainy, who is my sister's daughter; she is currently 7 years old and studying in kindergarten.

Describe a park.

模板套话：Well, the park I want to talk with you about is the Street Park on the opposite side of my neighbourhood, it is a handy place and only takes me 5 minutes to walk from my house.

注意：模板套话和第一问的答题时间请控制在 25 秒以内。

第二步

What

有关 What 的问题一般是必问的，回答模式可分为两种类型：总分举例子型和讲故事型。

总分举例子型

What special dishes do they serve?
What can you learn from this good student?
What kinds of things do you often buy from this shop?
What can you see from this garden?

总分举例子型，即按照总分结构进行举例。比如说：

What are the contents of this website?

总	There are heaps of/loads of/a variety of/a wide range of contents on this website,
分	including/such as/like search engine, video clip, music download service, maps and
收	you name it/some stuff like that/I can go on and on/to name but a few.

What special dishes do they serve?

总	Well, they serve a variety of special dishes,
分	such as spaghetti, pasta, steak, salad, milk tea and some stuff like that.

讲故事型

What does the movie talk about?
What did people do at the wedding?
What does this advertisement talk about?

故事的情节构成：故事背景、故事发展、故事高潮、故事结局。可使用以下的关联词：

- ✓ At the very beginning...
- ✓ After that/Afterwards/And then...
- ✓ During/While···
- ✓ Towards the end/In the end/Finally/Eventfully...

比如说：

What happened on this occasion?(生气的场合)

背景 Well, at the very beginning, I was standing in a queue at the airport waiting for taxi.

发展 During this period, every passenger was complying with the rule of "first come, first served", but for a middle-age man, he then tried to take advantage of rule-abiding people by jumping the queue.

高潮 I was so annoyed that I started a fight with him.

结局 Even though I was a little bit hurt, I was still proud of my act of doing something righteous.

Where

当考官询问有关地点的问题时，一般的回答有以下几种：

- ✓ This place is located/situated in…(具体的地点)
- ✓ This place is very handy, it is just on the ground floor/around the corner/on the opposite side of my community/in a shopping mall called Joy City...(形象地描述地点)
- ✓ It is only 5 minutes' walk/10 minutes' drive from...(时间量化地点)
- ✓ The place I want to travel to in the future is Las Vegas, which is a world-renowned gambling destination in the States.(使用从句介绍地理上的位置)

Who

当考官问到有关人物的问题时，请大家一定要记牢这个强调句型，并善加利用：It is…who…

- ✓ Who do you want to travel with?
  Well, it is my boyfriend who I want to travel with, since we had an appointment before.
- ✓ Who took this picture?
  Well, it was my father who took this picture, while I was riding a horse on the grassland.

When

有关时间的问题分为两种：以前发生的事情 (When did you travel to this place?) 和将来发生的事情 (When do you want to travel to this place?)

回答以前发生的事情一定要用过去式：

I went to this place several months ago when I was having a holiday.

回答将来发生的事情要用将来时或者虚拟语气：

I plan to travel to the States this coming September.(时间已定好)

Well, I haven't decided my future timetable yet, basically speaking, as long as I pass the IELTS examination, I would travel to the States.(去还是不去要满足一个条件)

How often

固定型：

Normally speaking, I often go shopping at Joy City during weekends, I go there once a week.

非固定型：

It depends, as long as I need to buy some daily necessities, Carrefour will be my priority.

It depends, as long as I am in the mood for pizza, Pizza Hut will be my first choice.

How much

知道价格的情况下：

Basically speaking, an iPad would cost me roughly 3,000 yuan.

不知道价格的情况下：

Frankly speaking, I have never done a market research before, so I have no idea how much it is.

注意：中间两问的回答时间请控制在 20 秒以内。

考场还原

Describe a restaurant.

You should say: where it is
how often you go to this restaurant
what special dishes they serve there.

模板套话 Well, the restaurant I want to talk about is called Pizza Hut, which is a western style restaurant, specialising in pizza and spaghetti. It is one of the most popular and famous restaurants in China these days.(15s)

地点 Speaking of location, it is on the opposite side of my university, which only takes me 5 minutes to walk there.(10s)

频率 When it comes to frequency, normally speaking, as long as I am in the mood for pizza, it would be my priority.(10s)

总分 Talking about special dishes, they have a wide range of selections, including pizza, spaghetti, pasta and so on.(10s)

牛刀小试（练习）

Describe something expensive you want to buy if you have the money.

You should say: where you can get it
how much it will cost
what you can use it for.

模板套话 Well, something expensive I want to buy is a compact vehicle called Smart, which is presented by Mercedes-Benz, and is currently the most popular car for fashion-conscious people.(15s)

地点 Regarding to availability, generally, it is available at venues like car dealers or private sellers.(10s)

价钱 In terms of price, honestly, I couldn't recall the exact price, yet I guess it is between 100,000 and 150,000 RMB.(10s)

用途 Speaking of usage, normally, I want to use it for a wide range of aspects, including commuting, travelling, moving and so on.(10s)

第三步

考生需要在 1 分钟之内给出议论，时间非常紧迫，考生不但要陈述观点，还要给出支持的理由。所以我们可以使用下面的总 - 分 3- 总结构：

总：*I...for some reasons.*
分 3：
1. ***Firstly, I feel/find that...is...***
2. ***by this I mean...***
3. ***Besides, I also consider that...is...***
4. ***simply because...***

5. ***Most importantly, I always believe that…is…***
6. ***this is due to the fact that…***

总：***Generally, that's why I'd like to…***

以上的总-分3-总结构中，重点是中间的三个分论点，也是我们所描述对象的三个属性(attributes)其中1、3、5是观点，2、4、6是分别支持的理由，也就是说考生需要给出三对观点和理由。

考场还原

Why do you want to eat in such a restaurant?

参考解析

当我们步入一家餐厅的时候，我们可以从多感官(multisensory)的角度来评价它：

What you see——decoration style, environment, hygiene condition

What you hear——background music

What you smell and taste——flavour of the food

What you feel——service, price and speed

What you comment——location, nutrition of the food served

Simon选取了其中的三个角度来论述，分别是flavour, environment和service，其中Simon的评价是：

Flavour——tasty(因为这里的食物和口味很正宗)

Environment——cosy and comfy(所以我用餐时心情很舒畅)

Service——hospitable(因为他们的态度都很友好)

So, that is why I like to…(所以我喜欢在这用餐)

参考答案

总：I love Pizza Hut for several reasons.

分3：

1. 观点1：Firstly, the food there is really tasty and flavourful.(美味)
2. 支持：

✓ 客观(总分)：It provides authentic flavour of Italian food, and they have all sorts of pizza, including Hawaiian, Aussie, Roast Chicken & Potatoes, Vegetarian, Meat Lovers, you name it.

✓ 主观：I am a big fan of pizza, and I am always mouth-watering about them.

3. 观点2：Besides, I also feel that the environment is fairly cosy and homey.(环境舒适)
4. 支持：

✓ 客观(举例)：The atmosphere is great, we can have different options when choosing a seat and it also leaves some privacy for talking, it is pretty customer-oriented.

✓ 主观：I have a fancy for peaceful places, occasionally, I'd like to read a magazine while eating my dinner.

5. 观点3：More importantly, I always believe that the staff there are quite hospitable.(服务态度)

6. 支持：
- ✓ 客观（解释）：They will give you reasonable advice and recommendations if you are uncertain about what to order, which is very considerate and a customer can feel very comfy in such an environment.
- ✓ 主观：I personally will focus more on positive attitude and good service, for if conversely, they might ruin the good mood for a great meal.

总：Generally, that's why Pizza Hut is my favourite restaurant.

从以上的讲解中我们可以发现以下几个特点：
1、3、5 就是参考解析中提到的三个观点。
2、4、6 则是支持的理由，我们对支持的理由做了如下技术处理：
客观：考生不能讲完一个观点后就紧接着讲另一个观点，考生首先要告诉考官这个观点是什么意思，让考官通过支持的理由有一个更直观的理解。客观描述一般有以下几种手法：

- ✓ 解释：simply because/mainly because/since they provide customer-oriented service...
- ✓ 记叙：the whole place is decorated in a bohemian style...
- ✓ 量化：it only costs me 30 yuan per meal on average...
- ✓ 举例 / 总分：they've got all I want, such as...

主观：讲完客观，考生还要联想到自己，告诉考官自己的切身感受等等，这样才是一个完整的逻辑。主观描述有如下几种：

- ✓ 自身的感受：Whenever I am tired from study, I'd like to kick back at this place.
- ✓ 自身的情况：You know, I am a poor student with tight budget, so 30 yuan per meal is really a bargain.（要经常提钱，讲大实话）
- ✓ 自身的爱好：I am personally a big fan of Italian food. In my spare time, I will learn how to cook them with a recipe.
- ✓ 自身的打算：You know, I plan to live in Australia for at least two years, and I have to get myself well prepared for that starting with food.

任何一个观点的支持理由都可以从客观和主观两个角度来说明。
So，我们再明确一下结构：
总 1
分 1：观点 + 支持（客观 + 主观）
分 2：观点 + 支持（客观 + 主观）
分 3：观点 + 支持（客观 + 主观）
总 2
除了以上的参考解析和答案外，我们还可以评价说：

- ✓ The decoration style is classy upscale.（高档）
- ✓ The environment is hygienic and sanitary.（干净卫生）
- ✓ The price is affordable and I could get a discount with student card.（价格适中）
- ✓ The location is convenient, and it is easy to find a parking space.（方便）
- ✓ The service is speedy, all orders can be served in 10 minutes.（上菜速度快）
- ✓ The food is rather nutritious with low calories and less oily/greasy.（营养不油腻）

考生可以根据自身的喜好，从以上的观点中选出三条组装成自己的答案。

注意：每个观点的回答大概占用 20 秒，所以第四问至少需要 1 分钟，加上前三问的 45 秒，刚好达到考官 1-2 minutes 的要求。在本书的第六章中，所有的答案都给出了讲解，均符合观点加支持的清晰结构。

牛刀小试（练习）

Describe your favourite shop.

You should say: what the shop specialises in
how often you go shopping at this place
what kinds of people will go to this place
and explain further why you like it.

参考解析

以一家电子商务网站 (B2C website) 为例，该网站主营家用电器，卖点是：

- ☆ quality guaranteed 保证正品
- ☆ lowest price 价格最低
- ☆ door-to-door service 送货上门服务
- ☆ cash on delivery 货到付款
- ☆ free shipping 全场包邮
- ☆ free gift-package 免费包装
- ☆ 7-day refund or return policy 7 天包退换
- ☆ 2-year warranty 2 年质保
- ☆ home-installation 上门安装

参考答案

模板套话 Well, my most favourite shop is called "360buy(名字不重要)", which is a kind of B2C website, specialising in home appliances, including TV sets, refrigerators or other electronic products. Besides, they also cover a variety of products, such as books, garments, snacks and so on.（总分结构回答第一问）

频率 Speaking of frequency, well, as long as I need to buy some daily essential appliances, it will be my first choice, so, it depends on my personal needs.

购物者 When it comes to shoppers, basically, it is attractive to many people, for example, homebodies, housewives, students, bargain shoppers, you know, people from all walks of life(各行各业的人).
（以上回答时间为 50 秒左右）

总 I have a fancy for shopping at 360buy for some reasons.

分 3	Firstly, I feel that... Besides, I also consider that... Most importantly/What matters most is that...
总	Generally, that's why...

回答 why 的时候，只需要讲到以下表格中的任意三个观点即可：

观点	客观 （陈述事实 + 解释观点 + 数字量化）	主观 （和个人的关系 + 个人的感受）
quality can be guaranteed	They promise once you bought a copycat, they would give you 10-time refund.（假一赔十）	So, for me, it is really trustworthy.（很放心）
price is lowest	The price is generally 1/3 less than the market price.	I am a bargain shopper, low price is very attractive.
delivery is speedy	Once you place an order, your item will be delivered within 24 hours.	Personally, I could not even feel the difference between shopping online and in a real store.
provide cash-on-delivery service	Once you make sure that the quality is what they have promised, then you can pay the money.	So, it is worriless for me.（免去后顾之忧）
shipping is totally free	Traditionally, I need to pay extra for the postage when I shop online.	It is really a money saver.
offer 7-day return policy	Within 7 days, for any dissatisfaction, your order can be refundable without any fuss.（无条件退款）	For clothes or other non-standard stuff, I could have a second chance to pick up.
provide home-installation service	Professionals could get everything done for me.	I don't need to worry about those technical issues.

本书第六章将按照这样的逻辑和方式对题库进行讲解，请大家务必做到对前三问轻车熟路，最后一问有理有据，列出论据 1、2、3。此外，时间一定要控制在 2 分钟之内。

第五章

Part Three 哲学思想的辨证与统一

Part Three 问题归类

所有 Part Three 的问题或多或少都可以归纳到以下几大范畴：

两个选一个

Do you prefer X or Y and why?

回答策略

A. 起——用考官的话直接回答问题，给出自己的立场或者观点（跟考官唱同一首歌）
B. 承——用 KISS(keep it simple and straightforward) 原则给出一个核心关键词（形容词或动词短语）进行逻辑上的支持
C. 接——用自己或者身边的例子给考官一个“看得见、摸得着”的体验
D. 反——从反证的角度做出假设
E. 转——考虑到事物的另一面，从而给出更全面、客观的评价
F. 合——告诉考官：我讲完了，这就是我的立场

起	Personally, I prefer X to Y,
承 1	simply because X is more...than Y.
承 2	Besides, through X, I could...（回答 Part Three 的问题时，观点要尽量多于一个）
接和反	For example, if I...
合	So, generally, I will go for X.

考题总结

Do you prefer eating at home or at restaurants?
Which one is more important, your relatives or neighbours?
Do you prefer reading newspaper or watching TV program?
Do you prefer travelling alone or with other people?

What do you prefer, a high salary or job satisfaction?
Do you prefer making a call or writing a letter?
Do you prefer watching foreign movies or Chinese movies?
Do you prefer several short holidays or a long holiday?

重要类

Is...important?

回答策略

直接反证：很重要，因为没有……就会……
Yes, definitely yes, I always believe that X is really essential and necessary for...,
since without (doing) X, we would...(严重后果)
Besides,...
So apparently, there is no doubt about the significance of (doing) X.

考题总结

Is computer important?
Is art important?
Is protecting animals important?
Is doing outdoor activities important?
Is reading important?

有关以上两大类问题的回答方案，Simon 在第三章 Part One 终极分类中做了详细地描述，请大家参考起 - 承 - 接 - 反 - 转 - 合高分公式练习以上考题。

流行类

What is the most popular...in your country?

“中国最流行的……是什么？”回答此类问题时，切勿给出一个覆盖所有人的答案。我们的策略是把中国人大概分成两个阵营，并且这两个阵营的喜好要有明显的差异，比如说：

youngsters and elders(音乐、体育、电影、旅游景点等)
men and women(休闲方式、购物等)
children and adults(阅读、感兴趣的新闻等)
students and office workers(AA 制、购物等)
northern Chinese and southern Chinese(主食等)

我们使用以下的这个结构来回答：

It depends(看情况)

For X(对于一种人来说)
I believe that they have a fancy for...(总述)
such as...(举例)
simply because they...

Yet for Y(对另外一种人来说)
I guess they tend to like...(总述)
including...(举例)
That's probably because they...

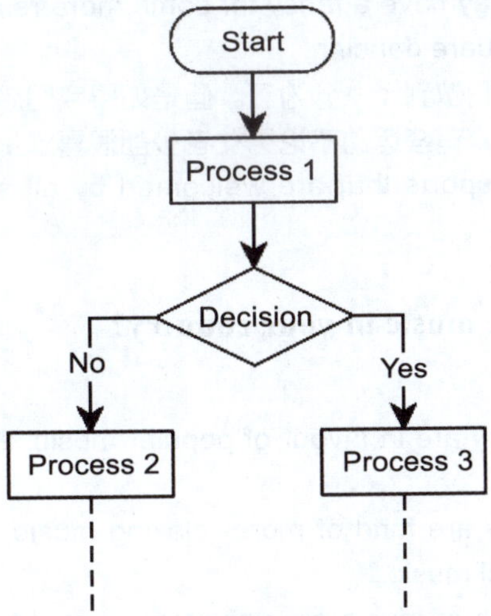

回答策略

一分为二，辩证统一：
It depends.
For X, I believe that...is the most popular one for them, such as...A, B, C and D, simply

because...

Yet for Y, I guess that they tend to choose..., including A, B, C and D. That's probably because they...

Meanwhile, there are...that are welcomed by all..., like...

考题总结

What is the most popular way of relaxing for Chinese?
What are the most popular travel destinations for Chinese?
What is the most popular sport in your country?
What is the most common accommodation in your country?
What is the most popular music in your country?

典型例题

What is the most popular sport in your country?

Well, it depends.

For youngsters, I believe that ball game is their most favourite sport, like B-ball, soccer, badminton, tennis, you name it.

Yet for elders, I guess they may have a fancy for some more relaxing sports, such as jogging, walking, doing Tai Chi and square dancing.

以上的回答已经很好，因为我们做到了一分为二。但是如果我们想拿更高分，还可以在此基础上做到合二为一。因为，在我国，有些运动不论男女老少都很喜欢：

Meanwhile, there are some sports that are welcomed by all age groups, like table tennis, swimming and cycling.

What is the most favourite music in your country?

Well, it depends.

For youngsters, I am sure they are in favour of popular music, like pop, rock, hip hop, fusion, funk and stuff like that.

Yet for elders, I suppose they are fond of more relaxing music, such as Chinese indigenous opera, red songs and classical music.

At the same time, some types of music are universally loved by all people, like light music, folk music and country music.

区别类

What are the differences between X and Y?

How could X differ from Y in...?

回答策略

回答区别类问题需要：

1. 熟背句型
2. 找到两者之间的不同之处（比如可以从城市大小、生活成本、生活压力、生活节奏、机会、设施、选择、空气、交通、空间等方面做论述）
3. 使用比较级

   Unlike X, Y tends to be more...（比较级）

   X is..., while Y is more likely to be...（反义词）

   Compared with X, Y is less likely to be...

   By this I mean...（进一步解释）

考题总结

What are the differences between men and women when considering relaxation ?

What are the differences between men's and women's shopping habit?

What are the differences between big shops and small shops?

What are the differences between living in big cities and living in small cities?

What are the differences between living in a big family and living in a small family?

What are the differences between elders and youngsters in ways of expressing anger?

What are the differences between single player sports and team sports?

What are the differences between watching live sports and watching on TV?

What are the differences between big weddings and small weddings?

What are the differences between Chinese movies and foreign movies?

What are the differences between self-teaching and being taught by teachers?

典型例题

What are the differences between big shops and small shops?

不同点：货量、价格、时间、距离、信誉、质量、规模等。

Well, compared with big shops, small shops definitely have smaller range of goods, since they only focus on daily necessities, like veggies, snacks, beverages, kitchen stuff and so on.

Besides, unlike small shop, big shop tends to have lower price due to their bargaining power(议价能力).

What's more, it may take a longer time to shop in a big shop, while a small shop is much handier. For example, suppose that I am cooking and I realise that I have run out of salt, and it is impossible for me to get it from Carrefour, since it is too crowded at the time, but fortunately, the grocery store on the first floor could help deliver it straightaway.

What are the differences between men and women in ways of expressing anger?

不同点：表达方式、表达途径、表达内容等。

Personally/As I see it/ From my point of view, there are a couple of/a variety of/heaps of/a few differences between them.(使用套句，可为自己争取 5 秒钟的思考时间)

Firstly, unlike women, men are more likely to express anger in a direct way, such as arguing and fighting.

Besides, I also consider that men tend to find a solution to the problem, while women choose to pour their heart out to a soul mate.

好坏处类

What are the pros and cons of...?

回答策略

任何事情都有两面性 (nothing is absolutely right or wrong)，但是总有侧重点。为了方便答题，无论是喜欢的居多还是讨厌的居多，我们都统一准备如下：

好处：依第一、二、三的顺序举 2-3 个观点。

坏处：举 1-2 个最显而易见的弊端。

三对好坏处类用词：advantages & disadvantages/benefits & drawbacks/merits & demerits

好处三点：Well,... is beneficial in a variety of ways.

Firstly,...

Besides,...

More importantly,...

坏处讲一到两点：Yet, when it comes to the drawbacks, I have to say that...

考题总结

What are the pros and cons of living with old people?
What are the advantages and disadvantages of traveling alone and with other people?
What are the advantages and disadvantages of raising pets?
What are the benefits and drawbacks of watching foreign movies?
What are the pros and cons of watching TV program for children?
What are the advantages and disadvantages of tourism?

典型例题

What are the pros and cons of living with old people?

Well, it is beneficial to live with old people for a variety of reasons
Firstly, they could take care of you, such as providing meals and doing laundry for you.(悉心照顾)
Besides, they could give you family companionship. Whenever you feel down, they could give you comfort, or provide recommendations and suggestions.(给予安慰和建议)
Plus, it is really important to have someone to sign for your parcels.(帮助接收包裹)
Yet, when it comes to the drawbacks, I have to say that (there probably will be)...

- less room for parties and home events.(活动空间少)
- old people might be talkative and wordy and they may keep talking all day long.(唠叨)
- they might interfere your personal affairs.(过多干涉)
- their timetable may not be synchronised with your daily schedule and you might be reluctant to make a change.(时间表有冲突)

What are the advantages and disadvantages of raising pets?

Well, raising pets is advantageous in a variety of aspects, such as...

- ✓ close/intimate companion of people—have fun together(亲密的伙伴)
- ✓ chase away loneliness—enrich your life(驱散孤独)
- ✓ more vibrant lifestyle—cheers you up when seeing them play around(生活乐趣)
- ✓ personal assistants—can be trained as guides for the blind, or for searching the survivals in a disaster.(导盲犬等)

Yet, when it comes to the disadvantages, I have to say that they might be...

- noisy—they might bark in the deep dark night, which can be disturbing and annoying(半夜吠叫)
- dangerous—mad dogs might attack hosts and passersby(疯狗)
- insanitary—they may spread diseases or infections/inappropriate for pregnant women and infants(不卫生)

messy—they might be messy by littering around(脏乱)

改变类

How has...changed recently in your country?

回答策略

在中国，考官喜欢问改变类的问题。他想知道人们以前是怎么做的，而现在人们的行为和想法又发生了什么样的变化。所以，我们需要：

- 针对以前和现在的不同情况举例子
- 指出今天的变化很大可能是由网络和科技造成的
- 指明今天人们的意识和价值观更加多元化 (diversified)

Generally speaking, people used to...in a traditional and conventional way, such as.... But now, an increasing number of people choose to..., including...(首先想到互联网和科技的影响)

考题总结

How has the relationship between neighbours changed recently in your country?
How has news report changed recently in your country?
How has the way of travelling changed recently in your country?
How has people's way of reading changed recently in your country?
How has people's way of listening to music changed recently in your country?
How has the wedding changed these days in China?

典型例题

How has people's way of communicating changed recently?

Well, in the past, people used to communicate with each other in traditional ways, such as making a phone call, writing letters or sending telegram.
Yet today, due to the proliferation of internet, people's way of communicating has been greatly transformed. Apart from traditional means, people now tend to communicate with each other on SNS(social network site), like Weibo, Renren, Twitter, Facebook and so on.(联想到新媒体)

How has family relationship changed recently in your country?

Well, in the past, family used to live under one roof, you know, they supported and took care of each other. Besides, they had more frequent contact with relatives.

Yet now, family member are easily separated, children tend to study, work and live far away from their parents, and they may even migrate to another city or country, thus the family relationship would not be as closely linked as before, and this leads to the phenomenon called the empty nest.

观点类

观点类的问题最难把握，考官主要是想听听考生对于一件事物的看法。Simon 在本书中将所有的观点类问题分为三种：

- **总分结构**
- **一边倒**
- **一分为二**

在详细解说观点类问题之前，我们先来复习一遍观点的常用表达：

- When it comes to.../Speaking of...
- I just think.../I always consider that...
- From where I stand, I feel that...
- From my perspective, I find that...

总分结构

What kinds of...are there/do people often...?

What are the reasons/values of...?

回答策略

回答总分结构类的问题需要罗列名词或者动名词，例如：

总：Well, people often do...for a variety of reasons...(将考官的问题转变成陈述句，后面加上 many/loads of/heaps of/a variety of/a wide range of 等)

分：such as/like/including...

考题总结

What are the reasons of shopping online?
What kinds of movies do children like to watch?
What kinds of shops are there near your house?
What kinds of advertisements are there in your city?
What kinds of things do people often lose?
What do people often celebrate in your country?
What are the common festivals in your country?
What kinds of roles do people play in a family?
Why do people care about their health?

典型例题

What are the factors people consider when buying a piece of furniture?

总 Well, speaking of buying a piece of furniture, I guess people would take a variety of factors into consideration, such as...（罗列名词，并最好给出支持的理由）

分
- room size and room layout 尺寸和布局
- colour coordination 颜色搭配
- price 价格
- design 设计
- quality 质量
- texture 质地

What are the efficient ways of learning English?

总 Well, talking about learning English, I consider there are many efficient ways, such as...

分
- soaking into a pure English environment by living in a native speaking country for a while.
- copying the way natives speak through watching TV programs or movies.
- getting started by studying an aspect of the culture, such as music, painting, literature and so on.

总分结构类问题中还有一种素质类

What are the qualities required to become a good...?

成为一个……应该具备……的素质？比如说成为一个 politician/leader/high-salary worker/celebrity/journalist/successful person...

回答策略

回答素质类问题时，需要使用以下结构：

- Firstly
- Besides/Plus...
- One more to add/mention...
- More importantly/most importantly...

例如：

Well, firstly, a qualified...should be...simply because...

Besides, they also need to be..., since...

More importantly, I always think...is essential for a...

考题总结

What qualities should a leader have?

What qualities should a traveller have?

What kind of people can become successful?

典型例题

What are the qualities required to become a good journalist?

Well, a good journalist should be responsible, since he must take responsibly for what he has reported.

Besides, a good journalist also needs to be insightful because the public want to know the truth and justice behind the stories.

Moreover, I always think that persistence is essential for a reporter; they should be able to overcome every kind of obstacle to draw the conclusion.

一边倒

Should (all) people do...?

回答策略

"一边倒"的问题一般都涉及社会主流价值观，考生在回答这类问题时，应明显地支持一方的观点。比如说：应该保护环境吗？应该坐公交车吗？应该多做户外运动吗？对此，考生的答案应当是肯定的：Yes, definitely yes, simply because...

在回答原因时，我们既可以从正向回答1、2、3点，也可以反证，即如果我们不这么做的话，会有……的后果，所以，我们应该……

考题总结

Should we protect the environment?
Should we protect animals?
Do we need to do outdoor activities?
Should parents control their children's time of using computers?

典型例题

Should parents control their children's use of computers?

Yes, definitely yes, I do believe that parents should have supervision on their children's use of computers.

正向证明：

- ✓ Firstly, children tend to lack the ability of telling right from wrong, they need adult's assistance to make judgments.（缺乏判断）
- ✓ Besides, some of today's websites contain inappropriate information for children, such as violence and pornography.（不良信息）
- ✓ Moreover, children are likely to be addicted to online games, which could bring them excitement and sense of content.（网游上瘾）

反向证明：

- ✓ Without parents' control, children are very likely to become addicted to...
- ✓ Without parents' control, children are more likely to be affected by some undesirable contents, such as...
- ✓ Without parents' control, children usually tend to spend an excessive amount of time on computers playing...

注意：有时，极端证明法能更好地解决此类问题。

Should all people take public transportation?

此题明显属"一边倒"类型的问题，Simon 以此题为例，用极端证明法来证明，假设所有的人都坐公交车，那么一切问题皆将迎刃而解。尽管在现实中这种情况不大可能发生，但是我们是为了证明观点。

Yes, definitely yes, if all people take public transportation, there would be less cars/much smoother roads/less gas emissions/less congestion/more efficient traffic control/less pollution...

又如：应该保护动物吗？

应该，因为如果不保护动物，可能就会破坏生态平衡，造成物种灭绝，甚至导致地球毁灭，还可能面临外星人接管地球的情况等等。所以，要保护动物。

一分为二

Is...always good for...?

回答策略

“一分为二”的问题通常存在争议，考官也没有所谓的判断对错的标准，因为每一种情况的存在都是基于某个环境和前提的，所以我们的策略是：

- ✓ 分两种情况
- ✓ 每种情况给出一个条件
- ✓ 每种情况给出一个结果

考题总结

Should parents buy expensive products for their children?
Should children learn how to play a musical instrument?
Do Chinese easily express their opinions?
Should public transportation be free of charge?
Is tourism always good for places?

典型例题

Is tourism always good for places? 请问旅游业一定是好的吗？

Yes, normally speaking, tourism could be a good thing for places, because it brings...

- money
- jobs

However, if we rely too much on tourism,

- the ecosystem might be destroyed.（破坏生态系统）
- local people's life might be disturbed.（打扰居民生活）
- the air may be polluted.（空气遭受污染）

Should all children learn how to play a musical instrument?

Well, it depends.
For kids who are interested, we should give them a try to see how good they can be, since interest is the best teacher.
Yet for those who are not interested, I don't think compulsory teaching will be a good idea, since people are born with different talents, and they might do better in sports or handicraft

rather than playing piano or violin.
So it totally depends on their preference and choices.

Should school libraries be free of charge?

No, I don't think that school libraries should be free of charge, simply because they need funding source to...
Yet for registered students, they should be free of charge, simply because those expenses have already been included in the tuition fees or miscellaneous fees(杂费).

技术点评：

有关免费不免费的问题也要一分为二来看待，因为任何一个机构或部门的运行都需要钱。资金有保障，机构或者部门才能：manage the whole system/pay the employees/maintain the system/pay tax/buy new facilities or equipment...
即使有政府的补贴 (subsidy)，机构或部门也不能对所有的人免费。所以，在回答的时候，我们可以把人分成两类，除了某一部分人，其他人都应该付费。比如说，以下设施应该对相应人群免费：
Library—registered students and their own staff(注册学生和教职工)
Park—taxpayers and local residents(纳税人和本地居民)
Public transportation—senior citizens and kids(老人和小孩)

Part Three 蕴含的社会动态 Societal Trends

Part Three 的问题通常充满了矛盾、对立和争议。在这一部分中，雅思考官最喜欢问的问题有如下几类：

年轻人和老人相处的问题

What are the pros and cons of living with old people?
How do young people treat their elders in your country?
What do you think of the problem of population aging?

家长和孩子互动的问题

Should parents give their children whatever they want?
Are today's children more stressed than before?
Should children do outdoor activities?
What are the pros and cons of watching TV programs for children?

男生和女生的思维与行为比较

What are the differences between men and women in ways of expressing anger?
What is the most popular way of relaxation in your country?
What are the differences between men and women in sports preference?

中西方的文化差异

What are the differences between Chinese movies and foreign movies?
What are the differences between Chinese music and foreign music?
What are the best ways for people to learn another language?

传统方式和互联网时代对比

How has the way of travelling changed in your country?
How has the way of finding a job changed in your country?
Do you like reading? And what's your favourite way of reading?
How has Chinese's way of travelling changed recently?

现代社会的热议话题

Why do some people like buying luxury goods/stuff?
Will iPad replace real/paper books?

对社会职业和品质的看法

What kind of qualities should a good leader have?
What are the qualities of a good journalist?
What kinds of people can become successful?
What kinds of people can earn a high salary?

政协委员提案

Should parks be free of charge?
Should libraries be free of charge?
Should public transportation be free of charge?
Should all people take public transportation?
Is tourism always good for places?
Should we protect animals?

第六章

雅思口语题库总结

第一节 Work and Study

Part Two

考场还原

核心话题

①喜欢的一门课：Describe your favourite subject.

②理想的工作：Describe your ideal job.

衍生话题

①喜欢的一门科学课：Describe your favourite science class.

②小时候想做的工作：Describe a job you wanted to do when you were young/little.

③想做的小生意：Describe a small business you want to do in the future.

分类剖析

学习类

喜欢的一门课

10 **Describe your favourite subject.**

You should say: what it is
what it is concerned with
when you learned it
and why you want to talk about this subject.

题目分析

- 基础学科：language, mathematics, literature, physics, chemistry, history, geography 等。
- 专业学科：management, psychology, philosophy, archaeology, economics, computer studies 等。
- 文体学科：fine arts, music, PE, specialty class 等。

喜欢的一门课可以和其他话题结合起来准备，比如：

喜欢的旅行 & history/culture/geography；
喜欢的书籍 & literature/philosophy/psychology；
成为金融业从业人士 & economics/finance/management/accounting.

参考答案

模板套话	Well, one of my favourite subjects is literature, which is the foundation and basis for almost every other subject.
内容	Basically speaking, literature covers a wide range of fields, including history, poetry, philosophy, novels, short stories, drama, language and so on.
时间	Speaking of when I learned the subject, I must say that I have been studying literature ever since primary school, and strictly speaking, the time I spend studying literature is not confined to any certain period, but every little drop of my life.
原因	I am partial towards literature for a number of reasons.
观点 1	As mentioned above, literature is an important aspect of a variety of educational programs.
客观	So, how could one read and write or communicate with others without being literate?
主观	Moreover, literature can help us be more educated and informed, and at the same time, can help pave the way for opportunities in study and work.
观点 2	Besides, I feel that literature can motivate a person to think critically/creatively/innovatively/independently/logically/systematically.
客观	Through studying history, religion, tradition and culture, one may develop a strong sense of logics, morality, etiquette（礼仪）, principle and so on.
主观	And that's really crucial for a person to function appropriately and effectively in society.
观点 3	More importantly, I always believe that literature contains the historical background of the time in which it was written,
客观	simply because literature is the record of the past, it is necessary for inheriting and passing on knowledge to the next generation.
主观	So, for me, I am quite interested in all aspects of the humanities, and literature helps me understand them more insightfully and thoroughly.

工作类

理想的工作

11 Describe your ideal job.

You should say: what this job is
where you will work at
what you will need to do this job
and explain further why you want to do this job.

题目分析

在雅思口语考试中，建议大家考虑以下几种职业：

- 旅游类：tour guide 导游　backpacker 背包客　adventurer 冒险家
- 环境类：volunteer 志愿者　environmentalist 环保人士
- 新事物类：hotel assessor 酒店评价员　island caretaker 岛主　fashion buyer 时尚买手

总之，理想的工作就是指能够实现自己的人生价值和理想，满足自己的兴趣，做自己喜欢的事情，同时还能 make a fortune 的工作，正所谓 kill two birds with one stone。

参考答案

模板套话　Well, the ideal job that I am dying to do is being a caretaker, to be more specific, an island caretaker, which was once called the best job in the world.

地点　Speaking of the location, I guess it depends, as long as there is an island with a stunning view and sensational shoreline, I'd like to devote myself to this job.

内容　When it comes to the job requirements/criteria, basically speaking, it calls for two main skills.

First, I have to speak fluent English or a local language, since I have to blend in smoothly with the local life.

Besides, it would be necessary for me to be a skilful swimmer, which is fundamental if I want to survive near the ocean.

More than that, creativity, passion, persistence and courage are also highly desirable to really do my job well.

原因　Island caretaker is my ideal job for the following reasons.

观点 1　Firstly, I am a big fan of the ocean and all kinds of water sports, like surfing, swimming, scuba diving, snorkelling, and being a caretaker is all about these things, and this job will really meet my recreational needs.

观点 2 Besides, I also think that the job is pretty easy, writing a weekly blog will be the main thing I need to do, beyond that, I could spoil myself as much as I like.

观点 3 Most importantly, the pay is incredibly attractive, it seems like if I stayed and worked for six months, I would receive $110,000, wow, that would be fantastic.

总结 In the end, though I am fully aware that this job is impossible for me, I am still longing for this kind of job, which is the perfect combination of having fun and making money. Generally speaking, that's why I want to talk about caretaking with you.

扩展阅读

The Best Job in the World (from ABC NEWS)

It's probably the best job in the world, now that the Australian tourism bureau has finally selected somebody to live on an island and write about life as a beach bum.

The new hire will get to live in a fantastic house on a paradise island in Australia's Great Barrier Reef for six months and get paid $110,000 to do it. The only requirement: write a weekly blog. That's right, weekly, not even daily.

Within the first 48 hours of the contest, the tourism group received more than 7,500 online applications. In the end, 34,000 people applied. Each made a 60-second video resume.

They were told to be creative and they were.

Sixteen finalists flew to Australia for the final, "gruelling" selection. Let's just say, it involved massages.

The job requirements are quite simple: The ability to speak English and swim.

The contest is part of a publicity stunt to drum up tourism in the area.

衍生题目

Describe a job that can make our world a better place.
Describe something you want to make a success of in the future.
Describe a job you wanted to do when you were little.
Describe a working place.
Describe a small but successful company.

让世界变得更美好的工作

12 Describe a job that can make our world a better place.

You should say: what it is
what the job involves
where the work is done
and explain further why the job could make our world a better place.

题目分析

考试中可以参考使用如下几种职业：

doctor 医生	teacher 老师	firefighter 消防员
artist 艺术家	designer 设计师	architect 建筑师
police 警察	volunteer 志愿者	celebrity 名人
entrepreneur 企业家	technician 技术人员	politician 政治家
UN Secretary General 联合国秘书长		businessman 商人

本题还可以结合理想的工作和喜欢的专业一起准备。

参考答案

模板套话 Well, the job I want to tell you about is being a doctor, which is one of the most essential and indispensable occupations in people's lives

内容 Regarding doctors' job, I reckon it covers a variety of fields, including dentist, psychologist, veterinarian(兽医), psychiatrist(精神科医师), nutritionist, and doctor of traditional Chinese medicine(cupping 拔火罐 /acupuncture 针灸 /massage 按摩 /skin scraping 刮痧).

Basically speaking, doctors aim to save people's lives, cure diseases and ease pains (救死扶伤).

地点 Normally speaking, they work at medical facilities, such as hospitals, nursing homes, clinics and treatment centres.

原因 I believe that a doctor is invaluable for the following reasons.

观点 1 Firstly, I think that doctors plays an important role in everybody's life.

客观 Without doctors, how could we be treated promptly and competently when we get sick?

主观 Being robust and healthy is quite fundamental for everyone's well-being, not to mention those who are facing the threats of death.

观点 2 Besides, I also think that doctors can provide security in the necessities of daily life.

客观 By this, I mean doctors are authoritative when making recommendations and giving advice on different aspects of life, such as nutritional advice, healthcare tips, diet therapy, or just common-sense of first aid.

主观	Undoubtedly, we live a more well-rounded and well-balanced life under doctors' instruction and practical guidance.
观点 3	More importantly, I always believe that psychologists are increasingly necessary in today's life.
客观	Obviously, people today tend to live an unhealthy lifestyle, and are more likely to live under all sorts of pressure or anxiety(焦虑).
主观	So, psychologists are more in demand than ever before to help and support those who are suffering from psychological and mental problems, like depression(抑郁症), insomnia(失眠), mental disorder(精神异常) and obsession(强迫症). They are crucial in exploring the causes, offering therapy, and providing systematic assistance to drag people out of suffering and pain.

想做的小生意

13 Describe a small business you want to do in the future.

You should say: what the business will be
where the business would be located
how many people it would need
and explain further why you want to do this.

题目分析

小生意的参考选项如下：

barber shop 理发店	hairdresser 理发师	butcher's shop 肉店
repair shop 维修店	car modification 汽车改装	mechanic 技工
bakery 面包店	pastry cook 糕点师	chef/cook 厨师
cafe 咖啡厅	barista 咖啡师	freelancer 自由职业者
florist's 花店	florist 花匠	bookstore 书店
nail salon 美甲店	milk tea shop 奶茶店	boutique 精品店
beauty parlour/salon 美容院	online store/e-store 网店	jewellery designer 珠宝设计师

想做的小生意应该符合以下属性：

- Profitable 可盈利的
- Personal interest 个人兴趣
- Flexible working hours 时间灵活
- Self-employed 自主经营
- Low threshold investment 低门槛投资
- Fast cost-recovering 成本回收快
- Promising market and highly demanded 市场前景好
- Targeted consumers 消费人群明确

回答这个题目时的场景有些类似于为自己的创业项目 (entrepreneurship program) 寻找一个风险投资人 (venture capitalist)。在这个过程中，需要向考官阐述以下几个方面的内容：

市场分析 market analysis　　行业预测 industry forecasts　　目标消费者 target consumer
个人优势 personal strengths　　盈利模式 profit model　　风险控制 risk management

当然，雅思口语考试重在语言，所以考生完全可以从个人情结和偏好 (personal attachment/sentiment/complex/preference) 入手，大胆做梦 (to be a dreamer)，为考官展现出小生意背后的梦想。

参考答案

模板套话	Well, the small business I want to do in the future is to open a cafe, specialising in espresso and cakes, which has been a long-time dream for me.
地点	Regarding the location, basically speaking, I guess it would be more appropriate to be located in a commercial complex or shopping mall, simply because our targeted consumers would be white collars, office workers, students and foreigners, who are more likely to be hanging around in such places.
员工	Speaking of the number of employees, normally, I can be the barista myself, but then, I will need one or two to give me a hand with serving or cleaning if necessary.
原因	Generally, there are a couple of reasons why I am longing so eagerly to own a cafe.
观点 1	Firstly, I consider that a cafe business calls for less investment and is less laborious.
客观	Compared with other small businesses, like a restaurant, it is less messy and troublesome; all I need to do is make a cup of drink for my guests.
主观	Since I have a strong preference for coffee, especially espresso, I would feel that I am doing something artistic and creative while I am making a cup of coffee.
观点 2	Besides, I also feel that the coffee shop sector will keep booming.
客观	Given that the westernised lifestyle is getting popular these days, espresso has become enthusiastically welcomed; the success of Starbucks is a good illustration.
主观	So, based on my market analysis, I believe that this business will be profitable with a short cost-recovery term.
观点 3	More importantly, this has been a life-long dream for me.
客观	I have always been dreaming that I could have my own little haven(小天地), where I could decorate and design in my favourite way.
主观	And you know, sharing with friends and catering to like-minded customers can be great things to do!
结论	So that's why I want to open a cafe.

Part Three

两个选一个

回答策略

高分公式：起 - 承 - 接 - 反 - 转 - 合

起：Personally, I think...

承：Simply because...

接：For example...

反：Without...

转：On the other hand,...

合：So generally,...

经典例题

14 **Which one is more important, salary or job satisfaction?**

起 Personally, I consider job satisfaction to be more important,

承和反 simply because if people don't like what they do, it will be a torture for them, and I don't believe that they would be persistent and productive under such a situation. So how can they become excellent and improve themselves?

转 Yet I do admit that salary is almost everyone's concern when they get a job, because people need to meet their expenses on a daily basis.

合 In conclusion, if I could only choose one out of the two aspects, I'd rather select job satisfaction.

流行类

典型问题

What are the most popular majors in your country?

What are the most popular jobs for young people in your country?

回答策略

一分为二，辩证统一：

Well, it depends.

For…, I consider…is quite popular for them, such as…, simply because…

Yet for…, I guess they might fancy…, including…, that's because…

For both,…

经典例题

15 What are the most popular jobs for young people in your country?

Well, it depends.

For boys, I feel that they are more likely to be concerned about which industry they are working in, or areas where they believe they will be successful sooner or later, such as banking, IT, engineering, construction and a mining company.

Yet for girls, I guess they tend to focus on job satisfaction and job content. Quite a number of girls dream of working in areas that are related to fashion or modern lifestyles, including fashion design, textiles, media specialist, hospitality sector and even show business.

For both, I think that being in business is pretty attractive, since young people nowadays long for financial freedom so that they can choose their favourite lifestyle and do whatever they want.

改变类

典型问题

How have the ways of finding a job changed?

How have people's ways of studying changed?

回答策略

对以前和现在的不同情况进行比较：

Generally speaking, people used to…in a traditional and conventional way, such as…

But now, an increasing number of people, especially youngsters tend to…in a more diversified way, including…, simply because our way of life has been deeply transformed by the internet and technology.

经典例题

16 How have people's ways of finding a job changed?

Well, people used to find a job in some traditional and conventional ways, like sending resumes to companies; being recommended by some acquaintances or looking for leads in newspapers or on notice boards.

But now, job hunters are more likely to turn to the internet for help, such as posting their CV on some recruitment websites or attending a job interview online.

More than that, it now is a trend to join a TV job-hunting show, which can greatly gain the publicity from audiences nationwide. However, the judges might be extremely critical and strict, since only one in a hundred can be chosen.

17 How have people's ways of studying changed?

Well, in the past, people used to study in traditional ways, such as attending a class and listening to teachers' lectures, or studying through reading books.

But now, an increasing number of learners are studying on the internet or through distance education(远程教育), and there is also a tendency for today's students to study in different countries.

观点类

典型问题

What kinds of subjects are useful?
Is equipment necessary for teaching?
What kind of people can earn a high salary and why do they deserve a higher salary?
What kinds of bosses are desirable for employees?
How could government help people to run a small business?

回答策略 1

总分结构：

- In terms of…, I think that…
- When it comes to…, I just think that…
- I feel/find that…
- Regarding…, my point is that…
- Personally, I believe that…

然后使用 Firstly, Besides 和 More importantly 来给出至少两个观点。

经典例题

18 What factors will people consider when seeking a job?

Personally, I believe that there are a variety of factors people will consider when hunting for a job.
Firstly, salary is the essential one that most people will consider, since they believe that their value can be judged by what they are paid.
Besides, job satisfaction is also vital, simply because people need to make sure that they will do their work with passion and energy.
Moreover, there are other important factors, such as…

- promotion opportunity 晋升机会
- training session 培训课程
- holiday period 假期时间
- welfare structure 福利结构
- working environment 工作环境
- colleagues 同事
- working hours 工作时间
- salary treatment 薪水待遇
- work location 工作地点

回答策略 2

高分公式：起-承-接-反-转-合

起：Personally, I think…

承：Simply because…

接：For example…

反：Without…

转：On the other hand,…

合：So generally,…

经典例题

19 Is working location important when people are seeking a job?

起 Yes, definitely yes, for most people, I think location is fairly significant,

承 mainly because it is directly related to the time you will spend commuting.

接和反 For example, if a person has to spend two hours commuting, I guess he is more likely to be frustrated and exhausted with the daily work. Personally, I would rather put that amount of time into my work.

合 So location is important.

20 Do you think that more and more people will work at home?

起 Yes, I do believe that an increasing number of people will be freelancers, working at SOHO(small office/home office),

承 since the internet has greatly changed the way people work today, and some jobs don't call for working in a fixed office, such as being a designer, writer, distance education instructor and even an accountant. As long as they can hand in their work by the agreed/consensual deadline, location isn't important any more.

接 Besides, efficiency is most people's first consideration, and working at home is very time-saving, money-saving and labour-saving. They could focus more on their work instead of facing congestion on the road.

合 Hence, I believe working at home is likely to become more popular.

总结

承、接、反、转是回答观点的四个角度，只要大家运用合理、符合逻辑，就可以随意组合，这样会产生许多意想不到的效果。

第二节 Media and Culture

Part Two

考场还原

核心话题

① 喜欢的电影：Describe your favourite movie.

② 喜欢的歌曲：Describe your favourite song.

③ 喜欢的书籍：Describe your favourite book.

④ 喜欢的电视节目：Describe your favourite TV program.

⑤ 喜欢的报纸或杂志：Describe your favourite newspaper or magazine.

⑥ 喜欢的广告：Describe your favourite advertisement.

⑦ 喜欢的异国文化：Describe a foreign culture that you are interested in.

衍生话题

① 智力竞赛节目：Describe a quiz show.

② 节目主持人：Describe a TV host.

③ 听外国音乐：Describe an occasion when you listened to a foreign music.

④ 想见的新闻人物：Describe a person in the news you want to meet.(详见人物类)

⑤ 新颁法律：Describe a new law that could make your life better.

分类剖析

媒体类

喜欢的电影

21 Describe a film you watched recently.

You should say: what the film is
when you watched this film
what happened in the film
and explain further why you found this film interesting.

题目分析

回答有关电影的问题时，考生可以从以下几个方面进行分析：

storyline/plot 情节	sound track 声带	costume 服装
special effect 特技效果	sound effect 听觉效果	visual effect 视觉效果
acting 演技	leading role 主角	supporting role 配角
dubbed movie 配音电影	subtitle 字幕	sequel 续集

参考答案

模板套话	Well, the movie that I am going to share with you is called *Real Steel*, which is a sci-fi movie starring Hugh Jackman, and it is nominated for the Academy Award for Best Visual Effects in 2012.
时间	I remember it was several months ago, when I watched it in the IMAX version at the cinema with my girlfriend.
内容	Basically, this movie combines different elements of drama, science-fiction, action and even fantasy. The story is set in the near future when the sport of boxing has gone high-tech, and a frustrated father called Charlie eventually won a comeback with his estranged son named Max after beating the most invincible robot with an abandoned robot Atom.
原因	I am greatly attracted by this film for a number of reasons.
观点 1	Firstly, the movie is full of fantasy and imagination.
客观	It is really amazing to watch a bunch of robots fight against each other; occasionally, the scene is so lifelike you doubt that you are watching a movie.
主观	Personally, I am a big fan of action and sci-fi movies, and this movie can really stimulate my hormones, and my mind was blown by its strong visual impact.

观点 2	Besides, I found that those actors' performances flawless.
客观	Audiences can be easily attracted by the movie, especially when the father and son teamed up together to win the final fight. It was particularly emotional when Max was claiming the challenge in the middle of the arena for the strongest Zeus.
主观	That was really contagious(有感染力的), and I even got goose bumps.
观点 3	More importantly, this is a Cinderella story, and is really inspirational.
客观	Atom, as a broken robot picked up from a trash field, eventually won the mission with courage and persistence, which is really encouraging and inspirational.
主观	I myself find that is quite motivating, since I learned that I should never ever give up, no matter how hard the situation is. Just as the movie's slogan says: Spirit is stronger than steel. And that's "Real Steel".
结论	So, that's why I want to share this movie with you.

Simon 的分享

如同讲故事，电影也需要分为：背景(时间/地点/人物)- 主线 - 结局

So, it is a challenging task to narrate the storyline of a movie in four or five sentences.

以下是描述电影三要素的必备句型(适用于所有讲故事类型)：

1. It is a...movie starring...(这是一部由……主演的……类型的电影)

   例如：It is a sci-fi movie starring Hugh Jackman.

   这是一部由休·杰克曼主演的科幻片。

2. The movie was nominated for the Academy Awards for...(这部电影曾经被提名为奥斯卡最佳……)

奥斯卡奖项包括：

✓ Academy Award for Best Picture	奥斯卡最佳影片奖
✓ Academy Award for Best Actor/Actress	奥斯卡最佳男主角/女主角奖
✓ Academy Award for Best Supporting Actor/Actress	奥斯卡最佳男配角/女配角奖
✓ Academy Award for Best Director	奥斯卡最佳导演奖
✓ Academy Award for Best Animated Feature	奥斯卡最佳动画剧情片奖
✓ Academy Award for Best Sound Mixing	奥斯卡最佳音效奖
✓ Academy Award for Best Sound Editing	奥斯卡最佳音效剪辑奖
✓ Academy Award for Best Visual Effects	奥斯卡最佳视觉效果奖
✓ Academy Award for Best Costume Design	奥斯卡最佳服装设计奖
✓ Academy Award for Best Makeup and Hairstyling	奥斯卡最佳化妆奖

3. The movie combines different elements of...(这部电影融合了……等元素)

   例如：The movie Titanic brings together different elements of disaster, romance and thriller.

   《泰坦尼克号》融合了灾难、爱情和惊悚等元素。

4. The story is set in...when...(这个故事讲述的是……，当时……)

例如：The story is set in World War I when the British were fighting against the Germans on the battlefield.

故事设定在一战期间，当时英国人和德国人正在战场上作战。

5. The story revolves around...（这个故事围绕着……）

例如：The movie revolves around the legendary life story of a guy called Forrest Gump.

这部电影是围绕着阿甘的传奇的一生来展开的。

以下是一些经典电影的故事梗概：

The Shawshank Redemption《肖申克的救赎》

Basically speaking, *The Shawshank Redemption* is a drama starring Tim Robbins and Morgan Freeman. It is a story of an innocent prisoner who was accused of being a wife murderer, and spent two decades in jail. He eventfully escaped from prison successfully.

Forrest Gump《阿甘正传》

Basically speaking, *Forrest Gump* is a comedy-drama starring Tom Hanks. The story is set in the latter half of the 20th century. It is a story depicting the legendary life of Forrest Gump, who is a naive and slightly slow-witted kid from Alabama. He has been witnessing, experiencing and being influenced by a series of significant events of the latter half of 20th century, including the Vietnam War, the hippie generation, the Watergate scandal and even the Ping Pong Diplomacy with China.

The Pursuit of Happiness《当幸福来敲门》

Basically speaking, *The Pursuit of Happiness* is a biographical drama starring Will Smith. The story is set in early 80s San Francisco. The story is about an on-and-off homeless father who has been through hard times struggling to provide a stable life for his son and himself. Eventually, his efforts paid off and he received a job offer as a stock broker.

Titanic《泰坦尼克号》

Basically speaking, *Titanic* is an epic romantic film starring Leonardo DiCaprio and Kate Winslet. It combines different elements of disaster, history, romance and thriller. The story is set in the year 1912, when the so-called Unsinkable Titanic was about to start her maiden voyage. It tells the story of a young artist and drifter called Jack, who ran into a gorgeous first-class passenger Rose, who was reluctant to marry a steel tycoon called Cal. Jack and Rose fell in love after a series of adventures on the ship, and eventually, Jack made a sacrificial effort to save Rose after the Titanic broke apart after hitting an iceberg.

Harry Potter《哈利波特》

Basically speaking, *Harry Potter* is a movie series starring Daniel, Rupert and Emma. It combines different elements of witchcraft, sci-fi, action and even fantasy. The story is about a wizard boy called Harry who, along with his friends, Ron and Hermione, goes on adventurous journeys to fight evil spirits and protect righteous fellows.

Kung Fu Panda《功夫熊猫》

Basically speaking, *Kung Fu Panda* is an animation movie set in ancient times of China. It is populated by taking animals, such as Panda, Tiger, Bunny, Wolf and so on. The movie combines different elements of fantasy, drama, action and comedy. The story revolves around a clumsy panda named Po, who courageously brings peace to the land by defeating the avenging and invincible snow leopard named Tai Lung.

Avatar《阿凡达》

Basically speaking, *Avatar* is an epic science fiction film starring Sam Worthington. It is set in the mid-22nd century when humans are mining a precious mineral on the planet of Pandora. The story is about Jake, a war veteran who gets called in to look for a valuable ore on Pandora in the guise of a native race called Na'vi. After understanding the secrets and spirit of Pandora and the Na'vi, Jake is torn by his conscience. Eventually, Jake, along with his righteous fellow human beings, leads Na'vi into victory by defeating and expelling those human colonists from the planet of Pandora.

Real Steel《铁甲钢拳》

Well, the movie that I am going to share with you is called *Real Steel*, which is a kind of sci-fi movie starring Hugh Jackman and this movie is nominated for the Academy Award for Best Visual Effects in 2012. Basically speaking, this movie combines different elements of drama, science-fiction, action and even fantasy. The story is set in the near future when the sport of boxing has gone high-tech. A frustrated father called Charlie eventually won a comeback with his estranged son named Max, after beating the most invincible robot with an abandoned robot Atom.

Braveheart《勇敢的心》

Basically speaking, *Braveheart* is an epic historical drama starring Mel Gibson. The film is set in the 13th century, when the Scottish were struggling against the rule of King Edward I of England. Mel Gibson portrays a Scottish warrior named William Wallace in the film, and sacrifices himself for the independence of Scotland.

Simon 的知识扩展

1. 好莱坞电影，无论是在表现形式上还是在故事情节的构架上，都试图向观众传达一种价值观，而这也正是考官所代表的西方人的主流价值观。考生只要抓住这些主线，就能够赢得考官更多的认同。好莱坞电影所传递的价值观包括：

   kindness 善良
   humanity 人性
   belief and faith 信念与信仰
   courage and persistence 勇气与坚持
   compassion 同情
   sacrifice and rebirth 牺牲与重生
   forgiveness and tolerance 宽恕与包容
   simple emotion and care 淳朴的情感与关怀

2. 国外电影的分级

G：General Audiences　　PG：Parental guidance

PG-13：Parents Strongly Cautioned　　R：Restricted

NC-17：No Children under 17

电影参考网站：www.rottentomatoes.com

喜欢的歌曲

22 Describe a song you have heard before.

You should say: what the song is
when you heard the song
who sang it
and explain further why you like this song.

题目分析

回答有关歌曲的题目时，考生可从以下几个方面进行分析：

lyrics 歌词　　melody/rhythm 旋律　　tune 调子

beat 拍子　　tempo/rhythm 节奏　　chorus 合唱 /solo 独唱

参考答案

模板套话	Well, the song I want to share with you is called *You Raise Me Up*, which is presented by a band named Secret Garden. This song is a real classic and has been covered(翻唱) by heaps of singers, like Westlife.
时间	I firstly heard this song when I was watching a TV program; it was the retirement ceremony for the F1 legend Michael Schumacher on CCTV 5. The moment they played this song as background music, I knew it was a perfect fit in that kind of atmosphere to commemorate this iconic star.
歌手	Speaking of the singers, just as I mentioned, it was originally performed by Secret Garden and has been covered by more than 100 singers in the world in different versions and styles.
原因	I am personally fond of this song for several reasons.
观点 1	Firstly, the music is really melodious and catchy.
客观	It mixes up different musical elements, such as the Irish ballad, bagpipes, violin and piano, and Secret Garden's resonant voice is a perfect complement for that music.
主观	Whenever this song is being sung, I cannot help but sing along with it.
观点 2	Besides, I find that the lyrics are totally and utterly encouraging and inspirational.

客观	As it says: when I am down and weary, you raise me up, and I can stand on mountains.
主观	For me, sometimes, it is inevitable to come across all sorts of frustration and failure in life, or just simply feeling physically weak or mentally depressed, this song is like a wake-up call to me, and it can drag me out of the low-points of life. After listening to it, I am able to cheer myself up, since it gives me courage and confidence.
观点 3	One more thing to add, this song was once covered by one of my most favourite bands called Westlife,
客观	which made it even more attractive and meaningful,
主观	since I could appreciate both of them at the same time.
结论	So, that's why I am sharing this song with you.

Simon 的知识补充

考生在回答有关歌曲的问题时，请尽量说出几句印象深刻的歌词（唱出来就算了），然后用以下的形容词来描述歌曲和歌词：

blue 忧郁的	penetrating 有穿透力的	soothing 舒缓的
refreshing 提神清新的	cheerful/joyful 愉悦的	uplifting/inspiring 令人振奋的
melodious 旋律优美的	nostalgic 怀旧的	sentimental 多愁善感的
calm 平静的	dynamic 有活力的	powerful 有力量的
realistic 写实的	energetic 充满活力的	passionate/enthusiastic 有激情的

motivating/encouraging/inspirational 鼓舞人心的

之后还可以用以下的句型来表示回忆，即这首歌曾在某个阶段带给自己特别的体验或者记忆：

Back then, I was a little bit frustrated and depressed/I was experiencing a downturn, and this song greatly empowered and inspired me, dragging me out of a low point in my life.

Simon 的知识扩展

You Raise Me Up

When I am down and, oh my soul, so weary;
When troubles come and my heart burdened be;
Then, I am still and wait here in the silence,
Until you come and sit awhile with me.

You raise me up, so I can stand on mountains;
You raise me up, to walk on stormy seas;
I am strong, when I am on your shoulders;
You raise me up... To more than I can be.

You raise me up, so I can stand on mountains;

You raise me up, to walk on stormy seas;
I am strong, when I am on your shoulders;
You raise me up... To more than I can be.

There is no life - no life without its hunger;
Each restless heart beats so imperfectly;
But when you come and I am filled with wonder,
Sometimes, I think I glimpse eternity.

You raise me up, so I can stand on mountains;
You raise me up, to walk on stormy seas;
And I am strong, when I am on your shoulders;
You raise me up... To more than I can be.
You raise me up... To more than I can be.

喜欢的书籍

23 Describe a book you want to read again.

You should say: what book it is and when you first read it
who the author is
what the book is about
and explain further why you want to read it again.

题目分析

回答有关书籍的问题时，考生可从以下几个方面进行分析：

content 内容
cover design 封面设计
author 作者
illustration 插图
chapter 章节

书籍分类如下：

detective novel 侦探小说
autobiography 自传
travel guide book 旅游指南
anecdote 趣闻轶事
science fiction 科幻小说
biography 传记
comic 漫画书
recipe book 食谱
time-travel novel 穿越小说
global history 全球通史
manga 日本漫画

参考答案 1

模板套话 Well, the book that I want to read a second time is the biography of Steve Jobs, who is a world-renowned entrepreneur and one of the most influential celebrities of this generation. I remember that the first time I read the book was several months ago, around October, 2011, when the book was published soon after the death of Steve Jobs.

作者　Speaking of the author, to be honest, I can't recall the name, since it is not the key point to me, but I do know that the author is a famous journalist who used to work for the *Time* magazine.

内容　This book summarises the whole life of Steve Jobs. From his childhood to his journey as a grown-up, from his experience at Apple Inc to his creative ideas to change the world, this book objectively and comprehensively presents to readers who Steve Jobs really was.

原因　I am longing to read it again for several reasons.

观点 1　Firstly, from this book, I can acquire well-rounded information about this amazing human being.

客观　I learnt that Steve was pretty ambitious when he was young, his life goal was to change the world, and I also learnt stories of how Apple's products have transformed and revolutionised our life, from reading to entertainment; from making a call to listening to music. He is such a visionary and a creative genius.

主观　After a closer look at Steve's life, I have to admit that he is really one of the most influential and greatest people of this generation.

观点 2　Besides, I also find that Steve is an inspiring mentor.

客观　He quitted university to find what he really loved, and he told us that we should listen to what our heart tells us instead of living in other people's lives. Even when he was experiencing the suffering of pancreatic cancer, he would insist on blowing his follower's minds at the Apple's conference.

主观　And his spirit will forever be the foundation of Apple and personally, he will be my impetus and strength as well.

观点 3　More importantly, I was reading the English version, which is a perfect way to absorb knowledge and improve my language level simultaneously.

客观　I learnt numerous useful words, phrases and expressions. Oh, plus, I would also occasionally listen to an audio version while I was doing something else.

主观　Definitely, my English listening comprehension was developed efficiently as well, simple because not only could I improve my reading ability, but I was also able to boost/enhance my listening English.

结论　Generally, it seems like I really must read this book again.

参考答案 2

模板套话	Well, the book I want to reread is called *Lonely Planet*, which is a travel guide book welcomed by backpackers around the world. It has versions for different countries and regions, covering a variety of information needed by travellers. I can still remember buying my first *Lonely Planet* in the Sydney version several years ago, when I was planning to take a trip to Australia.
作者	When it comes to the author, frankly speaking, I don't think there is only one writer for the whole series of books. The only thing I know is that the Lonely Planet Press has published more than 650 different theme books covering roughly 120 countries.
内容	This book basically aims to provide trip information for backpackers or other low-cost or tight-budget travellers around all the hot-spot countries, the information includes places of interest, recommendations, travelling tips, indigenous customs(本土风俗), itinerary planning(路线规划), financial-planning(预算规划) suggestions and so on.
原因	I am longing to read this book again for a number of reasons.
观点 1	Firstly, I feel that this book is very detailed and accurate.
客观	Just as I mentioned, this book offers every aspect of travel information for a traveller, and more importantly, the authors present first-hand experience, since they were travellers as well.
主观	As soon as travellers arrive at their destination, they will find themselves pretty familiar with the local situation, since they can preview what they are going to see with this guide book.
观点 2	Besides, this book is very attractive because it is easy to read.
客观	Apart from detailed tips, this book is beautifully illustrated, full of high-definition and up-to-date pictures, including hotels, restaurants, zoos and even street views on typical days.
主观	Readers' interests are greatly stimulated, since pictures are more convincing and direct to help people get to know a city.
观点 3	One more to add, the books in this series are pretty handy and light.
客观	Since the book is printed with the recycled paper, it is quite convenient to carry.
主观	They designed the book in a pocket size; you can easily put it into your bag and take it wherever you go. Most importantly, I have always dreamt of taking a round-world tour one day, and *Lonely Planet* is my guide and GPS for realising my dream.
结论	So, that is why *Lonely Planet* is the book I have always wanted to read a second time.

《孤独星球》这本书还可以扩展到喜欢的杂志（旅游杂志）和喜欢的电视节目（旅游节目）这两个话题上来。

Simon 的知识扩展

1. 书籍话题除了可以像电影话题一样叙述内容和进行论述外，还可以覆盖其他的属性，比如：
   strong readability 可读性强　　handy to carry 容易携带
   take some notes in the margin 在空白处做笔记
2. 孤独星球出版社简介：
   Lonely Planet is the largest travel guidebook and digital media publisher in the world. The company is owned by BBC Worldwide, which bought a 75% share from the founders Maureen and Tony Wheeler in 2007 and the final 25% in February 2011. Originally called Lonely Planet Publications, the company changed its name to Lonely Planet in July 2009 to reflect its broad travel industry offering and emphasis on digital products. After *Let's Go* Travel Guides, it was one of the first series of travel books aimed at backpackers and other low-cost travellers. As of 2010, it published about 500 titles in 8 languages, as well as producing TV programs, a magazine, mobile phone applications and websites.(from Wikipedia)
   孤独星球网站：www.lonelyplanet.com

喜欢的电视节目

24 Describe your favourite TV program.

You should say: what kind of TV program it is
how often you will watch it
what the TV program is about
and explain further why you like it.

参考答案

模板套话 Well, the TV program I want to share with you is called *Really For You*《非你莫属》, which is one of the most popular and famous job-hunting shows in China these days.

频率 The show currently airs on Sunday nights, so I watch this show once a week.

内容 Regarding the content of this show, basically speaking, a job-seeker is interviewed by a group of potential employers in several units, such as self-introduction, skills appraisal, job-hunting story and salary expectations.

结果 Eventually, those employers will make an evaluation after asking questions and sharing, to choose the talent they are looking for.

原因 I enjoy this show in particular for a number of reasons.

观点 1 Firstly, I consider that this show provides a great opportunity for me to get in touch with the job-hunting marketing.

客观 As a pending graduate(即将毕业的学生), I am about to start my working life this coming year,

主观 and it is really necessary for me to have a better understanding of all the diverse job opportunities and company cultures.

观点 2 Besides, I feel that the atmosphere is fairly intense.

客观 Occasionally, the job-seeker will be asked to answer many sorts of tricky and challenging questions, such as how would you solve some emergent situations or how to show leadership and management skills on a team.

主观 Sometimes I myself would get deeply involved in the topic as well, which always turns out to be stimulating and satisfying in the end.

观点 3 More importantly, I believe that this show is a touchstone(试金石) for me,

客观 since I continuously inspire and motivate myself by summarising and learning from those contestants' strengths and weaknesses.

主观 By learning from them, I prepare myself for the future job hunting.

结论 Generally, that's why this job-hunting show is one of my most favourite TV programs.

衍生话题——想见的新闻人物

25 Describe a person in the news you want to meet.

You should say: what the person does
how you came to knew this person
what you will ask when you have a chance to meet this person
and explain further why you want to meet this person.

(想见的新闻人物和节目主持人这两个话题可以结合起来准备)

参考答案

模板套话 Well, the person in the news I want to meet is Oprah Winfrey, who is a world-renowned talk show host, producer, actress and philanthropist. Her *Oprah Show* is regarded as one of the most successful and influential TV programs in history.

方式 Frankly speaking, I got to know her on a video clip when I was surfing the internet, but I can't recall precisely when I learned of her, since her show is not publicly televised here in China.

内容 Well, honestly, if I really had the honour and privilege of meeting her, probably I would ask how she can touch people's hearts so deeply when she is interviewing them. And that's what most people would ask as well.

原因　I want to meet her for a number of reasons.

观点 1　Firstly, I feel that Oprah is totally and utterly charismatic(有魅力的) and charming(人格魅力).

客观　For example, as a tough-guy figure on the big screen, Tom Cruise has never been moved and brought to tears on any show but Oprah's, so you can tell how good Oprah is at touching people's true feeling.

主观　From her show, I can feel that she is always sincere and considerate in the way she treats people around her. Her charming personality, her articulate expression and her charisma make her show greatly welcome and loved by audiences around the globe.

观点 2　Besides, I also consider that Oprah is quite versatile(多才多艺的).

客观　Apart from being famous with the Oprah Show, she is also able to host different shows in different styles, such as *Oprah's Big Give* and *Oprah's Favourite Things*.

主观　As one of her followers, I am impressed that her mind is so strong and she is courageous to build up such a big business empire with her bare hands(白手起家).

观点 3　More importantly, Oprah is a tough and diligent person.

客观　She has been through all sorts of ups and downs since she was little, I learned that she was even abandoned and suffered abuse. After years of frustration and diligence, she eventually cut a fine figure(崭露头角) in the TV industry.

主观　Her story encouraged me as well, and she is a perfect example of American dream, which is everyone can fully explore their potential and become richer regardless of social class or their birth circumstances, as long as they work hard.

结论　Generally, that's why I find my life inspired by this amazing human being—Oprah Winfrey.

Simon 的知识扩展

1. 电视节目可以和旅游、学习、想见的新闻人物等结合起来讲。当然，电视节目主要还是用来放松的：To relax and release pressure.
2. 老板想要的员工：What talents are employers looking for?

➢ Proficiency in languages (Mandarin, Cantonese, English, Japanese, Spanish, etc.)	语言能力
➢ Interpersonal-communication skills	人际交往
➢ Self-motivated	有上进心
➢ Goal-oriented self-starter	主动性强
➢ Team-work spirit and cooperation skills	团队合作

- Strong adaptability for different environments 适应能力
- Multitasking abilities 多任务处理
- Working under pressure 抗压能力
- Perspective taking 换位思考
- Time-management skill 时间管理
- Business ethics/etiquette 商业道德 / 礼仪

喜欢的报纸或杂志

26 Describe your favourite newspaper or magazine.

You should say: what it is
what information it contains
what kinds of people like to read it
and explain further why you like it.

题目分析

回答有关报纸或杂志的问题时，考生可从以下几个方面进行分析：

content 内容
section 版块
exclusive 独家的
headline 头条
presentation 表现形式
easy to read 易读性
handy 便携的
column 专栏
illustration 插图
informative 信息量大的
front page 头版
newsstand/newsagent 报摊

报纸 / 杂志类型

quality newspaper 优质报纸
times 时报
daily 日报
post 邮报
weekly 周刊
periodical 期刊

杂志名称

Vogue《服饰美容》
Vivi《昕薇》
Readers' Digest《读者文摘》
Cosmopolitan《时尚》
TopGear《汽车测试报告》
National Geographic《国家地理》
Esquire《时尚先生》
Hoop《NBA 时空》

报纸 / 杂志内容

profile 人物专访
special edition 特刊
express 快讯
street snap 街拍
outfit/dress 时装
gadget 小玩意
sneakers culture 球鞋文化
sport commentary 体育评论
in-depth reporting 深度报道
brief 摘要
cutting-edge 最新最潮的
accessories 配饰
life tips 生活贴士
domestic/international coverage 国内 / 国外报道
special coverage 专题报道
current affairs 时事新闻
gossip 八卦
women's fashion 女性时尚
cosmetics 化妆品
health care 健康保健

参考答案

模板套话 Well, the newspaper that I want to share is called *China Daily*, which is the most famous and popular English newspaper written and edited by Chinese. It is people's first choice when they want to read a newspaper in English in China.

内容 Basically speaking, it focuses on reporting current affairs in China as well as from around the world, just as others do, yet being in English make it unique, besides, it also covers a variety of topics, from sports express to culture insights, from technology to entertainment, from social events to all sorts of ads, you name it.

读者 Speaking of readers, I think quite a lot of people are loyal fans, including foreigners, students, white collar workers, officials, specialists and so on.

原因 I love *China Daily* for several reasons.

观点 1 Firstly, I feel that *China Daily* is pretty comprehensive.

客观 Just as I mentioned, it covers a wide range of topics, and all articles are written by a mix of Chinese and foreigners with different types of insights and opinions.

主观 Personally, It opens a window for me to the outside world. I can be frequently and promptly informed of all sorts of current affairs.

观点 2 Besides, I also think *China Daily* is a faithful English study helper.

客观 To learn another language, it is really important to input original expressions and ways of thinking, and *China Daily* is readily available in China for me to be immersed into(浸泡) a pure English environment.

主观 Currently, I am on my way to passing the IELTS, and reading it every day is beneficial to my reading comprehension, writing and even listening comprehension, because they have an audio version online now.

观点 3 Most importantly, *China Daily* has gone SNS(social network site 社交网络) now.

客观 This means I can download it or access its e-version, for example, reading it online or on my iPhone's App(应用程序).

主观 It is really time-saving and money-saving. When I take a ride on the subway or am travelling, I can read *China Daily* any time, anywhere.

结论 Generally, that's why I want to share *China Daily* with you!

文化类

喜欢的广告

27 **Describe your favourite advertisement.**

You should say: what it is
when and where you saw it
what the content of this advertisement is
and explain further why you like it.

题目分析

广告的选择应该符合以下几个方面：

- 内容在一分钟以内
- 故事主线清晰，四五句话能够概括
- 传递的信息符合主流价值观（人性、环保、生活态度等）
- 广告中有一个你最喜欢的亮点

广告应该从以下三个方面去分析：

- ✓ Idea 创意
- ✓ Presentation 表现手法
- ✓ Value 传达的价值

广告的种类：

ad/advertising/advert/advertisement 广告
public service announcement(PSA) 公益广告
classified advertisement 分类广告
TV commercial 电视广告
national publicity film 国家宣传片
banner ad 横幅广告
flyer 传单

参考答案 1

芝华士的广告——活出骑士风范 (Live with Chivalry)

广告内容　在一个帆船比赛中，当遇到暴风雨时，我们一定要加快速度，因为速度意味着胜利，胜利就意味着一切；但是有一种情况，我们会毫不犹豫的调转船头，那就是当我们发现有人落水了，即使落水之人是我们的对手；胜利？等救完人再说！

模板套话	Well, the advertisement I want to share with you is about a Scottish whisky called Chivas, which is one of the most prominent brands in my country these days.
时间和地点	I remember I first saw it a couple of years ago when I was watching a TV commercial; it left a lasting impression in my mind.
内容	The background of this advertisement is a sailing competition. One team was speeding up during a storm, aiming at winning the title—apparently, winning is everything for them. Yet there is one situation in which they would turn their boat around without any hesitation, which is someone falling into the water. Even though they are competitors, victory, compared with life, should be secondary. And eventually, they rounded up in a circle to salute to each other with Chivas. （视频地址：http://v.youku.com/v_show/id_XNjMwODg1MDA=.html 或者搜索芝华士——活出骑士风范）
原因	I want to share this TV commercial for a few reasons.
观点 1	Firstly, I feel that the idea is very creative.(Idea 创意）
支持	Since a sports event is appropriate for producing an atmosphere of conflict, audiences can understand the whole situation in just a few seconds.
观点 2	Besides, I also think that the presentation is quite dramatic.(Presentation 表现手法）
支持	On the face of it, the ultimate purpose of sailing is to win the competition, yet there is an unexpected ending, with friendship and humanity outweighing winning a trophy.
观点 3	More importantly, I believe that this advertisement has successfully conveyed a message, the spirit of chivalry, which is a matter of upbringing, loyalty and courage.(Value 传递的价值）
支持	The concept of chivalry is a core value we all appreciate.
结论	So that's why this TV commercial has left such a lasting impression on me.

公益广告

公益广告 (Public Service Announcement) 更能够联系到主流价值观，例如野生救援协会 (WildAid) 和地球一小时 (Earth Hour) 制作的宣传片就成功地向公众传递了环保、节约、可持续发展的观点。

Since environmental conservation and animal protection is such an important topic these days, those advertising can considerably raise people's awareness of sustainable development(可持续发展).

参考答案 2

野生救援协会——抵制鱼翅产品

广告内容	阿曼达是奥运会 200 米蛙泳金牌的获得者，在大海中，她拼命地向前游，因为前方有无数捕杀鲨鱼的鱼钩，她试图拿刀砍断这些绳索来拯救身后成千上万的鲨鱼。画外音：每年，有超过 4000 万的鲨鱼被杀害，你不必成为世界级的游泳健将来保护他们，你只需要拒绝和抵制鱼翅产品。在中国，有无数时尚事情可做，吃鱼翅汤绝对不应是其中之一。
记叙	Amanda Beard is the USA gold medallist for the 200 meter breast stroke (200 米蛙泳金牌获得者). She is swimming in the ocean with hundreds of sharks following after her. Ahead of her, there are countless fishhooks waiting to catch and slaughter sharks. Amanda is swimming as hard as she can to cut the cord to save them. The voiceover says: more than 40,000,000 sharks are killed each year. You don't need to be a world-class swimmer to rescue them. The only thing you need to do is to reject/boycott/refuse(抵制) consuming shark fin products. In China, there are hundreds of thousands of fashionable and cool things you can do, however, eating shark fin soup definitely should not be one of them. (视频地址：http://v.youku.com/v_show/id_XMTc4Njg1Njg4.html 或者搜索 Amanda Beard)
原因	I like this advertisement for a few reasons.
观点 1	Firstly, I feel that the idea and presentation are very creative.(Idea and Presentation 创意和表现手法)
支持	Animal protection is a big trend and theme in China these days. In only 30 seconds time, it illustrates to the audience that the number of sharks is greatly reduced and diminished due to slaughter by human beings, and the presentation is pretty direct and to the point(直中要害).
观点 2	Besides, I also believe that this ads conveys an important message, which is to avoid the consumption of shark fin product.(Value 传递的价值)
支持	It is really shocking that more than 40 million sharks are killed, and probably most of us don't realise, simply because we always take something for granted, and through this advert, I believe people's awareness can be raised. Just as it claimed: No buying, No killing(没有买卖就没有杀害).
观点 3	Most importantly, I was impressed by its closing words, which is there are countless fashionable things you can do in China, but eating shark-fin soup should not be one of them.(Striking Point 最大亮点)
支持	These words are fairly powerful, I made up my mind that I would answer the call(响应号召) to boycott(抵制) shark fin products, and do what I can to save them, simply because we share the same planet with animals, and we should live together harmoniously and peacefully. If animals all die out, no one will bail us out(拯救我们).
结论	So, this one is my favourite advertisement.

喜欢的异国文化

Describe a foreign culture that you are interested in.

题目分析

Foreign Culture 可以覆盖很多方面，在今天的生活中，对于某些文化，人们已经很难明确区分它究竟是中国所独有的，还是从国外引进的。但是，我们可以从兴趣爱好出发进行联想，因为这些都可能会是我们喜欢的异国文化，例如：

Movie—Hollywood culture; American TV series(美剧);Japanese Manga(日本漫画)

Music—hip hop; opera; musical; classic; blues; jazz; orchestra; symphony; country music

Simon 的分享

西方文化如下：

Gothic culture 哥特文化　　tattoo 纹身　　graffiti 涂鸦

X-sports 极限运动 (parkour 跑酷 /sky-diving 高空跳伞 /scuba-diving 潜水)

以下是一些异国文化的简介和盛行的原因：

1. 沙发客 Couch Surfing/ 背包客 Backpacker/ 青年旅馆协会 YHA(Youth Hostels Association)

简介

Couch surfing refers to travellers sleeping over at a friend's house during their trip, they can sleep in any available space in another' s house, including a bed, a couch or on the floor. Normally speaking, people can get to know each other and exchange personal information on the website in advance, and then, they can provide accommodation whenever they visit each other in a mutual way(相互的).

盛行原因

- ✓ It could help those round-world tour travellers with tight budget realise their dreams.
  可以帮助囊中羞涩的旅行者完成环游世界的梦想。
- ✓ Travellers could greatly blend in/fit in local life by living with local residents.
  旅行者可以更好地融入到当地人的生活中去。
- ✓ Travellers can explore and make meaningful connections with the people and places they encounter.
  旅行者可以深度探索所到之处并和所接触之人建立联系。
- ✓ They can share more about culture, tradition, lifestyle, food and values.
  他们可以更好地分享文化、传统、生活方式、食物和价值观。
- ✓ The distance between us can be shortened because of a couch.
  一张沙发拉近了彼此的距离。

2. 日本动漫 Japanese Manga/ 动漫真人秀 Cosplay

简介 Japanese Manga is a combination of comics and animation; it involves different themes and characters and styles, including science-fiction, fantasy, adventure, myth, fairy tale and so on.

简介 Cosplay (Costume Play) is a type of performance art, normally speaking, cosplayers will play a role from an animation or a comic book with identical costumes and accessories, to represent or express a specific character or idea.

盛行原因

✓ They can bring simple and straightforward joy.
它们能带来简单直接的欢乐。

✓ They can boost one's imagination and creativity.
它们能激发想象力和创造力。

✓ They can greatly arouse our emotions(激发情感), like happiness, anger, compassion, excitement, loyalty, sadness and disappointment.
它们可以激发我们的情感情绪，比如欢乐、愤怒、同情、兴奋、忠诚、悲伤和失望。

✓ It is a way to escape from daily life routines and clichés.
是暂避千篇一律的日常生活的方式和途径。

✓ The stories are lively and stimulating.
故事情节生动刺激。

✓ The music is melodious and soothing.
动漫音乐旋律优美、舒缓动听。

经典语录

✓ Detective Conan《名侦探柯南》
Enhances my observation and reasoning ability.
增强我的观察和推理能力。
There is no puzzle that cannot be solved.
世界上没有解不开的迷。

✓ Inuyasha《犬夜叉》
I wish you can be happy as much as possible, I don't know what I could do, but I will be with you forever.
我希望你快乐，希望你多多欢笑，我不知道我能做些什么，但我会永远陪在你身边。

✓ Naruto《火影忍者》
With a dream, there is nothing we cannot achieve.
只要有梦想就没有什么不可以。

✓ One Piece《海贼王》
I would never ever give up my dream, even if I risked losing my life for it.
我绝对不会放弃我的理想，即使我可能会因此而葬送性命。

✓ Card Captor Sakura《百变小樱》
It is miserable to lose something important in life, so we must learn how to cherish and value.
失去是一件很痛苦的事，所以我们要学会珍惜。

3. 拼车 Carpool/Carpooling/Car-sharing

简介 Carpooling is the sharing of a car during a journey, there will be more than one passenger to bear the cost.

盛行原因

✓ The cost of driving can be reduced, including fuel costs, toll fare and other expenses.
可以减轻费用，包括燃油费、通行费和其他费用。

✓ It is environmentally-friendly and sustainable, and produces less gas emission.
可以减少尾气排放，保护环境。

✓ Traffic congestion can be eased since there will be less cars on the streets.
可以减缓交通压力。

✓ People need a ride or lift instead of walking where public transportation is unavailable.
在公交不方便的区域，拼车是一种代步方式。

✓ It is cost-efficient and labour-saving during the Spring Festival migration.
春运期间可以省钱省力。

4. 星座 Constellation

Aries 白羊座	Taurus 金牛座	Gemini 双子座
Cancer 巨蟹座	Leo 狮子座	Virgo 处女座
Libra 天秤座	Scorpio 天蝎座	Sagittarius 射手座
Capricorn 摩羯座	Aquarius 水瓶座	Pisces 双鱼座
astrology 占星术	horoscope 十二宫图	prediction 预言
Mercury 水星	Venus 金星	Mars 火星
Jupiter 木星	Saturn 土星	Uranus 天王星
Neptune 海王星	Pluto 冥王星	

What is constellation? 什么是星座？

Well, basically, constellation is a system consisting of 12 astrological signs, and it is claimed to predict aspects of an individual's personality or characteristics, based on the positions of planetary bodies at the time of their birth. I like constellation studies, since many interesting coincidences occur with a person's situation and attributes（特征）. If you tell me your birthday, I can give you a fortunetelling analysis. I am not superstitious（迷信的）, I am just fascinated by those psychological points. For example, if you belong to...

Constellation	Positive Traits	Negative Traits
ARIES (March 21st - April 20th)	courageous, strong-willed, industrious, enterprising	moody, impatient, violent-tempered
TAURUS (April 21st - May 20th)	self-confident, steadfast, energetic, tidy, kind	obstinate, unforgiving, excessive
GEMINI (May 21st - June 21st)	skillful, humorous, persuasive	curious, restless, nervous, careless
CANCER (June 22nd - July 22nd)	sensitive, reasonable, home-loving	moody, irritable, domineering
LEO (July 23rd - August 23rd)	self-confident, courageous, aristocratic, idealistic	impulsive, domineering, hedonistic
VIRGO (August 24th - September 23rd)	tidy, industrious, calm, a keen intelligence	fault-finding, pedantic, materialistic
LIBRA (September 24th - October 23rd)	a feeling for beauty, wise, helpful, friendly	erratic, indifferent, love of convenience
SCORPIO (October 24th - November 22nd)	inquiring mind, determined, industrious	vindictive, lacking self-control, compulsive, unforgiving
SAGITTARIUS (November 23rd - December 21st)	openhearted, charitable, adventurous, enterprising	restless, stubborn
CAPRICORN (December 22nd - January 20th)	persevering, determined, serious, taciturn, shrewd	hard-hearted, obstinate, pessimistic
AQUARIUS (January 21st - February 19th)	kind, reliable, loyal	furious, unemotional
PISCES (February 20th - March 20th)	sensitive, placid, cheerful, warm-hearted	dreamy, restless, lack of self-confidence

From the website: http://www.englisch-hilfen.de/

Part Three

两个选一个

典型问题

Do you prefer watching movies at home or in a cinema?
Do you prefer watching sports events on TV or live?
Do you prefer listening to Chinese music or foreign music?
Do you prefer reading an electronic book or a real book?
Do you prefer reading a newspaper or a magazine?

回答策略

高分公式：起 - 承 - 接 - 反 - 转 - 合
起：Personally, I think...
承：Simply because...
接：For example...
反：Without...
转：On the other hand,...
合：So generally,...

经典例题

28 Do you prefer watching sports events on TV or live?

起 Personally, I prefer watching sports on TV,

承 simply because it is more time-saving, money-saving and labour-saving than watching them live.

接和反 For example, if I go to see them on the site, I may have to spend more money and time. More importantly, I may not be able to see the whole game from a better angle due to the crowd and distance.

转 Yet, when it comes to my favourite player or team, I might choose to support him on the site.

合 So generally, that's why I choose to watch on TV.

29 Do you prefer reading an electronic book or a real book?

起	Mostly, I prefer reading electronic books,
承	mainly because it is less laborious than reading real books and they are cost-free.
接 1	For example, I can download thousands of e-books onto my e-reader, and it seems like I am carrying a mobile library around with me.
转 2	Besides, it is really handy. If I take a train, I could flip through a random book with only my fingertip on my phone screen to kill time.
转	Yet, I do agree that the texture(质感) or feel of a real book is irreplaceable, especially for text books or books with illustrations.
合	So, that's why I love e-books more.

流行类

典型问题

What is the most popular music in your country?
What is the most popular TV program in your country?
What is the most popular reading material in your country?

回答策略

一分为二，辩证统一：
Well, it depends.
For…, I consider…is quite popular for them, such as…, simply because…
Yet for…, I guess they might fancy…, including…, that's because…
For both,…

经典例题

30 What is the most popular TV program in your country?

Well, it depends.
I think youngsters prefer watching relaxing shows, such as variety shows, Korean TV series, time-travel TV series(穿越剧), TV sitcoms(情景喜剧), talk shows or quiz shows, simply because they tend to catch up with the latest trends through those TV shows.
Yet for the elderly, I guess they might fancy serious or current-affairs related programs, including news reports, spy TV series(谍 战 剧), Peking Opera performances or just a

cooking show. That's because they have different preferences and daily activities.

改变类

典型问题

How have films changed over the years?
How has technology changed the way people listen to music?
How has advertising changed?
How has people's entertainment changed?

回答策略

对以前和现在的不同情况进行比较：
Generally speaking, people used to…in a traditional and conventional way, such as…
But now, an increasing number of people, especially youngsters tend to…in a more diversified way, including…, simply because our way of life has been deeply transformed by the internet and technology.

经典例题

31 How has the way of reading changed?

Well, people used to read in a traditional way, such as reading a book or newspaper.
But now, people tend to read in a more diversified way, since our life has been greatly transformed by the internet and new media, like reading an electronic book for free nowadays, or you can also choose to listen to an audio book while you are driving or doing something else. More commonly, an increasing number of readers choose new media as their daily information source, such as Weibo(micro blog), an online community or some other social networks.

区别类

典型问题

What are the differences between newspapers and magazines?
What are the differences between TV programs and radio programs?
What are the differences between Chinese music and foreign music?

回答策略

找到两者之间的不同之处，然后进行比较：
Compared with A, B tends to…
Unlike A, B is more/less likely to…
A is…, while B is more/less likely to…

经典例题

32 What are the differences between Chinese movies and foreign movies?

Well, compared with foreign movies, Chinese movies tend to be boring and monotonous. For example, our sci-fi movies are more likely to time travel to the past rather than to the future due to a lack of imagination and creativity.

Besides, Chinese movies are more commercial, while foreign movies provide a stronger cultural impact, such as documentaries and independent movies like *An Inconvenient Truth*《不可忽视的真相》or *Home*《家园》.

好坏处类

回答策略

好处：Doing…can be beneficial in many ways.
Firstly,…
Besides,…
More importantly,…
坏处：Yet, when it comes to the drawbacks, I have to say that…, and if we don't take steps, like…, it would be more serious.

经典例题

33 What are the pros and cons of watching TV programs?

Well, watching TV programs can be beneficial in many ways.

Firstly, it is an indispensable way to relax and have fun in today's world; since many sorts of TV programs are broadcast all over the place and people could easily find what they like.

Besides, through watching TV programs, we can keep up with the latest trends and current affairs very easily. You can just turn to the news channel, and you will know what is happening all over the world.

Yet, when it comes to its demerits, I have to say, some people might be addicted to it, like a couch potato, they are more likely to spend an excessive amount of time staring at the TV screen, which is really bad for their health physically and mentally.

观点类

回答策略 1

总分结构：

- In terms of..., I think that...
- When it comes to..., I just consider that...
- I feel/find that...
- Regarding..., my point is that...
- Personally, I believe that...

然后使用 Firstly, Besides 和 More importantly 来给出至少两个观点。

经典例题

34 How do TV programs influence children?

Personally, I believe today's TV programs have a great influence on children.
Firstly, they bring knowledge and information to children to help them understand the outside world. Through programs like *Animal World*, *Science Classroom* or travelling programs, their horizon can be broadened.
Besides, their imagination and creativity is also boosted with shows like cartoons, puppet shows(木偶剧), animation or fairy tale shows(童话剧). They can develop a sense of beauty and a sense of morality(道德观).
Conversely, children may also be influenced in undesirable ways. Some TV scenes are filled with violence and even pornography(暴力和色情内容), and children tend to imitate those dangerous behaviours which they learn from TV.
So we need to strictly examine TV programs to make sure they are appropriate for children.

回答策略 2

一分为二，分两种情况：
每种情况给出一个条件，每种情况给出一个结果。
Well, it depends.
For...
Yet for...

经典例题

35 Should libraries be free of charge?

Well, it depends.

For registered students or employees, library should be free of charge.

Yet for outsiders or the public, I don't think libraries should be free, simply because the library needs money for daily operations, like buying new books, paying workers, maintaining the facilities and so on.

第三节 People and Wildlife

Part Two

考场还原

核心话题

①小孩：Describe a child.

②老人：Describe an old person.

③好学生：Describe a good student.

④好朋友：Describe a friend of yours.

⑤领袖人物：Describe a (business/political) leader.

⑥新闻人物：Describe a person in the news you want to meet.（另见媒体类）

⑦家乡名人：Describe a famous person in your country.

⑧野生动物：Describe a wild animal.

对于人物类话题，考官会把问题集中在以下三个方面：

- Appearance 外貌
- Story 事迹
- Comment 评价

衍生话题

①有趣的老人：Describe an interesting old person.

②好驴友：Describe a person who you want to travel with.（另见旅游类）

③喜欢的动物：Describe your favourite animal in your country.

分类剖析

人物类

小孩

36 **Describe a small child you know.**

You should say: how old he/she is
what he/she looks like
what you often do together
and explain further why you want to talk about him/her.

相关词汇

smart/brainy 聪明的
naughty 淘气的
adorable/lovely 可爱的
courageous 勇敢的
curious 好奇心强的
annoying/disturbing 烦人的
active 活跃的
talkative 健谈的

参考答案

模板套话	Well, the small child I want to talk about is my niece called Rainy, who is the daughter of my sister's. She is currently eight years old, studying in primary school.
面貌	She is really adorable with sparkling eyes and rosy cheek. I really like her smile, because she smiles like an angel.
内容	We haven't seen each other a lot, but generally speaking, when we get together, we do a number of different things, such as playing a game, watching cartoons or hanging out in a park.
原因	I'd like to talk about my niece for several reasons.
观点 1	Firstly, I feel that Rainy is fairly smart.
客观	I can still remember when she was around her five or six, she was even able to learn English by herself through copying the way characters spoke in English animated cartoons.
主观	I was really amazed by her willingness to learn new stuff.
观点 2	Besides, I also think she is totally and utterly courageous.
客观	She takes part in all sorts of activities and events, like hosting a show, leading a group or helping other kids to finish tasks.
主观	I guess she does inherit some of my sister's traits, like getting along well with all sorts of people.

观点 3 客观	One more thing to mention, I always think that Rainy is a curious girl, because every time I see her, she keeps asking me all types of questions, even though some of them are quite childish and tricky to answer, like why the kangaroo had a pouch(育儿袋) or what are French fries made of.
主观	Yet I love to interact with my niece, when I am talking with her, I encounter a pure and simple mind, which is totally different from the adult world.
结论	And that's probably why I love kids and Rainy is the child I want to talk about to you.

老人

37 Describe an old person you want to talk about.

You should say: who the person is
how you knew this person
what you often do together
and explain further why you want to talk about this person.

相关词汇

knowledgeable 博学的	tough 坚强的	wise 有智慧的
kind 和蔼的	warm-hearted 热心的	amiable 和蔼可亲的
patient 有耐心的	sociable 爱社交的	generous 慷慨的
open-minded 思想开明的	conservative 守旧的	stubborn 顽固的
talkative/wordy 唠叨的	trendy/fashionable 潮的	amusing 风趣的
childish/babyish 孩子气的	bookworm 书虫	Mr. Know-All 无所不知的人
brainpower 智囊	soul mate 灵魂伴侣	inter-generation friendship 忘年交
mentor 良师益友	good-listener 好的倾听者	good-tempered/mild-tempered 好脾气的

参考答案

模板套话	Well, the old person I want to talk with is my grandfather, who is currently 75 years old, and he is one of the most important and influential people in my life.
过程	Well, just as I mentioned, he is my grandfather, so I have known him for my whole life.
内容	We often do a variety of things together, such as going fishing, chatting, watching TV programs and so on.
原因	Well, I'd like to talk about my grandfather with you for several reasons.
观点 1	Firstly, I feel that he is a knowledgeable person.

客观	He used to be a professor at a university, and he has been studying and reading all his life.
主观	So, whenever I have some questions, he will be the first one I turn to for help.
观点 2	Besides, I also think he is rather wise.
客观	He is always able to explain something complicated and difficult in an easy and simple way.
主观	For example, he gives me advice and suggestions when I come across frustration and downturns in life.
观点 3	More importantly, I always believe that he is a patient person.
客观	Ever since I can remember, he has never been mad with me no matter how naughty I used to be, and he is always nice and gentle to people around him.
主观	He is such a good-listener, and I am also willing to open my mind to share my concerns and worries with him.

形容老人的词汇和相对应的句型或短语

1. kind 善良的 /warm-hearted 热心的 /generous 慷慨的

   …be willing to give others a hand(乐于帮助别人)

2. sociable 爱交际的 /easygoing 随和的

   …get along well with all sorts of people(和各种各样的人都能友好相处)

   …would actively participate in events and activities(积极参加各种活动)

   …has strong organisational skills and people skills(有很强的组织能力和沟通能力)

3. tough 坚强的

   …has been through all sorts of ups and downs, such as…(经历了各种人生起伏)

   I really admire his/her toughness/boldness/optimism/tenacity.(我很钦佩他 / 她的坚强 / 魄力 / 乐观 / 坚韧)

4. amusing 风趣的

   …a person with a strong sense of humour(很强的幽默感)

   I never feel bored talking with him/her, since I can be amused by…(我总是被他 / 她的……逗乐)

以上内容可以用来形容大多数人物，当论述一个好学生或好朋友的时候，我们仍然可以使用这些词汇：knowledgeable, warm-hearted, patient, amusing, sociable…

除了以上内容和观点外，好学生、好朋友还应符合以下特质：

1. hard-working/diligent/industrious/studious 勤奋的，好学的

   He/She is always the first to come and last to leave.(他 / 她总是第一个来，最后一个离开。)

2. versatile/all-round 多才多艺的

   Apart from being excellent in…, he/she is also good at…(除了……优秀外，他 / 她还很擅长……)

3. smart/brainy 聪明的

He/She can get the hang of...in the shortest time.（他 / 她总是能在最短的时间内获得……的窍门。）

4. responsible 有责任心的
He/She is able to take responsibilities for...（他 / 她勇于承担……的责任。）

5. persistent 坚持的
He/She has often told me, we should persist until we succeed.（他 / 她常说：我坚持，我成功。）

6. common ground 共同点
We share many things in common./We have many common interests.（我们有很多相似之处。）

好学生

38 Describe a good student.

You should say: who the person is
when you knew him/her
what you learned from him/her
and explain further why he/she is a good student.

参考答案

模板套话和时间	Well, the good student I want to talk to you about is Rainy（尽量给出人名）, who used to be my classmate and desk-mate in high school. She was one of the most impressive friends of mine, a really excellent person.
内容	I benefited a lot from Rainy, learning from her attitude towards studying, her persistence, learning methods and how to be a responsible person.
原因	I'd like to talk about Rainy with you for several reasons.
观点 1	Firstly, I feel that Rainy was really diligent.
客观	I still remember she was always the first to come and the last to leave the classroom, even though she already ranked as a high-distinction/grade-A（拔尖的 / 优等的）student in class then.
主观	I was encouraged as well, she often told me that genius is 1% inspiration plus 99% perspiration, and I really admire and appreciate her diligence and boldness.
观点 2	Besides, I also consider that Rainy was totally and utterly brainy.
客观	She could get the hang of learning points in the shortest time, and after mastering those tricky concepts and formulas, she was also willing to give us a tutorial to help us.
主观	And I was the biggest beneficiary（受益人）, since I was the one who sat next to her, I still appreciate the valuable aid she gave me.
观点 3	What amazed me more was that she was so versatile.

客观　Apart from being excellent at her studies, she was also talented and good in other fields, for example, she was proficient(精通的) in English and Japanese; she held a tenth level certificate in piano, and more surprisingly, she was even good at Chinese calligraphy, how impressive that was!

主观　As her classmate and friend, she was the one I always wanted to be, and she was such a role model and benchmark for me to catch up with, until today, I have to admit she was motivating me to be excellent all the time.

结论　So, that's why when it comes to thinking of a good student, Rainy is the first person that comes to mind.

好驴友 Describe a person who you want to travel with

好驴友的特点一定要和旅行息息相关。

可选用的形容词包括 knowledgeable, amusing, generous, sociable, caring, considerate, responsible, easygoing 等。

除此之外，还可以选取以下具体的方面：

- good sense of orientation/direction　方向感很强
- experienced and a specialist in travelling　资深驴友
- have a common wish　共同的心愿

新闻人物

39 Describe a person in the news you want to meet.

You should say: what the person does
what make him/her appear in the news
what you want to say to him/her if you have a chance
and explain further why you want to meet him/her.

参考答案 1

模板套话　Well, the person I want to tell you about is Stephon Marbury, who used to be an NBA All-star and a member of the US dream team. Currently, he is the leader of Beijing's basketball team, the Beijing Ducks.

新闻性　I guess he gained his wide reputation and recognition soon after he won the title of CBA(冠军) by leading the Beijing team several months ago.

内容　As a die-hard fan(铁杆) of basketball, I have lots to say to him, and I want to tell him that I admire his courage and tenacity, I appreciate his devotion and diligence, and moreover, I like his humble and easygoing personality.

原因　I want to tell you about Marbury for a number of reasons.

观点 1　Firstly, I feel that he is totally and utterly professional and devoted.

客观	He has continually impressed people with his superior basketball skills and attitude, for every key moment, it is Marbury time, and he has repeatedly turned around the situation by his efforts(扭转局面).
主观	I learned that no matter how tough the situation is, we should not give up faith and confidence, and I believe that the harder you work, the luckier you'll be.
观点 2	Plus, I also consider that Marbury is pretty charismatic(有领袖魅力的).
客观	As the mainstay(中流砥柱) of the team, he is always encouraging/motivating/inspiring his teammates to play harder and become better, especially when the team was lagging behind, he showed strong leadership and united the whole team to fight as one.
主观	That's how a leader should be, influential and help to cheer his teammates up.
观点 3	More importantly, Marbury is an easygoing and open-minded person.
客观	Many are attracted by his optimism and positive attitude. Before he moved to China, he was experiencing a downturn in his life, he was abandoned by the NBA, and he was thinking of having a brand-new start here in China. Now he has completely changed the way people judge him, he isn't a "lone wolf" any more, he is trying to blend in with local life, such as trying food, learning a culture, and becoming a fan of the local football team.
主观	I can feel the inside passion and courage of Marbury, he inspired us as well, which is to believe that miracles happen every day, and yesterday isn't important, what we need to do is focus on today and look forward to tomorrow
结论	Generally, that's why Marbury is the person in the news I want to meet.

参考答案 2

模板套话	Well, the person in the news I want to meet is Lady Gaga, who is currently one of the most popular pop divas(流行天后) in show biz(演艺界) around the world. She started a brand-new and remarkable era of stylish storm.
新闻性	Lady Gaga, who is an American singer, songwriter, dancer and performance artist, is famous for her mind-blowing appearance and performance. Just as Lady Gaga claims: there is nothing to be afraid of.
内容	Honestly, if I really had a chance to meet her, I would probably feel nervous, since I always think of her as cool and mysterious. I would possibly ask her for an autograph or a picture.
原因	I fancy her for a number of reasons.
观点 1	Firstly, I really think she is phenomenal(现象的).

客观	Currently, even a lot of pop stars are imitating her style of dressing or her hairdo(发型), and she has been leading a brand new fashion attitude of boldness and freedom.
主观	I don't think I will copy her, simply because it is way too much(夸张) for me, but I appreciate her spirit and courage.
观点 2	Besides, she is talented as well.
客观	Since 2008, she has released several albums, receiving many positive reviews and much success. My favourite ones include *Just Dance* and *Poker Face*, and Lady Gaga has been nominated/awarded Grammy Awards(格莱美奖) and Billboard Music Awards(公告牌音乐奖) a number of times.
主观	I love her songs, they are quite cheerful and melodious, whenever I feel down, they cheer me up.
观点 3	More importantly, I have always considered Lady Gaga charitable.
客观	As a public figure, Lady Gaga is sympathetic to those who are suffering pain and disasters. For example, she called upon/on people to raise funds for the tsunami victims in Japan and she was even first place on the philanthropist list.
主观	She has been inspiring so many people, and I am no exception, but what I learned most is to have the courage to chase after my dream, to express myself in a unique and genuine way.
结论	Generally, that is why Lady Gaga is the one that fascinates me.

Simon 的分享

有关新闻人物等名人类的问题可能是最难讲也最宽泛的人物话题，其中包括：

actor/actress 演员（结合电影话题）	dancer/singer 舞者 / 歌手（结合音乐话题）
politician 政客	sports star 体育明星（结合体育话题）
entrepreneur 企业家（结合电子产品话题）	philanthropist 慈善家
artist 艺术家	architect 建筑师（结合建筑话题）

请考生结合领袖话题进行分析：Describe a leader.

一个球队的领队，一位有影响力的企业家或政治家，一位在某个领域有深远影响的人，甚至是一个学生会主席或班长，都应该是具备领导才能的领导人。

重点描述两个方面的内容：

1. 最大的成就、最大的特征、最有魅力的方面
2. 想见到他 / 她的最主要的原因

相关词汇和句型：

icon 标志	evergreen 常青树	legend 传奇
phenomenon 现象	one and only in my mind 我心中独一无二的	

1. **gifted/talented 有才华的**
He/She was born to be a…（他 / 她天生就是……）
He and his classic…left a lasting impression in our minds.(他所塑造的经典……深入人心。)
The image of Forrest Gump portrayed by Tom Hanks left a lasting impression on us.（汤姆 · 汉克斯所饰演的阿甘给我们留下了不可磨灭的印象。）
Michael Jackson's signature move(标志动作) Moon Walk(太空步) is one of the most breathtaking dance moves(令人激动的) in history.
2. **handsome 英俊的 /charming 迷人的 /gorgeous 极好的 /adorable 可爱的 /attractive or charismatic 有魅力的**
I was deeply mesmerised by his/her elegance and charisma/charm.（我被他 / 她举手投足间的优雅和魅力所折服。）
I could not take my eyes off him/her while he/she was…（当他 / 她在……时，我的眼睛简直不能从他 / 她身上移开。）
3. **charity 慈善 /charitable 慈善的 /philanthropist 慈善家 /donation 捐赠 /fundraising 筹款 /adoption 收养 /foundation 基金会**
They spare no effort in helping the needy, including…（他们不遗余力地帮助别人，包括……）
Bill Gates and his Bill & Melinda Gates Foundation(比尔和梅琳达 · 盖茨基金会) spare no effort in(不遗余力地) helping the poor children in Africa.
4. **tough 坚强的**
They have been through all sorts of ups and downs, from…to…; from…to…, eventually, they…(他们经历了各种各样的起伏，从……到……，从……到……，最终，他们……)
Barack Obama has gone through all sorts of ups and downs, from Jakarta to Hawaii; from juvenile delinquent(不良少年) to senator(议员); from a skinny boy(瘦弱少年) with a funny name(有趣的名字) "Barack" to the highest position in a country, he made history(创造了历史) in 2008 as the first African-American president of the United States; he has had such a legendary life experience.
5. **ambitious 雄心壮志的**
When he/she was…he/she made up mind to…（当他 / 她……时，他 / 她下定决心去……）
Eventually, they realised their dreams by…（通过……，他们最终实现了梦想。）
Bill Gates had a wish(愿 景) that one day, there would be a computer on everyone's desk, and he was in his twenties.
After becoming a billionaire(亿万富翁) in his thirties, Steve Jobs made up his mind(立志) to change the world(改变世界).

Simon 的知识补充

以下是一些名人故事，仅供参考：

1. Barack Obama

As the 44th president of the United States of America, Obama made history when he won the election in 2008. At the very beginning/At first/Initially, the reason that I adored/admired him was simply his legendary growth as well as his inspirational speech, as the first

African-American president. I was deeply impressed by his journey of growth, from Indonesia/Jakarta to Hawaii, from a juvenile delinquent to a community lawyer, a senator to the highest position in a country. However, far beyond that/as time goes on, I also find that he always spares no effort to take on serious issues such as the economy, the global financial crisis and wars in Iraq and Afghanistan. The recent Wall Street financial reform and medical reform was another good illustration of his tenacity and boldness/audacity as the national leader. Oh, I've never expected/dared to think that I would have a chance to meet up with him, however, that's the moment that I long for all the time. In my opinion, the best way to meet him would involve attending a speech/talk of his on site. His charisma, intelligence, and powerful speeches/messages have made him extremely popular with many Americans, not to mention me, one of Obama's hardcore followers.

2. Oprah Winfrey

As the evergreen tree among TV shows, Oprah Winfrey started a brand new era of talk show TV programming in a variety of ways. She is quite versatile at hosting different shows in different styles, including *The Oprah Show*, *Oprah's Big Give* and *Oprah's Favourite Things*; I find she's so fascinating not only because of her charming personality and articulate expression on stage, but also because of her insightful mind and skill at interacting with guests. For example, as the tough-guy figure on the screen, Tom Cruise has never been moved or touched to tears on any show except Oprah's, so you can tell how good Oprah is at touching the bottom of people's hearts. Given the surprisingly seamless appearance of her manifold enterprises, I admire her strong mind and courage in building up such a big business empire with her bare hands.

3. 悼念 Steve Jobs(10/5/2011)

Steve Jobs

1955-2011

Apple has lost a visionary and creative genius, and the world has lost an amazing human being. Those of us who have been fortunate enough to know and work with Steve have lost a dear friend and an inspiring mentor. Steve leaves behind a company that only he could have built, and his spirit will forever be the foundation of Apple.

奥巴马对乔布斯的悼念：

"Steve was among the greatest of American innovators—brave enough to think differently, bold enough to believe he could change the world, and talented enough to do it," Obama said in a statement.

奥巴马说："史蒂夫是美国最伟大的发明家之一，他勇于创新思维，相信自己可以改变世界，并且他的天资足以使他改变世界。"

The president said Jobs "transformed our lives, redefined entire industries, and achieved one of the rarest feats in human history: he changed the way each of us sees the world."

总统如是评价乔布斯："他改变了我们的生活，重新定义了整个行业，并取得了人类历史上少有的丰功伟绩——他改变了我们每个人看世界的方式。"

"The world has lost a visionary. And there may be no greater tribute to Steve's success than

the fact that much of the world learned of his passing on a device he invented," Obama said.
他还说："我们失去了一位梦想家。大半个地球上的人都通过他的一项发明获悉了他的逝世。对他而言，再没有比这更好的赞誉了。"

Simon 的备考建议：悼词是对一个人的生平和贡献最精华的总结。在此，我们可以通过苹果公司和奥巴马对乔布斯的哀悼来总结和提炼回答这个话题所需要的观点。总结后的观点同样适用于喜欢的电影和喜欢的书籍这两个话题，例如《乔布斯传记》。

扩展题目

Describe a person who influenced you.
Describe a person who taught you something useful.
Describe one of your neighbours.
Describe a person who has healthy lifestyle.（详见健康类话题）
Describe an adventurous person.
Describe two people from one family.
Describe a successful person.
Describe a TV host.（另见媒体类话题）
Describe a happy person.
Describe a popular singer group in your country.

人物类话题简明版（观点 + 支持）

观点 I think…	客观 (simply because/for example)	主观 (by this I mean/for me/ personally)
knowledgeable	He is Mr. Know-All.	Whenever I come across problems, he will be the first I turn to for help.
tough	…has been through all sorts of ups and downs, such as…	I really admire/appreciate his toughness and tenacity.
wise	He could always explain something difficult and complicated in an easy and simple way.	Occasionally, I would come across some bottlenecks in my life, and he is helpful to give me suggestions.
kind/warm-hearted	…would spare no effort to give others a hand, such as…	He is really a role model for me to learn from.
charitable	He and his…foundation managed to help the needy, such as donating money, raising funds for poor kids.	An increasing number of people have been influenced to take part in the charity organisation.

cool-minded	No matter how tough the situation is, he is able to **keep calm and come up** with a solution.	This is incredibly crucial for a person in the leader's position.
patient	He has never **been mad with** others.	People around him are impressed by his patience.
sociable/open-minded	...is able to **get along well with** all types of people.	His strong interpersonal communication skills makes me pretty popular among friends.
generous	He is the type of person who likes to **share with** others, not only in a material way, but also in many other ways, such as...	His willingness is really appreciated.
diligent	He is always the first to come to the classroom and the last to leave.	I was often told by him that genius is 1% inspiration and 99% perspiration.
persistent	It is hard for him to **waver(动摇) his mind** in pursuit of his goal. He believes that "I will persist until I succeed".	It seems that nothing could **quench(熄灭) his passion and desire** for success inside his heart. I like that.
smart	As a quick learner, he is able to **get the hang of(获得……的窍门)**...in the shortest time.	For the same question, he is more likely to have more creative and independent ideas.
versatile	**Apart from** being excellent in...he is **also** famous/good at...	He is the person I always want to be.
talented	It seems like he was born to be a...	I have to say that he probably is the most...person I have ever met.
amusing	He is full of a sense of humour; it is a treat talking with him.	Throughout the trip, I would never feel bored with his company.
optimistic	Although he might experience failure, he always has a positive attitude and **looks forward to** tomorrow.	I don't believe many can achieve that given that situation.
humble/modest	He is always **thankful** for what he got in his life and is **grateful** to people around him.	He told me that the sense of contentment is the source of being happy and cheerful.
responsible	If anyone on this team **blows things up(搞砸了)**, he boldly **covers** it up.	His sense of responsibility makes him a reliable and trustworthy person.

gorgeous/ charming	She is so glamorous(耀眼) under the spotlight, it seems like she was born to work in the show biz(演艺界).	I was deeply mesmerised by her, and she is my dream girl!
extraordinary performance skills	He and his classic image(经典形象) of…has left a lasting impression(深刻印象) in our minds.	Through his acting, people can easily become deeply involved in the movie.

野生动物类

40 Describe a wild animal.

You should say: where the animal comes from
when was the time you saw this animal
what the animal looks like
and explain further why you want to talk about it.

参考答案

模板套话 Well, the wild animal that I would describe is the national treasure of Australia, the koala, which is a kind of bear.

时间 Honestly, I have never had a chance to meet on of them. Personally, I believe that one day, my dream will come true. Currently, however, all my understanding of this lovable animal is from TV programs.

外形 Basically speaking, they have a charmingly naïve appearance. I fancy koalas simply because they are cute looking, with large ears and sleek fur, for every time I saw them, I couldn't help touching them eagerly.

原因 I love koalas for a number of reasons.

观点 1 Firstly, they are so special with interesting attributes.

客观 From what I can remember, they seem to be sleepy all the time and respond slowly to the outside environment. Normally, koalas only like eating the tasty but poisonous leaves from one particular indigenous tree. Koalas, however, are the only creature alleged to digest and absorb it. Isn't that amazing?

主观 If I had a chance, I would definitely test how long it takes for a koala to respond when I touch one.

观点 2 Besides, I also think that the koala is the symbol of Australia.

客观 Koalas are such fascinating creatures and only found on the Australian continent.

主观	I guess since studying in Australia is a long-time dream for me, the most suitable way to see them is to fly to this beautiful country.
观点 3	More specifically, I learned/found that the koala is one of the few mammals that has fingerprints.
客观	It is totally distinct from other animals.
主观	I guess there are numerous reasons for me to be into them, and one day, as I said, I will check it out on my own.
结论	So generally, that's why I want to talk about koalas with you.

野生动物类话题简明版（观点 + 支持）

观点	客观	主观
national symbol	It is the most recognisable（最知名）animal in...	I believe that when it comes to..., ...will be the first one coming up into people's mind, it is like an ambassador.
adorable	...is such a charmingly naive（憨态可掬）creature.	If I got a chance to see them, I don't think I could help touching them.
tough(wolf)	...is able to survive in harsh environment, like a desert or grassland（草原）.	So their tenacity is often praised by people.
qualified team player(wolf)	They have a strong sense of collectivity（集体感）for hunting or attacking.	Human beings even get inspiration from their organisation.
totem（图腾）	They are esteemed（被奉为）as a symbol of religion in areas like...	It is interesting to have...to represent their culture.
endangered species	Their race has been threatened with extinction（灭绝）in recent years.	Since we live on the same planet, protection and conservation should be a priority for us.
intimate companion(elephant)	They get along so well with humans, even giving us a hand with things like transportation and labour.	It seems they have a special way of communicating and understanding human beings.
smart(dolphin)	They imitate（模仿）people's behaviour and entertain us through performing.	It actually is amazing to see their performance at Sea World.

Part Three

改变类

How has the family relationship changed recently?

好坏处类

What are the pros and cons of watching TV programs for children?
What are the pros and cons of living with old people?

观点类

What are the qualities of a leader?
What kinds of people can become famous?
How do people become famous today?
What kinds of responsibilities should a leader take?
Do you want to be a leader and why?
Why doesn't someone want to be a leader?
What kind of skills should parents teach children?
What kind of roles should the elderly play in a family?
What is the attitude of young people towards older people in your country?
Do you think that old people should work?

Simon 的知识补充

1. 儿童类问题（回答有关儿童看电视、上网、买玩具、做课外活动和与人相处等问题）

Today's children might face the following problems:

sit in front of a computer all day long	宅童
watch an excessive amount of TV programs	沙发土豆

experience peer pressure to have better material goods 同龄人的攀比
lack interaction/communication/coordination with peers 缺少同龄人的互动
live under pressure from their parents 承受来自父母的压力
be asked to focus on academic fields only 被要求只是好好学习
be self-centred and spoiled 以自我为中心

They should:
interact/mingle/cooperate with their playmates 多和其他小孩子玩
have more outdoor activities 多做户外活动
get close to nature 亲近自然
develop extracurricular activities and hobbies 培养特长和爱好
be supervised and restricted from seeing negative information on the internet 远离不良网络内容
get in touch with a variety of knowledge to broaden their horizons 广泛尝试，扩展视野
learn how to respect, behave, and love in an appropriate way 学会如何尊重、表现和爱

2. 老人类问题（回答有关老龄化、与年轻人相处、老人的作用、老人的生活等问题）

Role of the elderly in a family:
providing suggestions and recommendations with abundant life experiences 给予意见和建议
taking care of the family 照顾好家庭
indispensable for household issues and decision-making 参与家庭决策
offering nurturing and cultivation 培养后代

Disadvantages of living with the elderly:
having different life timetables/schedules 作息制度不同
may have some conflicts 可能发生矛盾
might be too wordy, talking about the same topic repetitively 可能会唠叨
might interfere in young people's lives too much due to the different opinions 可能过多干涉年轻人的生活
there might be a generation gap 可能会有代沟
might be domineering 可能会很强势

3. 名人类问题（回答有关领导人的素质的问题）

A leader should possess skills like:
people skills 交际关系
organisation skills 组织能力
problem-solving skills 解决问题的能力
verbal skills 语言能力

And he/she should also be good at:
establishing a top-down organisational hierarchy 建立自上而下的组织结构
setting up a common goal 设立共同目标

building a team 组建团队
uniting subordinates 团结下属
making a judgment/adjustment based on the situation 根据形式做出判断 / 调整

And he/she should be:

- cool-minded 清醒冷静的
- generous 慷慨的
- a role model 榜样
- courageous 有勇气的
- considerate 体贴的
- devoted/dedicated 敬业的
- responsible 有责任心的
- visionary/forward-thinking 有远见的

核心词汇

描述一个小孩的模样

ponytail 马尾辫
chubby face 胖嘟嘟的脸
innocent smiling 天真无邪的笑容
freckle 雀斑
rosy cheek 红扑扑的脸颊
mixed-blood 混血儿
sparkling eyes 亮晶晶的眼睛
curly hair 卷发

描述一个人的身材

slim/skinny/bony 苗条的
overweight 超重的
stout/stocky 矮胖结实的
fat/plump 胖的
muscular 肌肉发达的
medium height 中等身材

描述一个人的外表

elegant/graceful 优雅的
glamorous 富有魅力的
appealing 动人的
sporty 有运动范儿的
gorgeous 灿烂的
catching 富有感染力的
charming 迷人的

描述一个人的性格

adventurous 爱冒险的
lively 活泼的
gentle 温和的
curious 好奇心强的
rational 理性的
frank 坦率的
caring 关怀的

评价一个人——积极面

knowledgeable 知识渊博的
aspiring 有抱负的
cool-minded 冷静的
career-minded 事业心强的
large-hearted 宽宏大量的
wise 睿智的
dedicated 敬业的
open-minded 思想开明的
well-organised 做事有条理的
strong-willed 意志坚强的
ambitious 有雄心的
warm-hearted 热心的
inner-directed 有主见的
determined 有决断力的
lenient/merciful 仁慈的

charitable 慈善的
straight/upright 正直的
courteous 有礼貌的
easygoing 随和的
introverted 内向的
faithful 忠诚的
frugal 节约的
humble 谦卑的
trendy/fashionable 潮的
smart/brainy 聪明的
gifted/talented 有才华的
considerate/thoughtful 体贴的
enthusiastic 满腔热情的
amiable 和蔼可亲的
audacious 无畏的
good-tempered 好脾气的
outgoing 外向的
punctual 守时的
tough 坚韧的
adorable 可爱的
industrious/diligent 勤奋的
amusing 风趣的
responsible 有责任心的
obedient 听话的，顺从的
passionate 充满激情的
visionary 有远见卓识的
patient 有耐心的
courageous 勇敢的
sociable 好交际的
extroverted 外向的
sophisticated 久经世故的
persistent 坚持的
modest 谦虚的
hard-working 努力的
studious 好学的
versatile 多才多艺的
charismatic 有领袖魅力的
energetic 充满活力的
generous 慷慨的

评价一个人——中性面

dominant 强势的
prudential 谨慎的
sensitive 敏感的
independent 独立的
strict 严格的
conservative 保守的

评价一个人——消极面

narrow-minded 狭隘的
talkative 爱说话的
childish/babyish 孩子气的
fussy 爱挑剔的，难取悦的
wordy 唠叨的
moody 喜怒无常的
stubborn 固执的

有用的短语

quick learner 学东西很快的人
good listener 好的倾听者
share the same interests/share many things in common/share much common ground 有很多相似之处
creative and innovative genius 创新性天才
inspiring mentor 鼓舞人心的导师

各种身份

patriot 爱国者
philanthropist 慈善家
Mr. Know-All 无所不知的人
hobbyist 业余爱好者
Little Monster Lady Gaga 的粉丝
pal/bro/mate/buddy/dude 哥们
indoors-man/indoors-woman/homebody 宅男宅女
patriotic 爱国的
trendsetter 达人 / 潮人
die-hard fan 忠实 / 铁杆粉丝
tech-head 技术迷
Bieber Fever 比伯粉丝
geek/nerd 极客 / 宅男
vegetarian 素食主义者
hipster 赶时髦的人
enthusiast 发烧友
iFans 果粉
bestie 闺蜜

第四节 Travel and Transportation

Part Two

考场还原

核心题目

① 未来想去旅行的地方：Describe a place you want to visit in the future.

② 想购买的车：Describe a vehicle you want to buy.

③ 喜欢的交通方式：Describe your favourite mode of transportation

衍生题目

① 好驴友：Describe a person you want to travel with.

② 过去的旅行：Describe some travelling you have done.

③ 想购买的昂贵品：Describe something expensive you want to buy.

分类剖析

旅行类

想去旅行的国家

41 **Describe a foreign country you want to visit.**

You should say: where you want to travel to
when you will travel
what you will do while you are travelling
and explain why you want to travel to this place.

参考答案

模板套句	Well, the foreign country that I want to visit is the States, which is one of the most attractive and fascinating travelling destinations for many backpackers, and I am no exception.
时间	I think after passing my IELTS examination this time(暗示原则), I'd like to take a tour around the states with my girlfriend/boyfriend/parents.
内容	During my travels, I definitely would spoil myself and take part in all sorts of activities and as many of them as possible, like driving from coast to coast, going shopping, visiting national parks, or hanging around those world-renowned universities.
原因	Well, I am dying to travel to the States for a number of reasons.
观点 1	Firstly, travelling to the States has been a long-time personal wish.
客观	Since I was little, American culture has been influencing us in almost every field, including movies, music, sports, arts and even cartoon characters, so if I have a chance, it will be great to have first-hand experience of it on my own.
主观	For example, I am a big fan of the New York Knicks, watching an NBA live game at Madison Square Garden(MSG) is a must-do activity, hopefully my dream can come true one day.
观点 2	Besides, there is a wide range of cultural and natural heritage that deserves a look.
客观	Those must-see destinations include Yellowstone Park, Grand Canyon,Las Vegas, Disneyland Theme park, Hollywood and you name it!
主观	I believe that my mind can be blown and my horizon can be greatly broadened.
观点 3	More importantly, I am about to study in the States, and I am longing to have some experience beforehand.
客观	You know, like the American accent, local food and customs, living habits or just the view, my dream is to study and live in this country for a while, and travelling definitely is a part of my future plans.
主观	And then, I reckon that life would be much easier and smoother after I set out on my brand new life journey.
结论	So, generally speaking, that's why I want to talk about this country with you.

顺便准备

未来想去的国外景点：Describe a place in a foreign country that you want to travel to in the future.

考官会重点注意三项内容：

1. Must-do activity 一定要做的事情

比如说：...is a paradise for shopping, luxury goods are cheaper than here in China.
A friend of mine is living there, and I could have a free tour guide to show me around.
Paris is the city of romance, grabbing a cup of coffee at a corner cafe is a must-do activity.
I am deeply mesmerised by the culture of...

2. Must-see destination 一定要看的景点

以下是一些国家著名的旅游景点：

➢ **United Kingdom**

Big Ben 大本钟
Buckingham Palace 白金汉宫
River Thames 泰晤士河
London Eye(Ferris wheel) 伦敦眼
The British Museum 大英博物馆
Westminster Abbey 西敏寺
Tower of London 伦敦塔
Stonehenge 巨石阵

➢ **Australia**

Opera House 悉尼歌剧院
Harbour Bridge 海港大桥
Great Barrier Reef 大堡礁
Uluru 乌卢鲁巨石
Blue Mountains 蓝山
Great Ocean Road 大洋路
Twelve Apostles 十二门徒石

➢ **Canada**

Rocky Mountains 落基山脉
Niagara Falls 尼亚加拉大瀑布
Banff National Park 班夫国家公园
Yukon River 育空河

➢ **France**

Louvre 卢浮宫
Eiffel Tower 艾菲尔塔
Notre-Dame de Paris 巴黎圣母院
Seine 塞纳河
Champs Elysees 香榭丽舍大街

➢ **Japan**

Tokyo Tower 东京塔
Mount Fuji 富士山
Nagoya 名古屋
Osaka 大阪
Kyoto 京都
Hokkaido 北海道
Sakura 樱花
Hot Springs Hotel 温泉酒店

➢ **United States**

Empire State Building 帝国大厦
Times Square 时代广场
Statue of Liberty 自由女神
Central Park 中央公园
Hollywood Walk of Fame 星光大道
Beverly Hill 比利佛山
Sunset Strip 日落大道
Golden Gate Bridge 金门大桥
Fisherman's Wharf 渔人码头
Silicon Valley 硅谷
Madison Square Garden 麦迪逊广场花园
The Metropolitan Museum of Art 大都会博物馆

3. Must-have experience 一定要尝试的经历

考题训练

Describe some travelling you want to do in the future.
Describe a city you want to travel to.
Describe a trip you have taken before.
Describe an occasion when you got a bit angry.
Describe something expensive you want to buy.

好驴友

42 Describe a person who you want to travel with.

You should say: who the person is
where you want to travel to
when you will travel with this person
and explain further why you want to travel with this person.

参考答案

模板套话	Well, the person I want to travel with is my girlfriend, who is my perfect travel mate no matter where I am going to go.
地点和时间	Frankly speaking, we have several options for our destination, depending on our budget and time availability, I guess, probably, as long as I could pass the IELTS this time, she could accompany me on a trip to Japan or Korea.
原因	I want to travel with my girlfriend for a number of reasons.
观点 1	Firstly, my girlfriend is pretty knowledgeable in history, culture and traditions of different places and proficient in languages.
客观	She has a combined degree in cross-cultural studies and English; besides, she even took Japanese as a second language.
主观	So, throughout the trip, I guess I would feel relieved and trouble-free going around with her.
观点 2	Besides, I also feel that my girlfriend is totally and utterly sociable and easygoing.
客观	It seems like she could get along well with all types of people, since she is interested in dealing with people, especially new friends.
主观	During a trip, people skills actually are really vital, as no one knows what and who they might encounter, so I am pretty confident that we can handle different situations.
观点 3	More importantly, I always believe that my girlfriend and I are the best partners.

客观	It is going to be a wonderful journey with my girlfriend, we are both generous people, we can share everything during a trip, from bills to budgets, from ideas to laughter, from happiness to bitterness, that would be so memorable and unforgettable.
主观	I actually can't wait for another great travelling experience.
结论	So, generally, that's why she is the one I want to travel with.

交通类

想购买的车

43 Describe a vehicle you want to buy.

You should say: what kind of vehicle it is
how much it will cost
what you will mainly use it for
and explain further why you want to buy this vehicle.

汽车作为交通类的核心话题，还可以结合以下问题进行思考：
Describe something expensive you want to buy.
Describe something you want to buy from a foreign country.(例如在国外上学需要买车)
Describe a form of transportation.

参考答案 1

模板套话	Well, the vehicle I want to buy is a compact vehicle called Smart, which is one of the most popular urban cars presented by Mercedes-Benz.
价格	Honestly speaking, I have no idea about the precise price, yet I guess the range is between 100,000 and 200,000 RMB.
用途	Generally speaking, I need a Smart mainly to ride instead of walking(代步工具), for daily commuting(日常通勤)in the city, or probably I could also do a part-time job while I am studying overseas.
原因	I am interested in Smart for a number of reasons.
观点 1	Firstly, I feel that Smart is pretty handy.
客观	Smart is probably the smallest car on the market, it can be easily handled and controlled in all sorts of situations, such as parking and especially parallel parking.
主观	Personally, I am a rookie driver, so Smart could perform perfectly in some congested cities like Beijing.
观点 2	Besides, I also think that Smart is totally eco-friendly,

客观	simply because Smart would consume less fuel and produce less gas emissions(尾气排放) than other vehicles, so it is definitely fuel-saving.
主观	Given that today's petro prices have been skyrocketing, it is money-saving as well to drive a Smart around.
观点 3	More importantly, Smart is quite fashionable and trendy.
客观	Smart has been favoured by quite a number of young people because of its adorable car body and streamlined design.
主观	And I am no exception; I believe it will be eye-catching for passersby.
结论	Generally, that's why I want to share Smart with you.

参考答案 2

观点 1	Firstly, I feel that an SUV is really spacious and multifunctional,
客观	simply because an SUV has more leg room for passengers, apart from driving to work, It is also capable of(胜任的) moving and carrying.
主观	For example, I could carry my whole family around for commuting or travelling to different places.
观点 2	Besides, I also think an SUV is quite tough.
客观	An SUV can perform excellently on all types of road conditions, such as on-road and off-road mode.
主观	I often dream of taking a self-drive tour to Tibet with my friends, and an SUV is the perfect vehicle for realising my dream.
观点 3	More importantly, I believe that an SUV is quite safe.
客观	An SUV provides better and more reliable protection, such as a well-rounded airbag, more durable outer covering and a solid body.
主观	So it would be trustworthy and also, it represents a freestyle way of life, especially for today's young people.
结论	Generally, that's why I want to describe an SUV to you.

交通类话题简明版（观点 + 支持）

观点	客观	主观
a ride instead of walk	It is much easier to get around in a city.	I could save time and my labour.
handy	...convenient to park and parallel park.	I am a green hand at driving, so compact vehicle is easier to handle.

fashionable	The car is adorable with a streamlined design(流线形设计), it is a young people's favourite.	And it has always been a dream for me to have one.
eco-friendly	It consumes less fuel than any other vehicles.	So it is fuel-saving and money-saving.
spacious	It is suitable for carrying the whole family around.	I am a driver who fancies more leg-room in a car.
bold engine	It has a lot of power(动力) with an acceleration time(加速时间) of 2.8 seconds for 0-100m.	I believe that I would have an incredible experience achieving this.
tough	...is excellent in different road conditions, including on-road mode and off-road mode.	Taking a self-drive tour to Tibet is always my dream.
safe	It could provide me with all-round protection, such as air bags, better shield and strong steel.	I guess nothing is more important than being safe when you drive a car.

Part Three

改变类

回答策略

对以前和现在的不同情况进行比较：

Generally speaking, people used to...in a traditional and conventional way, such as...

But now, an increasing number of people, especially youngsters tend to...in a more diversified way, including..., simply because our way of life has been deeply transformed by the internet and technology.

经典例题

44 How has people's way of travelling changed?

Well, people used to travel in a traditional way with some limitations, for example, they tended to make a trip around China by train or inter-city bus. But now, they are more likely to travel self-sufficiently, and besides, foreign trips are getting popular, those tropical islands with exotic sensations are extremely appealing for many Chinese, like the Maldives, Tahiti, Bali, Fiji and so on.

流行类

回答策略

一分为二，辩证统一：

Well, it depends.

For…, I think…is quite popular for them, such as…, simply because…

Yet for…, I guess they might fancy…, including…, that's because…

For both,…

经典例题

45 What are the most popular travelling destinations in your country?

Well, it depends on the different age groups.

I believe young people prefer travelling to big cities, like Hong Kong and other international cities, since they can enjoy themselves by shopping, playing in a Theme park or experiencing something stimulating and intriguing

Yet for elderly, I guess they will likely choose places with stunning natural scenery, like some famous mountains and small villages.

Besides, quite a number of aged Chinese have a special sentiment towards those "Red Holy Lands", where our Communist forefathers used to fight and live, like Yan'an or Jing Gangshan.

好坏处类

回答策略

好处：Well…is beneficial in a variety of ways,

Firstly,…

Besides,…

More importantly,…

坏处：Yet, when it comes to the drawbacks, I have to say that…

经典例题

46 Is tourism always good for places?

Tourism can be a good thing for places, since it can boost the local economy and increase employment.
Yet if we rely too much on tourism, the local life and ecosystem might be undermined/disturbed, because more tourists means more littering and more interruption.
So, we need a bit of balance for that. For example, we could put a number restriction on tourists or raise people's awareness of eco-protection.

What are the advantages and disadvantages of tourism?(参考上题)

观点类

回答策略

高分公式：起-承-接-反-转-合
起：Personally, I think...
承：Simply because...
接：For example...
反：Without...
转：On the other hand,...
合：So generally,...

经典例题

47 Should all people take public transportation?

起 Yes I believe that all people should take public transportation as much as possible,

承 simply because it is money-saving and environmental-friendly since less gass emissions will be produced and it may promote the efficiency of traffic, because it carries more passengers at a time.

反 If all people take public transportation, there will be less vehicles on the road, so traffic congestion will be avoided and eased, undoubtedly road travel will be much smoother.

合 So taking public transportation should be encouraged.

48 Should public transportation be free of charge?

逆向思维：

起	No, I don't think that public transportation should be free of charge.
承和反	simply because if we run the system for free, there will be less money for the daily expenses, including buying new buses or trains, paying employees, maintaining and repairing the infrastructure. So the consequence is that service quality will be lowered, the system will be less reliable and tend to be out of control.
合	So it is better if it is reasonably charged and managed.

第五节 Shopping and Lifestyle

Part Two

考场还原

核心话题

① 喜欢的商店 / 购物场所：Describe your favourite shop/place for shopping.

② 想购买的奢侈品：Describe something expensive you want to buy if you have the money.

③ 想去国外购买的产品：Describe a product you want to buy from a foreign country.

④ 电子产品：Describe an electronic product.

⑤ 家具：Describe a piece of furniture.

⑥ 想购买的车：Describe a vehicle you want to buy.（另见交通类话题）

⑦ 喜欢的餐厅：Describe your favourite restaurant.

⑧ 喜欢的国外食物：Describe your favourite foreign food.

⑨ 新颁法律：Describe a new law that can make our life better.

衍生话题

① 喜欢的交流方式：Describe your favourite way of communicating with your friends.

② 喜欢的网站：Describe your favourite website.

③ 喜欢的建筑：Describe your favourite (modern) building.

④ 收到的礼物：Describe a gift you received from others.

⑤ 送出的礼物：Describe a gift you gave to others.

⑥ 遗失物品：Describe something you lost.

⑦ 喜欢的着衣风格：Describe your favourite clothing style.

⑧ 特殊场合的衣装：Describe a piece of clothing for a special occasion.

⑨ 特殊聚餐：Describe a special meal you want to have with others.

⑩ 庆贺场合：Describe an occasion when others celebrated for you.

⑪ 亲手做的东西：Describe something you made by yourself.（例如烹饪）

分类剖析

购物类

参考解析

想买的东西可以是一件产品，也可以是一个梦想，比如环球旅行的梦想或者出国留学的梦想，另外还可以是一笔教育投资。

在国外想买的东西应该或多或少具备以下几个条件：

1. 价格比国内便宜
2. 货物种类比国内齐全
3. 没有假货
4. 限量版，国内没有卖
5. 买了之后要在外国使用，比如说留学期间购买的车。

电子产品和奢侈品这两类可能符合以上要求，所以我们的话题准备可以集中在：

✓ an electronic product 电子产品
✓ luxury stuff 奢侈品
✓ a vehicle(另见交通类话题)
✓ a house(另见房屋类话题)

购物场所的问题可以集中在：

◆ 一个商店 / 购物中心
◆ 你喜欢的服装款式
◆ 电子产品

电子产品

49 **Describe an electronic product.**

You should say: what it is
what you can use it for
how much it will cost
and explain further why you want to talk about it.

题目分析

电子产品相关词汇：

laptop 笔记本	smart phone 智能电话	desktop 台式机
projector 投影仪	all-in-one machine 一体机	ultrabook 超级本
RAM 内存	processor 处理器	hard-disk 硬盘
screen 屏幕	case 机箱	mouse 鼠标

keyboard 键盘
stereo speaker 环绕音响
USB flash disk/USB drive/USB stick U 盘

摄影相关词汇：

aperture 光圈
wide-angle lens 广角镜头
telephoto lens 长焦镜头
zoom lens 可变焦的
filter 滤光镜
shutter 快门tripod 三脚架
flashlight 闪光灯
DSLR(digital single lens reflex) 单反相机

有关电子产品外观的形容如下：

trendy/fashionable/stylish/eye-catching/posh 时髦的，吸引人的
the surface is sleek and neat 表面光滑整洁
ultra-thin design and metallic body 超薄设计和金属机身
brand-new and cutting-edge 最新款

有关电子产品价格的描述如下：

pricy/costly/cost a fortune 昂贵的
moderate/reasonable/affordable/economical 价格适中的

有关电子产品的使用评价如下：

informative 信息量大的
capacious 容量大的
intelligent 智能的
durable 耐用的
innovative 创新的
practical 实用的
handy/mobile/portable 便携的
multifunctional/versatile 多功能的

参考答案

模板套话　Well, the electronic product I want to buy is called Macbook Air, which is called “the thinnest laptop in the world”, another masterpiece created by the mighty Steve Jobs.

功能　It can apparently function like other computers, so I can use it for studies, entertainment, personal communications and playing computer games.

价格　Frankly speaking, I could not recall the accurate price, I guess the price range is around 10,000 Yuan.

原因　Well, I want to buy a Macbook Air for several reasons.

观点 1　Firstly, I need a laptop because it is a necessity.

客观　Since I am about to study overseas, a laptop is an essential equipment. Without a computer, how could I hand in my assignments and prepare my class presentations?

主观　This computer provides me with all the office software and applications, it is also durable with a standby time/battery life of more than 7 hours, and I can bring it with me to the classroom as a notebook.

观点 2	Besides, I feel that it is multifunctional and versatile.
客观	Apart from studying, I could use it in a variety of ways, such as listening to music, watching movies, chatting with my friends and surfing on the internet.
主观	Today, it seems like a laptop is a survival tool for everyone, especially for senior netizens(网民) like me.
观点 3	Most importantly, Macbook Air is highly distinctive for its mobility.(便携性)
客观	As Steve Jobs himself said: it is so thin that you could not even feel it, it is even lighter than a magazine, I could put it into my pack without effort.
主观	Plus, I am deeply fascinated by its sleek and neat appearance with a shining apple logo in the middle of the front.
结论	Generally, that's why Macbook Air is the one I am longing for all the time.

Smart phone/Electronic dictionary/Recorder/Video game player 都可以从以下四个角度进行描述：

- Necessity 必要性
- Multifunctional 功能强大
- Handy gadget 携带方便
- Fondness 喜爱程度

电子产品购物类话题简明观点（观点+支持）

观点	客观	主观
necessity	Without it, I couldn't do…,	Since I am going to study overseas, it is a must-have gadget(必备的电子设备) for me to survive on a daily basis.
multifunctional	Besides doing A, I could also do B, C and D.	It is an all-in-one device for me.
handy/portable	It is thin and light, which can be easily put into my pocket,	especially when I take a trip or studying overseas, I could carry it with me easily wherever I go.
trendy/ fashionable	The exterior design is cutting-edge and catching.	As a fashion-conscious(紧追潮流的) person, it is always a dream to have a…

innovative and creative	It is full of high-tech designs and functions, such as a multi-touch screen(多点触摸屏), all-glass surface(全玻璃表面), man-machine interactive device(人机互动设备), built-in sensor(内置传感器), apps(应用程序).	I believe this is the most amazing...so far.
reasonable/affordable price	Normally, the price is about...on the market.	As a student-class consumer, it suits me pretty well.

想去国外购买的产品

50 Describe a product you want to buy from a foreign country.

You should say: what that is
where you can buy it
how much it will cost
and explain why you need to buy it from another country.

题目分析

国外产品，尤其是国外的奢侈品种类如下：

hand bag 手提包
belt 皮带
purse 女用钱包
bracelet 手镯
sunglasses 太阳镜
jewelry 珠宝
platinum 白金
diamond 钻石
wristwatch 腕表

对奢侈品的形容：

dandy 华丽的
luxurious 奢华的
delicate 精致的
aristocratic 贵族的
mysterious 神秘的
timeless 无限的
indescribable 难以形容的
irresistible 难以抗拒的
classy 高档的
prestigious 有声望的
time-honored 历史悠久的
avant-garde art 艺术先锋
dazzling 闪耀的
unparalleled/incomparable 无与伦比的

参考答案

观点 1	Firstly, I feel that the luxury goods there are genuine and authentic(正宗的).
支持	I believe that it is impossible for me to come across knockoffs (山寨货), and the quality will be reliable and trustworthy.
观点 2	Besides, I also think that the price of luxury goods is greatly attractive.

支持	Normally speaking, the price will be 1/3 less than China's market price, when it comes to the sale season or promotion, I might encounter an even lower price. I am a bargain shopper, and I can spoil myself shopping.
观点 3	More importantly, I could have a wider range of selection in a foreign country.
支持	It is more likely that I find some limited editions available, which is rare in China. Normally they have new arrivals available earlier as well. So, it is really advantageous.
观点 4	One more to add, they provide door-to-door service.
支持	They promise that the ordered items will be delivered overnight, which vastly enhances users' shopping experience. And besides, we could escape from the crowds and fatigue of shopping and getting around, so it is time-saving and labour-saving. With a click of my mouse, shopping is just as easy as it sounds.

以上给出的观点 1、2、4 恰恰符合今天很多电子商务网站 (B2C/C2C) 的特点，比如某家电商所发布的一则广告中给出的广告语就是：

- 保证正品
- 价格最低
- 隔夜到达

通过这一话题，考生可以顺便准备商店 (shop)、网站 (website) 甚至是广告 (advertisement) 类的话题。

一家实体店

51 Describe a shop you want to talk about.

You should say: what the shop is and what the shop specialises in
how often you go to this shop
what kinds of people go shopping there
and explain further why you want to talk about this shop.

参考答案

模板套话	Well, my favourite shop and the one I want to talk about is called ZARA, which is a wellknown Spanish brand-name. It is currently one of the hottest and most popular fashion retail shops in China. It specialises mainly in men's and women's fashion, including clothes, accessories, shoes, boots, and other fashionable gadgets; they even have a section for kids.

频率	Normally speaking, whenever I am in the mood to go window-shopping, ZARA is my priority.
顾客	When it comes to other shoppers, I guess it is welcomed by people from all walks of life(各行各业的人), such as trendsetters/hipsters/stylists(潮人), students, white collars, housewives and so forth.
原因	I like ZARA for a couple of reasons.
观点 1	Firstly, their costume design and quality is highly selective and tasteful(有品位的),
客观	simply because most of the clothes are designed by famous European designers, and they provide cutting-edge fashion and elegant designs in the first place.
主观	Personally, I really appreciate the originality and freshness of the design.
观点 2	Besides, I also think that ZARA is a relaxing place to hang around.
客观	The whole decor and lighting is pretty sensational, the layout of the shop is customer-oriented(以顾客为导向的), you can easily find what you are looking for.
主观	The shopping atmosphere is pretty soothing, even the background music boosts my shopping appetite.
观点 3	More importantly, I always believe that the staff there are quite hospitable.
客观	They offer a one-month return or exchange guarantee, which means if you are unsatisfied with what you bought, your money can be refunded(可退款的) without any fuss(没有任何麻烦),
主观	then I won't regret any impulsive buying(冲动购物), as long as I keep the tag and receipt(标签和发票).

顺便准备

一个购物场所：Describe a place where you can go shopping.

生活方式类

喜欢的着衣风格

52 Describe your favourite clothing style.

You should say: what that is
what kinds of clothes does this style include
how often your wear it
and explain why you like it.

题目分析

不同风格的衣装：

leisurewear 休闲服
leggings 紧身裤
cardigan 开衫
skinny jeans 塑腿仔裤
sneaker 运动鞋
flip-flop 人字拖
scarf 围巾
wedding dress/gown 婚纱
sporty 运动服
down jacket 羽绒服
pullover 套头衫
shorts 短裤
slippers 拖鞋
jersey 球衫
glove 手套
tuxedo 无尾礼服
T-shirt T恤
hoodie 帽衫
V-neck 鸡心领
pyjama 睡衣
sandal 凉鞋
belt 皮带
bowtie 领结

参考答案

模板套话和种类	Well, my favourite clothing style is casual clothing, which includes a wide range of selections, such as T-shirts, jeans, sporty outfits and so on.
频率	Basically speaking, I wear them almost every day, since I am still a college student, and casual clothes fit my status pretty well.
原因	I like wearing casual clothes for a few reasons.
观点 1 客观	Firstly, I consider that casual clothes are pretty comfortable/cosy/flexible, simply because wearing casual clothes like T-shirts and shorts help me cope freely with my daily life issues, like walking, jogging, climbing stairs and so on.
主观	I am a sporty person, if I wear formal clothes like a suit, it would really make me feel uncomfortable.
观点 2	Besides, I also feel that a casual clothing style is appropriate for me to fit in/blend in with my age group.
客观	For most of my peers at school, casual clothes are mainstream for them.
主观	And wearing clothes with designs or graphic patterns makes me look more confident and energetic.

观点 3	Most importantly, the biggest reason for casual clothes is that they are totally and utterly affordable.
客观	Normally, a T-shirt only costs me roughly 50 Yuan.
主观	And I can easily catch up with the cutting-edge trend without paying a fortune.
结论	Generally, that's why I want to talk about casual clothes.

顺便准备

特殊场合的衣装：Describe a piece of clothing you will wear on a special occasion.

Simon 的知识扩展

Group Buying/Purchasing 团购

简介：Group buying means if a certain number of people are signing up for the same item, the discount or price reduction will be available for all.

盛行原因：
1. It has great money value, which is attractive for bargain shoppers.（优惠的价格）
2. Those group buying websites provide refund service after they expire.（支持过期退款）
3. The business provides undifferentiated service.（商家提供无差异化的服务）
4. Heaps of updated information comes up all the time.（每日有大量商家信息更新）
5. It makes a triple-win situation for merchants, group buying websites and consumers.（实现三赢的局面）

喜欢的餐厅

53 Describe your favourite restaurant.

You should say: what it is and where it is
how often do you go there
what kind of food do you have there
and explain why you like this restaurant.

题目分析

餐厅种类和名称如下：

cafeteria/buffet restaurant 自助餐厅
eatery/canteen 餐厅
western-style restaurant 西餐厅
Szechuan-style cuisine 四川风味
Sushi Train 回转寿司
food court 美食广场
bakery 面包店
theme restaurant 主题餐厅
chafing dish restaurant 火锅店
Mini Hot Pot 迷你涮涮锅
snack bar 小吃店
cafe 咖啡馆

参考答案

模板套话	Well, the restaurant I want to talk about with you is called Sushi Train, which is a Japanese style restaurant specialising in sushi and sashimi. The location, basically, is pretty handy, which is the ground floor of a shopping mall called "New Gate", and it only takes me 5 minutes to walk from where I work.
频率	Normally speaking, whenever I am in a rush for lunch, it is my first choice, since I only have one hour for the lunch break.
食物	Apart from severing sushi, they also provide a variety of special dishes, such as sashimi, udon noodle, miso soup and so on.
原因	I love Sushi Train for several reasons.
观点 1	Firstly, the food there is really healthy and nutritious.
客观	Since it is made of rice, veggies and seafood, it provides all sorts of nutrition, such as vitamins, protein and energy.
主观	In such a short time, I don't fancy junk food, and sushi meets my requirement for nutrition.
观点 2	Besides，I also feel that the environment is fairly customer-oriented.
客观	It is a kind of buffet with a revolving conveyor presenting all types of sushi in front of every customer.
主观	I don't need to take time to order or wait, it is ready-to-serve.
观点 3	More importantly, I always find the location handy,
客观	simply because I need to finish my lunch as soon as possible, so my selection is confined to the same building where I am working.
主观	It only takes me two minutes by elevator, so it is actually relaxing to eat at such a place.
结论	Generally, that's why Sushi Train is my favourite restaurant.

顺便准备

特殊聚餐： Describe a special meal you want to enjoy with other people.

You should say: what the meal is
where you want to have this meal
who you want to enjoy it with
and explain why you want to talk about this meal.

喜欢的国外食物

54 Describe your favourite foreign food.

You should say: which country does it come from
where you can get it
what kind of food it is
and explain further why you like it.

题目分析

国外的食物种类有很多，以下列举一些以供考生参考：

spaghetti 意大利面	pasta 通心粉	lasagna 千层面
steak 牛排	sushi(roll) 寿司（卷）	sashimi 生鱼片
sake 清酒	sushi train 回转寿司	tempura 天妇罗
udon 乌冬面	miso soup 味增汤	teriyaki 照烧
bibimbap 石锅拌饭	kimchi 泡菜	cold noodle 冷面
fried rice cake 炒年糕	barbecue 烧烤	curry 咖喱
Pat Thai 泰式炒米粉	Tom Yam Kung 冬阴功汤	kebab 土耳其烤肉

参考答案

模板套话	Well, the foreign food I want to share with you is sushi, which is the symbol of Japanese food, it is regarded as the most healthy food in the world.
地点	Basically, it can be easily found in many kinds of places, mainly at Japanese restaurants, or at convenience stores, supermarkets and cafeterias.
内容	The food is a combination of different veggies and seafood with rice, such as cucumber, seaweed, salmon, shrimp and so on.
原因	I love sushi for several reasons.
观点 1	Firstly, I think sushi is pretty handy.
客观	Sushi comes in a roll or in a box, it is very convenient to take away.
主观	Occasionally, I need to hurry to class, so I can finish my lunch as soon as possible.
观点 2	Besides, I also think sushi is nutritious.
客观	It provides us with all sorts of daily essential nutrition, such as vitamins, protein, minerals, fiber, and it is low in fat and calories.
主观	I am currently trying to lose weight, so it is perfect to feed myself and worry-free regarding weight gain.
观点 3	Most importantly, I always feel the price is totally and utterly affordable.

客观	It only costs me roughly 20 yuan for a mean on average, and it is a real bargain compared with other options.
主观	I am a poor student with limited pocket money and on a tight budget, so the cheaper, the better.
结论	Generally, that's why I want to talk about sushi with you.

顺便准备

亲手做的东西：Describe something you made by youreIf.

寿司的制作工艺

Step One: place a bamboo mat on the table.（放一个竹垫）
Step Two: nori, which is a thin sheet of seaweed, is ideal for rolling sushi.（铺上海苔）
Step Three: spread sticky rice evenly on the nori.（放上米饭）
Step Four: put vegetables(cucumber; avocado; carrots) and sashimi-grade fish(salmon; squid; jellyfish; cuttlefish) onto the rice.（铺上不同的蔬菜和海鲜）
Step Five: wrap it into a roll and cut it into pieces with a sharp knife.（卷起来，然后切段）
Step Six: dip them with the wasabi and soy sauce.（蘸着芥末和酱油）

Part Three

两个选一个

典型问题

Do you prefer buying domestic goods or imported goods?
Do you prefer eating at home or at a restaurant?
Do you prefer shopping online or at a real shop?

回答策略

高分公式：起 - 承 - 接 - 反 - 转 - 合
起：Personally, I think…
承：Simply because…
接：For example…
反：Without…
转：On the other hand,…
合：So generally,…

经典例题

55 Do you prefer shopping online or in a real store?

起	Well, mostly, I prefer shopping online,
承	simply because it is very convenient to shop online, prices are lower, the quality is trustworthy and the delivery service is quick.
接	For example, the price is 20 % less than the market price, besides, something you ordered in the morning, you can get delivered the following day.
反	If I go window-shopping to real stores, it might be a lot of trouble, since I will have to visit different places, but if I shop online, I can save time by doing comparison sitting in front of a computer.
转	Yet, for some items, like clothes, I guess it is more reliable to try them on to decide which size fit me best.
合	So generally, online shopping is more desirable.

改变类

典型问题

How has people's way of shopping changed?
How has people's way of eating changed?

回答策略

对以前和现在的不同情况进行比较：
Generally speaking, people used to…in a traditional and conventional way, such as…

But now, an increasing number of people, especially youngsters tend to…in a more diversified way, including…, simply because our way of life has been deeply transformed by the internet and technology.

经典例题

56 How has people's way of shopping changed?

Well, people used to shop in traditional shopping places, like a department store, a grocery or a street stall(路边摊).

But now, consumers' shopping habits have been transformed by the internet and e-commerce, and more people tend to shop on the internet or go shopping in foreign counties, such as the States or France.

区别类

典型问题

What are the differences between men's and women's shopping habits?

What are the differences between shopping online and shopping at a real store?

What are the differences between big stores and small stores?

回答策略

找到两者之间的不同之处，然后进行比较：

Compared with A, B tends to be…

Unlike A, B is more/less likely to be…

A is…, while B is more/less likely to be…

经典例题

57 What are the differences between men's and women's shopping habits?

Compared with men, women are probably more partial towards shopping, and they are more willing to spend an excessive amount of time on shopping.

Unlike women, men are more likely to be target-oriented or purpose-driven when they go shopping, and they might find shopping laborious.

Men probably have more interests in stuff like electronic products or cars, while women focus more on household stuff or clothes.

观点类

典型问题

Is it popular to buy imported goods in your country?
Why do some people like buying luxury goods?
Why do some people like shopping online?
Do people today eat too much fast food?
Should children learn how to cook?

回答策略

总分结构：

- In terms of..., I think that...
- When it comes to..., I just think...
- I feel/find that...
- Regarding..., my point is that...
- Personally, I believe that...

然后使用 Firstly, Besides 和 More importantly 来给出至少两个观点。

经典例题

Why do some people like buying luxury goods?

人们喜欢购买奢侈品的原因可能是：

- ✓ peer pressure 攀比
- ✓ celebrity effect 明星效应
- ✓ values advocated by brand culture 品牌背后的价值观
- ✓ symbolise social status/wealth/power 象征社会地位 / 财富 / 权力
- ✓ perfect match for one's temperament 与自己气质匹配
- ✓ stand for premium quality and workmanship 代表一流的质量和做工
- ✓ people can have a strong sense of fulfilment 一种成就感
- ✓ chase after the high ROR(return of return) or ROI (return on investment) 追求高回报率
- ✓ might appreciate with time 有升值的空间
- ✓ a way of rewarding or stimulating 一种自我激励的方式

核心词汇

购物饮食

shopping mall/center 购物中心
convenience store 便利店
online shopping 网上购物
stall 小摊
boutique 精品店
fruit market 水果市场
snack bar 小吃店
cafeteria/eatery/canteen 餐厅
counterfeit/copycat/knockoff 山寨货
commercial complex 商场
grocery store 杂货店
group purchase 团购
auction 拍卖
name brand 名牌
food court 美食街
bakery 面包店
take-away 打包
department store 百货商店
outlets 品牌折扣店
purchasing agent 代购人
flea market 跳蚤市场
luxury goods 奢侈品
buffet 自助餐
cafe 咖啡厅
feast 盛宴

衣服

leisurewear 休闲服
leggings 紧身裤
cardigan 开衫
skinny jeans 紧身牛仔裤
sneaker 运动鞋
flip-flop 人字拖
scarf 围巾
wedding dress/gown 婚纱
sportswear 运动服
down jacket 羽绒服
pullover 套头衫
shorts 短裤
slipper 拖鞋
jersey 球衫
glove 手套
tuxedo 无尾礼服
T-shirt T 恤
hoodie 风帽衣
V-neck 鸡心领
pyjamas 睡衣
sandal 凉鞋
belt 皮带
bow tie 领结

食物

congee 粥
cookies/biscuit 饼干
preserved egg 皮蛋
soy milk 豆奶
lolly 棒棒糖
sweet dumpling 元宵
yum cha 广式饮茶
instant noodle 方便面
spring roll 春卷
appetiser 开胃菜
soybean milk 豆浆
steamed bun 馒头
rice dumpling 粽子
dim sum 点心
sausage 香肠
shark fin 鱼翅
egg tart 蛋挞
yoghurt 酸奶
steamed stuffed bun 包子
wonton 云吞
preserved vegetables 酱腌菜

肯德基 / 麦当劳

Big Mac 巨无霸
Family Big Box 全家桶
Mashed Potatoes 土豆泥
set meal/combo 套餐
pudding 布丁
straw 吸管
French fries 炸薯条
Nugget 上校鸡块
Sprite 雪碧
sundae 圣代
ketchup 番茄酱
Cheese Burger 芝士堡
Chicken Drumsticks 小鸡腿
ice-cream cone 甜筒
milk shake 奶昔
beverage 饮料

外国餐

spaghetti 意大利面	pasta 通心粉	lasagna 千层面
steak 牛排	sushi(roll) 寿司（卷）	sashimi 生鱼片
sake 清酒	sushi train 回转寿司	tempura 天妇罗
udon 乌冬面	miso soup 味增汤	teriyaki 照烧
bibimbap 石锅拌饭	kimchi 泡菜	cold noodle 冷面
fried rice cake 炒年糕	barbecue 烧烤	curry 咖喱
Pat Thai 泰式炒米粉	Tom Yam Kung 冬阴功汤	kebab 土耳其烤肉

营养类

nutrition 营养	nutritious 营养的	healthcare products 保健品
organic 有机类	carbohydrate 碳水化合物	vitamin 维生素
protein 蛋白质	fiber 纤维	energy 能量
fat 脂肪	calorie 卡路里	antioxidant 抗氧化剂
calcium 钙	Low GI 低血糖	oily 油的
greasy 油腻的	MSG(monosodium glutamate) 味精	

hogwash oil/second-hand cooking oil 地沟油

家具

bunk bed 高低床	closet/wardrobe 衣柜	shoe rack 鞋架
swivel chair 转椅	nightstand 床头柜	dresser 化妆台
bookcase 书柜	wine cabinet 酒柜	drop-leaf table 折叠桌
folding guest bed 折叠床	sofa bed 沙发床	IKEA 宜家

ready-to-assemble furniture 自行组装的家具

第六节 Fitness and Environment

Part Two

考场还原

核心话题

① 健康的生活方式：Describe a person who has a healthy lifestyle.

② 积极的转变：Describe a positive change you want to make in your life.

③ 喜欢的户外运动：Describe your favourite outdoor activity.

衍生话题

① 对健康有益的事物：Describe something good for your health.

② 对健康有益的活动：Describe something you do to keep healthy.

③ 保护环境的行动：Describe something you can do to protect our environment.

④ 一种噪音：Describe a kind of noise.

分类剖析

健康类

健康的生活习惯和积极的转变

Describe a healthy lifestyle and a positive change.

题目分析

好的生活习惯和积极的转变可以从以下几个方面进行分析：

* 生活规律 (regular life routine and biological clock)

以前	I used to stay up till late night and oversleep in the morning.
现在	But now I want to maintain a disciplined lifestyle, which is early to bed and early to rise.
好处	I could recharge my battery completely and be more vitalised for the whole day's activities.

* 劳逸结合 (achieve a balance between work and rest)

以前	I used to be sedentary, sitting in front of a computer screen all day long and avoiding outdoor activities.
现在	But now I need to breathe more fresh air and stretch out my body by doing some aerobic exercise, such as jogging, cycling or just walking.
好处	It is a great opportunity to get in touch with nature and keep fit.

* 健康饮食 (well-rounded dietary habits or eating patterns)

以前	I used to be addicted to junk food, which is pretty oily and greasy.
现在	But now I am thinking of changing my diet pattern, and I ought to have more veggies and less meat/more home-made food and less eat-out/more organic foods and less man-made ones.
好处	It is surely beneficial for my cardiovascular system and reduces stress on the body.

* 与人沟通 (interpersonal communication)

以前	I used to be a nerd living in my own sphere, and not blending in with other fellows.
现在	But now I am longing to interact/mingle/share/get along with different types of people, enjoying each other's company.
好处	I believe that I could enlarge my social circle and find a sense of belonging.

* 远离不良习惯 (keep away from bad habits)

以前	I used to be addicted to such things as smoking, alcohol and gambling.
现在	But now I would like to quit them, and escape from the control of those bad habits.
好处	I am able to have physical fitness and mental wellness.

一个按照健康生活方式生活的人，就应当具备以上的几个特点。

相关词汇：

regular exercise 经常锻炼
aerobics 有氧运动
sedentary lifestyle 久坐的生活方式
health overdraft 透支健康
brain worker 脑力劳动者
fitness centre/gym 健身中心
organic food 有机食物
binge drinking 酗酒
overweight 超重
hogwash oil 地沟油
MSG(monosodium glutamate) 味精
well-balanced and well-rounded 均衡和全面的

喜欢的户外运动

Describe your favourite outdoor activity.

题目分析

与户外运动相关的词汇如下：

backpacker tour 背包游
self-driving tour 自驾游
jogging 慢跑
hiking 徒步旅行
climbing mountains 爬山
camping 露营
cycling 骑自行车
playing hula hoop 呼拉圈
walking 散步
dog walking 遛狗
skateboarding 滑板
playing paintball 彩弹射击
sandbagging 沙包
orienteering 定向越野
rafting 漂流
going fishing 垂钓
surfing 冲浪
BMX(bicycle motocross) 小轮车
parkour 跑酷
aerobics 有氧运动
playing Tai Chi 打太极拳
martial arts 武术

户外运动的好处：

- keep fit and relieve stress(保持健身和减压)
- provide us a great opportunity to escape from daily life routine/cliché and crowds(远离千篇一律的生活 / 城市的喧嚣)
- provide aerobic exercise and fresh air(有氧运动和新鲜空气)
- get a sense of freedom by returning to nature(体验回归自然的自由感觉)
- Some outdoor activities, like paintball, orienteering and rafting, call for cooperation and coordination among team members. We cultivate friendship and team spirit through reaching a common goal regardless of age and occupation.
  某些户外运动，如彩弹球、定向越野和漂流，都需要团队合作。通过这些户外运动，我们培养了不同职业和年龄阶段的人的友谊和团队合作精神。
- People enjoy exploring the unknown and wilderness, simply because some outdoor activities are full of challenges, freshness and stimulation, such as a backpacker tour, mountain climbing or a self-driving tour.
  人们被探索未知的活动，如背包游，爬山和自驾游所带来的挑战和新鲜感所深深吸引。
- Through outdoor activities, we can overcome our inner fears and gain confidence and self-belief.
  通过户外运动，我们可以克服心中的恐惧，收获自信。

以下户外运动话题均可以结合自行车运动来回答：

- Describe an outdoor activity. ——户外骑自行车
- Describe something you can do to protect the environment.——绿色出行，保护环境 / 低碳和零排放 (low-carbon and zero-emission)
- Describe what you would do if you had one-day off.——周末骑自行车出游，远离城市喧嚣 (escaping from urban life)
- Describe a sport you like to watch.——环法自行车赛：最有影响的自行车赛事 (Tour de France: the most influential cycling sport event)
- Describe your favourite transportation/a vehicle you want to buy.——自行车也属于交通工具，还不怕堵车 (avoiding traffic congestion)

自行车运动的好处：

- perfect way of getting aerobic exercise(有氧运动)
- eco-friendly, responding to the call of living a low-carbon and zero-emission lifestyle(响应低碳生活的号召)
- appreciating the view better on a tour in the open air(更好地欣赏沿途风景)
- avoiding traffic congestion(避免堵车)
- a ride instead of walking for short-distance commuting(短途代步工具)
- a foldable bicycle is handy to carry around(折叠自行车很便携)
- affordable(买得起)

环保类

保护环境的行动

Describe something you can do to protect our environment.

题目分析

今天，我们处在微环保时代 (micro environmental protection era)，只要从自己做起、从身边力所能及的事情做起，我们就可以尽一份环保之力，例如：

- turning off unnecessary light whenever possible(关掉不必要的灯)
- avoiding disposable utensils to prevent plastics pollution, including chopsticks and take-out boxes(拒绝使用一次性餐盒和筷子)
- using fabric shopping bags instead of plastic bags(布袋替代塑料袋)
- using public transportation as much as possible(尽量使用公共交通)
- using the stairs instead of the lift(爬楼梯替代乘电梯)
- rubbish recycling and separation(使用垃圾回收和分类)
- car pooling(拼车)
- raising people's awareness of preserving water and forest resources(提高节约水资源和森林资源的意识)
- rejecting the consumption of bottled water and chewing gum(拒绝瓶装水和口香糖)

一种噪音

Describe a kind of noise.

You should say: where the noise comes from
how you feel about the noise
how you deal with it
and explain why do you want to talk about it.

题目分析

防止噪音的措施：

- complaining to the person who made the noise(向当事人抱怨)
- making a complaint or calling a newspaper hot-line(向报社投诉)
- installing double-paned/double-glazed window(安装双层窗户)
- wearing a noise-proof earplug(戴防噪耳塞)
- moving away from the noisy neighbourhood(搬家)

噪音的危害：

Noise poses a great threat to our lives.

- Noise can impair hearing.
  噪音可以损害听力。
- It can interfere with people's sleep, especially late at night.
  噪音会影响人们的睡眠，尤其是在深夜的时候。
- People might get furious because of the noise.
  噪音会让人发怒。
- People's wellbeing can be undermined and psychological problems caused.
  噪音会破坏人们的幸福生活并导致心理疾病。
- Noise can upset the whole neighbourhood.
  噪音会影响整个邻里。

Part Three

流行类

典型问题

What is the most popular way of keeping healthy in your country?
What are the common noises where you live?
What is the most popular way of relaxing in your country?

回答策略

一分为二，辩证统一：
Well, it depends.
For…, I think…is quite popular for them, such as…, simply because…
Yet for…, I guess they might fancy/have a fancy for…, including…, that's because…
For both,…

经典例题

58 What is the most popular way of keeping healthy in your country?

Well, it depends on the different age groups.
Young people fancy keeping fit in more energetic ways, like playing sports and taking part in all sorts of social events.

Yet the elderly might choose from a wider range of selections to keep healthy, like having a more well-rounded diet or recipe, or focus more on healthcare products, like fish oil, vitamin pills and things like that.

改变类

典型问题

How has people's way of exercising changed in your country?
How has people's way of keeping healthy changed?

回答策略

对以前和现在的不同情况进行比较：
Generally speaking, people used to…in a traditional and conventional way, such as…
But now, an increasing number of people, especially youngsters tend to…in a more diversified way, including…, simply because our way of life has been deeply transformed by the internet and technology.

经典例题

59 How has people's way of exercising changed?

Well, people used to exercise in traditional ways, like taking outdoor actives or doing a physical job.
Yet, now, people have a wider range of selections, such as body-building at a gym or fitness centre; besides, some ways of exercising are becoming popular among urbanites(都市人), including yoga, salsa, Pilates and so on.

观点类

典型问题

Do you think that today's people get enough exercises?
Should public sports facilities be free of charge?
How can children be encouraged to adopt healthy habits?

How could government promote a healthy lifestyle?
What's the source of city noise?

回答策略

总分结构：

- In terms of..., I think that...
- When it comes to..., I just think that...
- I feel/find that...
- Regarding..., my point is that...
- Personally, I believe that...

然后使用 Firstly, Besides 和 More importantly 来给出至少两个观点。

经典例题

60 How could government promote a healthy lifestyle?

Well, from my perspective, I believe that government can do lots of things to encourage the public to live a healthier life.

Firstly, they should instil the concept and idea of a healthy lifestyle in a number of ways, such as making TV programs to teach healthier eating and show the importance of getting physical exercise.

Besides, government also needs to establish well-equipped sports facilities for the public, including basketball courts, parks, stadiums, gymnasiums and other leisure facilities.

At the same time, these facilities need to be affordable to encourage more people to take advantage of them.

More importantly, they should also put on more restrictions on the consumption of tobacco and alcohol, or prohibit advertising campaigns for those products.

第七节 Housing and Places

Part Two

考场还原

核心话题

① 理想的居所：Describe your ideal housing.

② 美丽的公园/花园：Describe a beautiful park/garden.

③ 历史建筑：Describe a historical building.(结合旅游类话题)

④ 现代建筑：Describe a modern building.

衍生话题

① 喜欢的房间：Describe your favourite room.

② 小时候住的地方：Describe the place you lived during your childhood.

③ 安静的地方：Describe a peaceful place.

④ 傍水之地：Describe a place near a lot of water.

⑤ 想购买的昂贵物：Describe something expensive you want to buy if you have the money.

⑥ 户外放松的地方：Describe an open-air place you can relax yourself.

⑦ 休闲中心：Describe a leisure centre.

⑧ 对公众开放的地方：Describe a place open to the public.

⑨ 常去的地方：Describe a place you have often visited.

⑩ 一条街道：Describe a street.(结合商业步行街或者户外休闲)

分类剖析

参考解析

房屋和地点类话题主要集中在以下几个方面：

- House(户内)
- Park/Garden(户外)
- Building(建筑)

房屋类

理想的居所

61 Describe your ideal housing.

You should say: what it is and where it is
what kind of rooms it have
what the surroundings look like
and explain further why this house is ideal.

题目分析

回答这道题需要考生充分发挥自己想象力。当我们可以任意地选择居住地点和环境的时候，我们首先要能想象出一个具体的画面。比如说，我们可以想象居住地点在：

city center 市中心
seaside 海边
half way up a hill 半山腰
farm 农场
pasture land 牧场
resort 度假胜地
multicultural area 多元文化的地区

我们还可以想象居住环境是：

remote/distant 人烟稀少的
vibrant/dynamic 热闹的
serene/tranquil 安静的
convenient/handy 方便的

下面，我们来看一则摘自 www.domain.com.au 的房产信息，然后从中寻找一些灵感：

Perfectly poised to offer a lifestyle of absolute convenience, this two bedroom apartment presents an ideal opporturnity for market newcomers or investors to secure a superbly central, sought-after address promising rapid, direct access to the CBD. Set on the ground floor of a security block, surrounded by vibrant landscaped gardens, the apartment offers exceptional scope to update and personalise its comfortable, original interiors to taste.

从上则房产信息中，我们可以总结出以下句型和词汇：

perfectly poised to offer…	极佳的位置，可以提供……
market newcomers or investors	市场新人和投资者
a superbly central, sought-after address	绝对中心的、受欢迎的位置
ground floor	一楼
surrounded by…	被……所围绕
exceptional scope	绝佳的余地和范围
update and personalise	更新和改造
interior	内部

下面，我们再来看一座房屋的卖点介绍：

* Lounge enclosed by floor-to-ceiling glass
* Sunny undercover garden balcony
* Leafy garden views from most rooms
* Eat-in kitchen with modern appliances
* Original bathroom w/ bath and shower
* Double bedrooms, master with built-in
* Internal laundry, linen cupboard, LUG
* Steps to train station, shops and cafes

从上面的卖点介绍中，我们可以总结出以下句型和词汇：

lounge enclosed by…	客厅被……所环绕
floor-to-ceiling glass	落地窗
sunny undercover	阳光棚
leafy garden views	郁郁葱葱的花园景色
eat-in kitchen	可放餐桌吃饭的厨房
modern appliances	现代化电器
built-in/internal	内置的
linen cupboard	亚麻橱柜
steps to …	距离……仅有几步之遥

相信考生在看完以上原汁原味的描述后，应当知道该怎样回答前三问了。更重要的是，考生还能够提前熟悉国外租房或买房的常用表达，以便今后更快、更容易地融入当地生活。

回答这一道题，考生需要注意的是：

✓ 脑海中要形成一个理想居所的具体画面
✓ 要包含里外所有元素
✓ 要使用 would, could, might, should 等词汇

参考答案

模板套话	Well, the ideal house I want to tell you about is a villa, and I am always dreaming of living in a peaceful place near the sea, where I could breathe fresh air and enjoy an ocean view every day. To be more specific, the location I have in mind is Bondi Beach, which is one of the most famous beaches in Sydney. It is a convenient distance from every kind of public facility, such as the hospitals, schools, shopping malls, transportation and so on.
布局	Basically speaking, apart from the bedroom and living room, I'd like the interior laid out according to different functions. For entertainment, I want to have a video game room and a home theatre; for study, there should be a small library and a sunroom for reading; most importantly, it is really necessary to have a balcony to have a stunning ocean view from where I live.
环境	Just as I mentioned, I fancy a tranquil exterior environment, so when I step out of my house, I can feel happy walking around a garden with some features such as a pond, several vegetable plots and so on.
原因	I want to live in such a place for a few reasons.
观点 1	Firstly, I feel that such a place is my life-long dream.
客观	I have always had a vision that one day I could live away from the noisy city, in a tranquil and serene community, and it would be much better if I could have a great ocean view or garden view the second I open my window in the morning.
主观	I believe that I would be in a good mood as well.
观点 2	Besides, I think I could live a self-sufficient lifestyle.
客观	By this I mean, I could grow vegetables and fruits by myself, given that the food safety issue has been increasingly serious in China these days, we have been suffering from all sorts of poisonous foods.
主观	It will be fun and secure at the same time.
观点 3	Most importantly, I have always believed that such a place will be my haven.
客观	Given that I love playing video games and sports, I am longing for an entertainment room and basketball court in this house, or in my spare time, we could have a barbecue party in the yard.
主观	So, I could spoil myself and share great times with my friends and family member, since it would be spacious enough to accommodate all of them.
总结	Generally speaking, that's why I want to live in my ideal place.

与理想的居所紧密相关的是公园或花园的话题，因为后者对户外环境的描写也可以用来描述理想的居所。

地点类

美丽的公园/花园

62 Describe a beautiful park/garden.

You should say: where it is
what it looks like
what people do in this place
and explain why you like this place.

题目分析

花园里的元素：

blossoms 花丛
fountain 喷泉
bench 长椅
path 小路
woods 树林
pond 池塘
rockery 假山
shrub 灌木丛
pavilion 亭子
stream 小溪
swing 秋千

公园里的活动：

exercising 锻炼
going jogging 慢跑
flying a kite 放风筝
playing hide-and-seek 玩捉迷藏
having a picnic 野餐
dog walking 遛狗
going fishing 钓鱼
morning reading 晨读
taking a nap 打盹
cycling 骑自行车

下面，我们来看一个告示牌。这个告示牌矗立在悉尼歌剧院 (Sydney Opera House) 旁边的皇家植物园 (Royal Botanic Garden) 里面。上面的第一句话“Please walk on the grass”深深地吸引了许多人。我们可以从这个告示牌学到许多原汁原味的表达方式。比如说：...smell the roses, hug the trees, talk to the birds and picnic on the lawns.

从上面的告示牌中，我们可以总结出以下词汇：

botanical garden 植物园	domain 领域	preserve 保护
Palm Grove Centre 棕榈林中心	sponsor 赞助者	benefactor 捐助者

至此，我们已经积累了足够的词汇来回答前三问，即描述公园/花园的环境和人们的活动。而对于为什么要来这个地方，我们可以通过以下的一个流程图来做一些讨论：

原因：I like this place and we need some outdoor places to do activities because in our normal life, people get used to…（人们习惯过着一种……的生活方式）

⇨ **People get used to living a sedentary lifestyle（人们习惯了久坐不动的生活方式）:**
表现：

✓ sitting in front of a computer all day long	电脑前坐一整天
✓ living an indoor lifestyle, to be a homebody	宅在家里
✓ being stuck in an office or classroom all the time	习惯于呆在办公室或教室里
✓ seldom interacting with peers	很少和其他人互动
✓ easily get into a bottleneck in life or study	生活或学习中常遇到瓶颈

⇨ **In this situation, we need (to)（这样的情况下，我们需要）:**

✓ fresh air	新鲜空气
✓ contact with nature	跟自然的接触
✓ an opportunity to appreciate the beauty surrounding us	欣赏周围的美景
✓ switching our mood	换一种心情
✓ escaping from our daily life routines/city crowds	远离千篇一律的生活/城市的喧嚣

⇨**So, we should（所以，我们应该）:**

✓ get/walk around	到处走走
✓ stretch out	伸伸胳膊动动腿
✓ pack a bag for hiking	背上背包去远足
✓ interact with friends and family	和家人或朋友互动
✓ get some exercise	做运动

⇨ **Then we could (get)（然后，我们可以）:**

✓ relaxation	休闲放松
✓ inner peace	内心的平静
✓ keep fit and be in good shape	保持健康和良好身材
✓ be inspired and in a good mood	获得灵感和好心情
✓ be revitalised and recharged	重新焕发活力
✓ sharing moments with loved ones	和家人朋友一起分享

以上的分析还可以用来回答旅游和健康类话题。

参考答案

模板套话	Well, the beautiful garden I want to share with you is the one in my community, which is only a five-minutes walk from where I live.
环境	In the garden, well, during spring and summer, you can see a lot of beautiful flowers, such as peonies, cherry blossoms, daisies and so on. Besides, it is enclosed by all sorts of trees and shrubs; in the middle of the garden, there is a wooden bridge with a stream flowing beneath it. Yet in autumn and winter, it has nothing but bare-branched trees.
活动	The garden is really essential for local residents' activities. People do lots of activities here, such as playing Tai Chi, walking their dogs, playing games and reading a book.
原因	I like this garden for a number of reasons.
观点 1	Firstly, this place is very peaceful and refreshing.
客观	The aroma and fragrance of those flowers provide me with tremendous freshness and purity.
主观	Every morning, when I am walking through it, it puts me into a good mood for a brand new day.
观点 2	Besides, I also feel I can relax in such a place.
客观	This place is like an oasis in the middle of the city. You know, we get used to living a sedentary lifestyle, and we need to get some fresh air by doing some outdoor activities.
主观	Whenever I have a bottleneck in my studies or life, I like to get around and be inspired by nature, which is also a good way of relaxing.
观点 3	More importantly, the public needs such a place for leisure activities.
客观	Local residents, especially kids and senior citizens, need a place and room for sharing and interacting, and this garden is the perfect place.
主观	It is always good to see people relaxed and happy in this garden, and having contact with nature is always an important thing for city dwellers.
结论	Generally, that's why I find this garden very impressive.

历史的建筑

63 Describe a historical building.

You should say: what it is and where it is
when it was built
what kind of building it is
and explain further why you like to talk about it.

题目分析

中国古建筑种类：

temple 庙
monastery 寺院
palace 宫殿
bell tower 钟楼
drum tower 鼓楼
pagoda 塔
attic 阁
pavilion 亭
cave 洞穴
academy of traditional learning 传统书院

中国历史遗迹：

Summer Palace 颐和园
Forbidden City 紫禁城
The Temple of Heaven 天坛
Terra-Cotta Warriors 兵马俑
Su Zhou traditional garden 苏州园林
Mogao Grottoes 莫高窟
The ancient town of Lijiang 丽江古镇
The storied building of Fujian 福建土楼

古建筑结构：

structure 结构
layout 结构
rooftop 屋顶
ornamental column/pillar 华表
memorial archway 牌坊
stone tablet 石碑
stone guardian lions 石狮
brick and tile structure 砖瓦结构
wooden structure 木质结构
courtyard building 庭院式的建筑

对历史建筑的描述应该集中在：

- 历史渊源 historical background
- 建筑特点 main characteristics
- 名气地位 reputation and fame

参考答案

模板套话 Well, the historical building I want to share with you is the Great Wall, which is one of the most famous old constructions in China, and it is also the must-see travel destination for almost all foreign visitors who come to China. The actual location of the Great Wall is along the east-to-west historical borders of northern China. It is spread out among several provinces of China. However, the most famous and well preserved Great Wall is located in Beijing, in the north of the city.

时间 Its origin goes back to as early as 7th century BC. The emperor Qin Shi Huang made the most famous one during 221 BC, and then the Great Wall was reconstructed and rebuilt by a number of dynasties over the following centuries.

功能 Its construction is basically bricks, stones or wood. Initially, the wall was built for the protection of northern borders from the invasion of other ethnic groups. The Great Wall could probably also be used as a way of transportation across the country.

原因	I like to talk about the Great Wall for a few reasons.
观点 1	Firstly, the Great Wall is an amazing and magnificent building.
客观	It is regarded as one of the seven wonders of the world. According to some sources, the Great Wall can even be spotted/recognised from outer space by astronauts as a man-made object.
主观	I have been there once. When I was on top of the Wall, I had a far-ranging(广阔的) view for hundreds of miles, it was one of the most breath-taking scenes I had ever seen.
观点 2	Besides, I also feel that the Great Wall is the symbol of Chinese culture.
客观	For thousands of years, the Great Wall has symbolised the spirit of the Chinese. Because of its greatness and majesty(雄伟壮丽), it represents the integrity and tenacity(坚忍不拔) of the Chinese.
主观	That's why we are all proud of the Great Wall.
观点 3	More importantly, I feel that the Great Wall is attractive for visitors from all over the world.
客观	Just as a proverb says, "One cannot claim himself as a true man unless he has reached the Great Wall(不到长城非好汉)."
主观	And I believe that if you ever go there, you will definitely be impressed and amazed.
结论	So generally, that's why when it comes to old buildings, the Great Wall is the first one that comes up in my mind.

现代的建筑

64 Describe a modern building.

You should say: what it is and where it is
what kind of building it is
what it looks like
and explain why you want to talk about it.

题目分析

现代建筑相关词汇如下：

gymnasium 体育馆
stadium 体育场
skyscraper 摩天大楼
exhibition center 展览中心
commercial complex 商业综合体
museum 博物馆
art gallery 艺术馆
mansion 大厦
real estate 房地产
cityscape 城市景观
skyline 天际线
memorial hall 纪念堂
observation/viewing deck 观景台
Central Business District 中央商务区

对现代建筑的描述应该集中在：

- 外观 exterior appearance
- 内部 interior design
- 功能 function and purpose

参考答案

模板套话 Well, the modern building I want to tell you about is called the Bird's Nest, or also officially known as the National Stadium, which is one of the most recognised buildings in China these days. It is located in Beijing, and it used to be the host stadium for the 2008 Beijing Olympic Games.

功能 Its purpose, apart from hosting the opening ceremony, was to hold all the track-and-field sport events. Currently, several years after the Olympic Games, the Bird's Nest is often used for holding concerts(演唱会) or soccer matches.

外观 Basically, it looks like a bird's nest from a distance, but when you approach it, you see it is made of steel and concrete(钢筋混凝土). As the Olympic Stadium, it has a capacity of more than 90,000 people.

原因 I'd like to talk about it for a few reasons.

观点 1 Firstly, the design is pretty meaningful.

客观 The initial design of a bird's nest stands for a cradle, which is the vehicle for creating new hope. And now, it is the symbol of Beijing, since the image has been deeply rooted in people' minds.

主观 I like it, because it is full of inspiration and creativity, and it has won awards as one of the most impressive buildings in the world.

观点 2 Besides, I also feel that it is a symbol of China.

客观 As it were the first Olympic Games ever held in China, the year 2008 greatly inspired and encouraged the Chinese. This event left a lasting impression in our mind, and the Bird's Nest is more like a totem or representative than just a building.

主观 Even today, this building always reminds us of the pride and glory we used to have.

观点 3 More importantly, I feel the Bird's Nest is a great leisure centre for the public.

客观 After the Olympic Games, it was converted into a leisure and sports complex, we can listen to a concert or watch a football game there. Besides, many kinds of leisure events are being held quite often as well, last winter, we went to the "happy ice and snow season", which was a snow carnival(嘉年华) with all sorts of winter games and festivities.

主观 The building itself has been given different roles at different times, which is a great way to appreciate the different aspects of a building.

结论 So generally, that's why I want to talk about the National Stadium.

总结

分析完以上的四道房屋地点类核心话题，请大家再去思考一下房屋地点类的所有衍生话题，它们基本上都可以回归到我们以上的论述中，包括：

a place near water　　a peaceful place　　a favourite room
a leisure centre　　an open-air place　　a street
a place to listen to music　　a place where you can learn history

Part Three

两个选一个

典型问题

Do you prefer living in a big city or in the countryside?
Do you prefer relaxing at home or outside?

回答策略

高分公式：起 - 承 - 接 - 反 - 转 - 合
起：Personally, I think...
承：Simply because...
接：For example...
反：Without...
转：On the other hand,...
合：So generally,...

经典例题

65 Do you prefer relaxing at home or outside?

起　Well, mostly, I prefer relaxing outside,

承　simply because I would like to wind down by being involved with others through activities like playing ball, going shopping and travelling.

接 For example, I am a big fan of swimming, and it is apparently impossible for me to relax at home.

反 If I try to relax at home, the only entertainment for me is to surf the internet or watch TV programs. Actually I am already bored with being a couch potato.

转 Yet, I do agree that sleeping at home is an efficient way of relaxation.

合 But, generally, I prefer the latter one to the first one.

改变类

典型问题

How has people's way of relaxing changed recently?
How have people's living conditions changed recently?

回答策略

对以前和现在的不同情况进行比较：
Generally speaking, people used to…in a traditional and conventional way, such as…
But now, an increasing number of people, especially youngsters tend to…in a more diversified way, including…, simply because our way of life has been deeply transformed by the internet and technology.

经典例题

66 How has people's way of relaxing changed recently?

Well, in the past, people used to relax in a traditional way, such as by playing cards, watching TV, reading the newspaper or doing sports.
But now, an increasing number of people, especially youngsters tend to kick back on the internet, including playing computer games, surfing the internet, catching up with their friends and so on.
Besides, today's people have a wider range of selections for their amusement, like travelling to different countries, playing mafia or paintball, or some other similarly trendy activities.

流行类

典型问题

What is the most popular way of relaxation in your country?

What is the most popular outdoor activity in your country?

回答策略

一分为二，辩证统一：

Well, it depends.

For…, I think…is quite popular for them, such as…, simply because…

Yet for…, I guess they might fancy/have a fancy for…, including…, that's because…

For both,…

经典例题

67 What is the most popular outdoor activity in your country?

Well, it depends.

I think men prefer something more energetic, such as playing basketball, soccer, extreme sports, and activities like that.

Yet women might fancy relaxing activities, including playing badminton, walking, jogging and so on.

区别类

典型问题

What are the different ways of relaxing between youngster and elders/men and women?

What are the differences between Chinese architecture and foreign architecture?

What are the differences between historical buildings and modern buildings?

What are the differences between indoor activities and outdoor activities?

回答策略

找到两者之间的不同之处，然后进行比较：

Compared with A, B tends to be…

Unlike A, B is more/less likely to be…

A is…, while B is more/less likely to be…

经典例题

68 What are the differences between historical buildings and modern buildings?

Unlike historical buildings, modern buildings tend to be more practical, since people need to live and work in well-equipped and well-furnished modern buildings, like residential hall, office building and so on.

Compared with modern buildings, historical buildings have more value in regard to culture, tradition and custom, including temples, drum/bell towers and ancient palaces.

More than that, historical buildings are more likely to be traditionally designed and built, with more decoration, while modern buildings tend to be plainer and more westernised, such as skyscrapers, commercial complexes, art galleries and so on.

对比的方面包括：

- 外观 exterior appearance
- 内部功能 inside function
- 价值 value
- 历史 history
- 作用 purpose

好坏处类

典型问题

What are the pros and cons of old buildings?

What are the pros and cons of living in a big city?

回答策略

好处：Doing…can be beneficial in many ways.

Firstly,…

Besides,…

More importantly,…

坏处：Yet, when it comes to the drawbacks, I have to say that..., and if we don't take steps, like..., it would be more serious.

经典例题

69 What are pros and cons of old buildings?

Well, basically, old buildings can be beneficial in some ways, such as preserving culture and tradition.

Besides, it is also advantageous in disseminating knowledge, since an old building is a faithful monument for preserving what transpired in the past.

Yet I have to say old buildings might spoil the appearance of the cityscape. In addition, old buildings can't be efficiently utilised, since today's people focus more on living and working. Sometimes what they need cannot be provided by old buildings.

观点类

典型问题

Should the government and media encourage old people to get involved in outdoor activities?

Should people partake in outdoor activities?

Should public leisure centres be free of charge?

Why don't some people like doing outdoor activities?

What kinds of factors will people consider when they choose housing?

回答策略 1

一分为二，分两种情况：

每种情况给出一个条件，每种情况给出一个结果。

Well, it depends.

For...

Yet for...

经典例题

70 Should public leisure centres be free of charge?

No, I don't think that they should be free of charge, simply because they need a funding

source for management and maintenance. Besides, income is also needed for updating equipment and facilities.
Yet for certain groups of people, it is unreasonable to charge them, such as local residents and senior citizens, since they should take advantage of social benefits.

不应该免费，因为它们需要钱来满足以下需求：

management and maintenance	管理和维修
buy equipment and facility	更新设备和设施
pay for employees	发薪水
miscellaneous expenses	其他费用

但是，对于有些人来说应该免费，例如：

taxpayer	纳税人
indigenous residents	本地居民
senior citizens and kids	老人和儿童

回答策略 2

总分结构：
总：Well, people often…for a variety of…(将考官的问题转变成陈述句，后面加上 many/loads of/heaps of/a variety of/a wide range of 等)
分：such as/like/including...

经典例题

71 What kinds of factors will people consider when they choose housing?

Well, basically, people will take a number of factors into account when they buy houses, such as…

✓ location	地理位置
✓ price	价格
✓ house quality	房屋质量
✓ property developer	地产开发商
✓ room layout	房屋布局
✓ interior design	内部设计
✓ neighborhood landscape	小区环境
✓ property service management	物业管理
✓ supporting facilities	周围配套设施

第八节 Memories and Experiences

Part Two

考场还原

核心话题

① 兴奋的经历：Describe an exciting experience.

② 特殊场合的穿戴：Describe a piece of clothes or jewellery you wore on a special occasion.

③ 历史事件：Describe a historical event.

④ 经历的坏天气：Describe a bad weather you have experienced.

⑤ 一场婚礼：Describe a wedding.

⑥ 喜欢的照片：Describe your favourite photo.

⑦ 他人为你庆贺的场合：Describe an occasion when others celebrated for you.

⑧ 生气的场合：Describe an occasion when you got angry.

⑨ 丢失的东西：Describe something you lost.（结合电子产品话题）

⑩ 听外国音乐的场合：Describe an occasion when you listened to a foreign music.（结合音乐话题）

⑪ 获得他人帮助的经历：Describe an occasion when others helped you.（结合丢失的东西）

⑫ 家里的旧物件：Describe something old you kept in your family.

⑬ 电话对话：Describe a conversation over the telephone.

⑭ 获得的礼物：Describe a gift from others.

⑮ 收到的一封信：Describe a letter you received.

⑯ 人生最困难的时刻：Describe the most difficult time in your life.

⑰ 团体项目：Describe a group activity you joined with others.（结合旅行类 / 学习类话题）

⑱ 参加过的体育运动：Describe a sport or match you took part in before.（结合运动话题）

⑲ 童年旅行：Describe a journey you took in your childhood.

⑳ 童年时喜欢的书：Describe a book you liked to read in your childhood.

㉑ 童年故事中的人物：Describe a character in a childhood story.

㉒ 童年喜欢的玩具：Describe your favourite toy in your childhood.

㉓ 童年喜欢的游戏：Describe a game you liked to play in your childhood.

㉔ 童年乐事：Describe a happy childhood event.

衍生话题

① 让你开怀大笑的事情：Describe something that made you laugh.

② 需要礼貌的场合：Describe an occasion when you needed to be polite.

③ 体育赛事：Describe a sports event.

④ 超出预期时间的旅行：Describe a trip that was longer than your expectation.

⑤ 迟到的经历：Describe an occasion when you were late.

⑥ 家庭事件：Describe a family event.

⑦ 在家经历的有趣生活：Describe an interesting life you had before in your family.

⑧ 特别的生日庆祝：Describe a special birthday celebration.

⑨ 一种噪音：Describe a kind of noise.

⑩ 一天中最喜欢时刻：Describe your favourite time of day.

⑪ 他人的帮助：Describe support you received from others.

⑫ 收钱做礼物的经历：Describe an occasion when you received money as a gift.（结合出国留学或者压岁钱）

⑬ 他人的建议：Describe a piece of advice from others.

⑭ 曾经参加的俱乐部或小组：Describe a club or group you joined before.

⑮ 喜欢的天气：Describe your favourite weather.

分类剖析

参考解析

回忆和经历类话题可以说是 Simon 总结的八大核心场景中最天马行空的一类，因为考官可以针对考生的回忆和经历设计出无数个问题来。对于这类问题，考生很难把握，但仔细观察后，我们会发现考官的提问只针对两个方面：

1. What happened then（当时发生的事情）
2. How you felt then（当时的心情）

在备考时，考生要将主要精力集中在这两个方面。首先，考生要学会讲述一个发生在过去的事情，因此考生要特别注重过去时态的运用，这也会是考官重点注意的方面。

讲故事时会用到的关联词：

At the very beginning 最开始
And after that/Afterwards 后来
During/While… 在……期间
At the same time/Simultaneously/Meanwhile 同时
Since then/Ever since… 从那时起
In the end/Eventually 到最后

经历场合类

收到的一封信

72 Describe a letter you have received.

You should say: when that was
who wrote it
what the letter said
and explain further why you want to talk about it.

题目分析

书信种类：

love letter 情书　offer 通知书　business letter 商业信函
letter of complaint 抱怨信　invitation letter 邀请函　congratulation letter 祝贺信

故事情节：

我花了一个月的时间来整理我的留学申请材料，这期间我感到非常辛苦。最终，我拿到了我想去的那所大学的录取通知书，尽管是有条件的录取 (conditional offer)，但我仍然很激动，因为我看到了希望。但同时我也很担心，因为如果三个月内我不能通过雅思考试的话，我会很被动，所以我下定决心这次一定要通过雅思考试。（跟目前的实际情况结合起来会更有画面感）

故事情节构成：

故事背景（把考官带到故事中）
故事高潮（让考官听到重点）
故事结局（考生想表达的观点）

参考答案

模板套话	Well a letter I once received was the offer from Manchester University last month, which was very meaningful and exciting for me.
故事背景	At the very beginning, I had decided to study overseas; Manchester was my first choice, simply because I am a die-hard fan of Manchester United, and I was dreaming of having a chance to watch a soccer game at Old Trafford, which is the home court of MU.
故事发展	And then, I began the laborious preparation. I collected all the information they needed for my application, including my undergraduate transcript, three letters of recommendation, my personal statement, my study plan and things like that. It took me a month to do that, and I realised that studying overseas was not as easy as I thought.
故事高潮	Afterwards, one day on a weekend, I checked my email on my mobile phone while I was watching a film, and the moment I got my conditional offer from UM, I couldn't help being excited. Meanwhile, I got a lot of details about this offer, I learnt my study schedules, my tuition structure and subjects curricula.
故事结局	Back then, I had a strong feeling that all my efforts had paid off.（故事讲完了，接下来，考官想知道的是你为什么要讲述这封信。这时，你需要更多地描述自己当时的心情。在这一过程中，我们可以参照戏剧元素，例如冲突、起伏、纠结、圆满结局等。所以，拿到这封信之后，你的心理过程可以是：excited → worried → motivated → determined）
兴奋	At the very beginning, I was really thrilled, since I was on track to realise my dream.
担忧	Yet meanwhile, I was a little bit worried that the courses at UM might be demanding and I would need to work harder.
激励	Afterwards, I realised that only if I passed my IELTS examination in 3 months' time with a 6.5, could I get my full offer, so there was still a long way to go.
坚定	Eventually, I made up my mind that I wouldn't hold back no matter how difficult it would be. And I believe my dream will come true one day.
结论	So, that is why I want to talk about it.

心情相关词汇总结如下：

兴奋的，高兴的：excited/surprised/thrilled/cheerful/joyful
满足的：satisfied/blessed/favourable
感激的：grateful/thankful/appreciative
下决心的：determined/unwavering
受鼓舞的：motivated/encouraged/inspired
感动的：moved/touched/impressed
同情的：compassionate/sympathetic
焕发活力的：revitalised/refreshed/recharged
受打击的：frustrated/stricken
生气的：upset/mad/offended/provoked/furious
尴尬的：embarrassed/awkward
无奈的，无语的：speechless
绝望的：hopeless/desperate
失望的，失落的：disappointed/low/downhearted
忧郁的，沮丧的：blue/depressed
压力大的：stressful
紧张的：nervous/tense/strained/uptight
倒霉的，不幸的：hapless/unlucky/unfortunate
讨厌的：annoyed/disturbed/bothersome
难过的：grieved/sad/gloomy
害怕的：fearful/scared/frightened
惭愧的：ashamed
后悔的：regretful
寂寞的：lonely/isolated
烦恼的：worried
疑惑的：confused/perplexed
担心的：bothered
纠结的：entangled

电话对话

73 Describe a conversation over the telephone.

You should say: when that happened
who called
what you said to each other
and explain further why this conversation left an impression on you.

题目分析

电话对话有以下几种情况：

job interview 面试　　harassment call 骚扰电话　　a quarrel 一次争吵
discussion on a certain topic 讨论某个话题

故事情节：

我申请了曼彻斯特大学，校方也给了我一次电话面试的机会。由于申请竞争激烈，所以我特别想表现好自己，但是我从来没有电话面试的经历，而且还是英文电话面试。所以一开始时，我特别紧张。但是，后来我发现校方代表非常的友善，我们聊了很多关于学校和我的个人经历的话题，我感到很放松。后来我也认为我很有希望被录取，所以这次电话面试让我非常的难忘。

参考答案

故事情节	Well, the telephone conversation I want to tell you about is a telephone interview I had several months ago, when I was talking with a guy called Mark, the representative from the University of Manchester.
故事发展	We had an appointment to have an interview at 5pm in the afternoon, which was 9am in the UK. We had a discussion about a variety of issues. Firstly, I gave a brief introduction of myself, then I stated my study plan and my future career goals. After that, I was asked to give a personal statement and towards the end, I asked him a lot of questions about Manchester, including local life, local weather, facilities, my accommodation arrangements and so on.
故事结局	Eventually, I was told that I was quite promising as one of their future students. I was so excited. It was the first time I had had an interview over the telephone, and it was unforgettable. （情绪变化：super nervous → relaxed → content → excited）
紧张	At first, I felt extremely nervous, since it was my first interview, and it was in English. So I was worrying that I might screw it up（搞 砸）, and I was dying to have a chance to study at Manchester.
放松	During the conversation, however, I found the interviewer called Mark was actually fairly nice and gentle. He was always encouraging me to keep talking and sharing, I felt pretty relaxed, and my previous nervousness just disappeared.
满意	Afterwards, I could feel that he was satisfied with my performance, and I was glad my preparation had paid off.
兴奋	Towards the end, when I was told I was promising, and could move to the next stage, I was very excited.
结论	So, that is why it left a lasting impression in my mind.

总结

有的同学可能会问：讲故事和分享心情难道不能同时进行吗？在此，我要说的是，尽管事情的发生和情绪的产生是同时进行的，但考官的问题却有四问。所以，在回答前三问时，请大家尽量平白直序地讲述故事的背景、发展、高潮和结局。等回答最后一问时，再重点述说当时的情绪波动。总结来说，请大家尽量分成两个部分来讲述。

生气的场合

74 Describe an occasion when you got a bit angry.

You should say: when that was
where that was
what happened then
and explain further how you felt about that.

题目分析

生气的原因一般包括：

- ✓ be deceived 被欺骗
- ✓ be betrayed 被背叛
- ✓ be misunderstood 被误解
- ✓ be annoyed by the misbehaviour 被错误的行为激怒
- ✓ be ignored/overlooked/neglected 被忽视
- ✓ out of patience 失去耐心

考生在考试中需尽量选取一个听起来比较正义的生气原因 (righteous anger)，比如说旅游时被骗了、买东西被骗了、看他人插队很生气等。

故事情节：

有一次坐飞机回北京，我在距离登机还有半个小时的时候被通知由于航空管制，航班被无限推迟。一开始时，大家都很配合，但是 5 个小时过去后，依然没有人给予我们任何答复。所以，我很生气，最后我们多等了 8 个小时才起飞，每个人都身疲力竭了。

参考答案

模板套话 Well, the occasion when I was angry was several months ago, when I was about to board a flight at the airport.

故事背景 I was waiting in the lounge to return to Beijing. Before the departure time, we heard on an announcement that our flight had been delayed due to the air control/snowstorm/lightening/dense fog.

故事发展	We had been waiting hopelessly for departure by the hour in the lounge.
故事高潮	During the waiting period, the airline staff just told us that nobody could do anything about air control, and with that excuse, our time had just been meaninglessly wasted.
故事结局	Eventually our flight took off 8 hours behind schedule. That's my most unforgettable memory of getting angry. (情绪变化：understandable→impatient→angry→frustrated and desperate)
理解	In the beginning, it was commonly understandable to experience flight delay, and all the passengers were quite cooperative,
不耐	yet five hours later, we started to be angry, simply because we were put aside without any concern on the part of the staff. At the very least, we should have been taken care of, like arranging accommodation, offering compensation, arranging an alternate flight or being provided some refreshments, but no one did.
生气	Many who were held up had important issues, such as working, signing a contract or attending a meeting, and when we tried to communicate with the air company, we were told that there was nothing they could do.
沮丧	That made us feel so hopeless, and we were all totally pissed off by their neglect, sloppy management, slow reaction, indifference and buck passing.
结论	Eventually, we felt nothing but desperate, and finally the flight took off, eight hours later than the set time.

他人为你庆贺的场合

75 Describe an occasion when others celebrated for you.

You should say: when that was
what the celebration was for
what you did
and explain further why you want to talk about it.

题目分析

他人为你庆贺的场合可能包括以下几种情况：

birthday 生日　　promotion 晋升　　enrollment 入学
winning a competition 获胜　　mission accomplished 完成某个目标

故事情节：

在我小的时候，我的爸爸送我去美术班学习国画。刚开始我感到很无聊很枯燥，所以每天逃课。但是，当我逐渐认识到只有黑白两色就能够画出那么美的景色时，我开始欣赏国画的价值。后来，我还拿了奖。作为奖励，爸爸很用心地把我所有的作品做成了一个作品集送给我。直到现在，我都依然珍藏着，这是我童年美好的回忆。

参考答案

模板套话	Well, the celebration I want to share with you happened in my childhood, when I was about 10 years old. My father celebrated my winning a painting competition.
故事背景	My father had sent me to a painting school to learn Traditional Chinese painting.
故事发展	After being sent to a tutorial, I started to skip class because I found it was boring. But gradually, I learned to appreciate the beauty of it.
故事高潮	A year later, I was even given an award in a drawing competition. My father was so happy that he decided to give me a surprise: a delicate portfolio(精美的作品集) with all my paintings in it.
故事结局	To this day, I keep it as a treasure. Not only is it a record of a childhood memory, but it is also an encouragement for me to work hard. (情绪变化：uninterested → interested → awarded → encouraged)
不感兴趣	At the very beginning, I wasn't interested in drawing at all, but my father was a big fan of traditional Chinese painting, and he hoped that I could develop my talents in that.
有兴趣	I gradually realised that it was really amazing to create something so beautiful just with two colors, white and black. After that, I applied myself to painting.
回报	After winning the prize, even though it was at a low level, I felt a sense of fulfillment.
鼓励	My father's special gift left a lasting impression on me and gave me a lasting memory.
结论	So that's why I really appreciate that meaningful celebration.

一个婚礼

76 Describe a wedding you attended before.

You should say: when you went to this wedding
who the new couple was
what people did at this wedding
and explain further why you want to talk about this wedding.

题目分析

婚礼相关词汇：

bridegroom/groom 新郎	bride 新娘	best man 伴郎
bridesmaid 伴娘	vow 誓词	wedding march 婚礼进行曲
wedding dress/gown 婚纱	exchange rings 交换戒指	feast 盛宴
live band 现场乐队	honeymoon 蜜月	

婚礼事宜：

➢ making marriage vows	婚礼誓词
➢ bowing down to parents	拜父母
➢ sharing the love journey	分享相爱旅程
➢ giving and receiving rings	交换戒指
➢ having a feast	举行盛宴
➢ proposing a toast	祝酒
➢ teasing the new couple	闹洞房

故事情节：

我曾经做过一次伴郎，我对那次的经历有很深刻的印象，因为那是我唯一一次参加婚礼。婚礼的仪式尽管很俗套，但是我的感触颇深，因为新郎是我最好的朋友。我对他们的感情历程比较了解，所以在婚礼上我特别感动，也衷心地祝福他们。在这场婚礼上，我见到了许多很久没见面的朋友，我们都聊得特别开心，我们度过了难忘的一天。

参考答案

模板套话	Well, the wedding ceremony I want to share with you was my best friend Michael's, it was the first time I had been a best man.
故事背景	Michael and I have been life-long friends since childhood, so we have known each other for more than two decades. When he invited me to be his best man, I agreed without any hesitation.
故事发展	We had a memorable and busy day back then, which was in last October. The ceremony procedure was quite conventional, just like others, we had different activities, including saying vows, sharing stories, bowing down to parents, proposing toasts and so on.
故事高潮	Since we met a lot of friends, we turned the wedding into a big reunion party, everyone had a good time.
故事结局	That was a beautiful memory. (情绪变化：nervous → tired → touched → blessing → happy)
紧张	At the very beginning, I was quite nervous, since I had never been a best man before, and it seemed like I was going to have a big day.
疲惫	Before the ceremony, we had laboriously decorated and planned everything.
感动	During the ceremony, they recalled their love journey, they were bonding together after experiencing all sorts of ups and downs, and I was deeply touched and moved.
祝福	As their best friend, I just wanted to express my wholehearted blessing and best wishes to them.
高兴	Eventually, we all got drunk, but it was one of the most unforgettable moments of my life.

Simon 的知识扩展

威廉王子和凯特王妃的誓词：

I, William Arthur Philip Louis, take thee, Catherine Elizabeth to my wedded wife, to have and to hold from this day forward, for better, for worse: for richer, for poorer; in sickness and in health; to love and to cherish, till death us do part, according to God's holy law; and there to I give thee my troth.

誓词中，绿色文字部分就是广为人知的经典句：无论是顺境或是逆境、贫穷或是富有、疾病或是健康，都相亲相爱、不离不弃。这恰恰是描述婚礼时最核心的部分，请大家在考试时一定要能够非常熟练地讲述出来。

顺便准备

特别的家庭事件：Describe a special family event.

家庭照片：Describe a family photo.

同一家庭的两个人：Describe two people from one family.

人生最困难的时刻

77 Describe the most difficult time in your life.

You should say: when that was
what happened
how you dealt with the difficult time
and explain further how you felt at that moment.

题目分析

讲故事一定要和自己的生活经历结合起来，这样才能够思如泉涌。

故事情节：

为了实现出国留学的梦想，我一直在为通过雅思考试而努力。两年内我考了五次雅思，但迄今为止，我每次都是 5 分的成绩。我“杯具”地向各位烤鸭证明了：雅思真的是一个“标准化考试”。朋友还称我为“雅思考试铅笔收集者”，并且坚信我会收集所有颜色的铅笔。理想很丰满，现实很骨感，我遇到了人生最困难的时刻，因为我真的不知道该怎么办了。这次是我第六次进行雅思考试，我坚信，我的努力一定会有回报的！

参考答案

故事背景 I guess for each person, there will be countless things that happen every day, but the most difficult thing that has ever happened to me is the one I am experiencing right now—taking the IELTS examination.

故事发展	I want to talk about this simply because I have taken the IELTS five times, and every time, I only got five points. I have to say that IELTS is really a standardised test. Honestly, once I thought of quitting and I hated IELTS.
故事结局	However, this is the sixth time, I don't want to be a loser, probably I will end up with five again, yet I won't give up before trying again. (情绪变化：determined → unconfident → laborious → frustrated and hopeless → motivated → persistent)
决定	After deciding to go overseas to study, I faced a tough task, which was passing the IELTS with a score of 6.5 for my masters degree, and I was determined to achieve that.
缺乏信心	When I was in high school, English had been my weakness since I wasn't really into it, so I lacked confidence.
努力	Afterwards, I believed that as long as I put my mind to it, I would make it.
沮丧和绝望	Yet no matter how hard I tried for the last five times, the score of five was the only number I ever got. I was greatly frustrated and hopeless. I have never experienced something as difficult as that in my life.
鼓舞和坚持	Eventually, a teacher of mine gave me a lot of suggestions and encouragement. He told me that as long as I persist, one day I would be successful. I personally believe that my efforts will pay off sooner or later.
结论	So, that's why I am here today to fight for my dream.

兴奋的经历

78 Describe an exciting experience.

You should say: when that was
what happened
how you felt
and explain further why you felt excited.

题目分析

故事情节：

我非常喜爱打篮球，并且加入了大学的篮球队。尽管我不是首发并且从来没上过场，但是我一直在不停地努力练习。有一次，在球队落后的情况下，我出乎意料地被教练替换上场。一开始的时候，我特别紧张，还犯了规并且遭遇到了很强的防守。但这些更加激起了我的战斗意志。最后时刻，我们赶上了比分，我甚至还投中了压哨球。全场观众都在为我们欢呼，我简直无法想象还有什么比这一时刻更令我兴奋的了！

参考答案

故事背景	Well, the exciting experience I want to tell you about happened several years ago when I was studying in university. I was playing on a basketball team with a bunch of my classmates.
故事发展	At first, I wasn't a starter in the game and actually I rarely had a chance to play on the court due to my incompetence. Yet, once in a game, when the team was lagging behind, I was called unexpectedly by the coach.
故事结局	Although I was fouled and blocked by our rivals, I managed to play with my teammates, and eventually, I even made a buzzer-beater(压哨球) to win the game. It was such a big turnaround. (情绪变化：anxious → nervous → impatient → thrilled → unforgettable)
忧虑	In the beginning, when I was sitting on the bench witnessing our team being left behind, I was pretty anxious, yet I couldn't do anything for the team.
紧张	Unexpectedly, I was called to switch one of the starters, I was so nervous, since I had been longing for this moment all the time, and it came to me so suddenly.
急躁	The moment I stood on the court, I made some mistakes since I wanted so badly to contribute.
兴奋	Later on, we made great chemistry in the team, and gradually we caught up with the other team.
难忘	Eventually, we were only one point behind. During the last second, I even shot the buzzer-beater, and we won, so you can imagine everyone went nuts, it was so unexpected.
结论	So it is wonderful for me to recall such an exciting moment.

备考策略

Step One: 写下多于六个表达情绪的形容词（用箭头表达）

Step Two: 用中文把故事的过程梳理一遍

Step Three: 弄清故事情节构成 (At the very beginning; Afterwards; Towards the end)

Step Four: 使用过去式！！

回忆类

童年故事中的人物

Describe a character in childhood story.

题目分析

童年故事相关词汇：

fairy tales 童话
fable 寓言
proverb 谚语
Anderson 安徒生
Mickey Mouse 米老鼠
Donald Duck 唐老鸭
Pinocchio 匹诺曹
Popeye 大力水手
Tom and Jerry《猫和老鼠》
Mermaid《美人鱼》
The Frog Prince《青蛙王子》
Little Red Riding Hood《小红帽》
Three Little Pigs《三只小猪》
Cinderella《灰姑娘》
The Smurfs《蓝精灵》
Snow White and the Seven Dwarfs《白雪公主和七个小矮人》

参考答案

故事背景	Basically speaking, as the main character in this story, a kid goatherd(牧羊人) found herding sheep was quite boring/humdrum/vapid(无趣的).
故事发展	So one day, he decided to make fun of the other sheepherders/farmers by shouting loudly "wolves' coming!". Everyone else believed him and rushed to him but found nothing. The boy enjoyed cheating others a lot. The same thing happened again the following day.
故事高潮	Unfortunately, the third time he shouted, his lie met up with reality.
故事结局	As no one would trust him anymore, he helplessly watched all of his sheep being eaten as the wolves' dinner.
感触	At the very beginning, I was told this story by my mum, and I was utterly afraid of telling a lie. From then on, I promised to myself that the word cheating had been deleted from my life dictionary, since I knew that it would bring baneful consequences, especially in some emergency situations.

童年喜欢的游戏

Describe a game you liked to play in your childhood.

题目分析

Simon 在国外时被同学邀请去玩一种叫做躲避球 (dodge ball) 的游戏，Simon 看了一局就明白了，这不就是丢沙包嘛。如此，Simon 发现原来丢沙包在国外也这么流行。所以，考生可以拿它来回答童年喜欢的游戏这一道题。

丢沙包还可以用来回答以下题目：

- ✓ Describe your favourite sport/game in your childhood.
- ✓ Describe your favourite outdoor activities.
- ✓ Describe something you can do with others.
- ✓ Describe your favourite toy in your childhood.
- ✓ What are the differences between toys of today's children and toys of children in the past?

丢沙包的游戏过程：

1. 分组

Two teams play the game, it starts with one team standing in the middle of the court, with the other team standing on two sides of the court.（一组站中间，一组站两边）

2. 玩法

The players who stand on the sides shoot the ball at the ones in the middle.（两边的人向中间的人丢沙包）

3. 结束

Once you were hit, you were out.（中间的人被击中就下场）

喜欢丢沙包游戏的原因：

1. It involves a lot of team work spirits/cooperation/interaction/coordination skills, which greatly boosted my physical and mental development.（团队合作精神的培养）
2. It generated genuine friendship at that moment, I learnt how to interact/communicate with other peers through playing with them.（培养友谊）
3. It is an unforgettable memory of my childhood, and keeps reminding me of my carefree childhood experience.（童年的回忆）

Part Three

两个选一个

典型问题

Do you prefer writing letters or emails?
Do you prefer making phone calls or sending text messages?
Do you prefer big weddings or small weddings?

回答策略

高分公式：起-承-接-反-转-合
起：Personally, I think...
承：Simply because...
接：For example...
反：Without...
转：On the other hand,...
合：So generally,...

经典例题

79 Do you prefer writing letters or emails?

起 Well, I personally prefer writing an email,

承1 simply because it is more money-saving/time-saving/labour-saving than writing a letter.

承2 Besides, emailing is the most common way for today's people to communicate with each other.

接和反 For example, currently, I am applying for foreign universities, if I sent a letter to professors overseas, it might take at least a week, and all my applications would be delayed.

转 Yet, on some special occasions, I do agree that writing a letter is more appropriate, such as a wedding invitation or love letter.

合 But, for the most part, I guess email is handier.

区别类

典型问题

What are the differences between men and women/children and adults in expressing anger?
What are the differences between big weddings and small weddings?
What are the differences between pictures and paintings?

回答策略

找到两者之间的不同之处，然后进行比较：
Compared with A, B tends to be...
Unlike A, B is more/less likely to be...
A is..., while B is more/less likely to be...

经典例题

80 What are the differences between big weddings and small weddings?

Well, whether it is a big wedding or small wedding totally depends on the...

- ✓ budget 预算
- ✓ preparation time 准备时间
- ✓ number of guests 宾客人数
- ✓ availability of wedding venue 可选择的婚礼场地
- ✓ preferences of both families 双方家庭的意愿

改变类

典型问题

How has the wedding changed recently in China?
How has people's way of communicating changed?

回答策略

对以前和现在的不同情况进行比较：
Generally speaking, people used to…in a traditional and conventional way, such as…
But now, an increasing number of people, especially youngsters tend to…in a more diversified way, including…, simply because our way of life has been deeply transformed by the internet and technology.

经典例题

81 How has the wedding changed recently?

Well, in the past, due to the limitation of materials, people used to have their wedding celebration in the traditional ways, such as inviting friends or relatives to a hotel or home.
But now, people are more likely to spend a fortune on a series of celebrations and events, including holding a ceremony, going on a honeymoon holiday and taking expensive wedding photos.
Besides, more new couples tend to have a wedding that is distinct from others, like holding an undersea wedding, taking a wedding tour or inviting celebrities to come along and perform.

观点类

典型问题

What do people usually lose?
Is the crime rate increasing in the place where you live?
Do people pass old things on to the next generation in your country?
What is the value of old things?
Why do people celebrate weddings?
What kinds of bad weather are there in your city?
On what occasions will people receive money as a gift?
Should people always express their anger when they feel upset?

回答策略

总分结构：
总：Well, people often…for a variety of...(将考官的问题转变成陈述句，后面加上 many/loads of/heaps of/a variety of/a wide range of 等)
分：such as/like/including...

经典例题

On what occasions will people receive money as a gift?

Well, normally speaking, people usually receive money as gifts in the following ways…

- lucky money during spring festival 压岁钱
- a subsidy from a relative for going to college 上大学时亲戚给予的鼓励
- financial support from parents for education 父母提供的教育经费
- rewards for competitions or praise 比赛或者表彰的奖励
- donations from others 他人的捐赠
- compensation or complement 补偿

第七章

高分词汇替换表

词汇替换表

核心话题词汇

Work and Study

温馨提示：左边为学生常用词汇　右边为雅思高分词汇

beneficial	rewarding	有好处的
It is rewarding to learn a foreign language.		
good future	promising	有前途的
I believe that I would have a promising future with this major.		
popular	prevailing	流行的
This major is prevailing, since this industry has a high demand for...		
laborious	backbreaking	劳累的
After a day's backbreaking work, I really need relaxation.		
high salary	well-paid job	高薪的
After graduation, I could get a well-paid job.		
office worker	clock/card puncher	上班族，打卡一族
I don't want to be a card puncher, I want to be a freelancer.		
seek a job	job-hunting	找工作
Being proficient in languages makes me competitive in the job-hunting market.		
job-centered	career-oriented	以职业为导向的
Our study plan should be career-oriented.		

difficult	tricky/challenging	困难的
Studying alone in a foreign country is an apparently challenging task.		
ask for a lot	demanding	要求高的
This job is demanding, so I have to learn new knowledge every day.		
case study	scenario analysis	案例分析
Let me give you a scenario analysis, from one thing…from another…		

Media and Culture

relaxing	soothing	放松的
Light music is pretty soothing.		
funny	hilarious	好笑的
This comedy is nothing but hilarious.		
exciting	dynamic	动感的
Youngsters have a fancy for dynamic music.		
enjoyment	blast/treat	享受
What a treat to enjoy his show.		
lively	energetic	活泼的
Rock makes me feel more energetic.		
electronic magazine	e-zine	电子杂志
An increasing number of people choose to read e-zines.		
electronic book	e-reader	电子书
E-book is a necessity for killing time while I am taking the subway.		
recent news	current affairs	时事新闻
We could keep up with current affairs through Weibo.		
reporter	journalist	记者
Honesty is the bottom line of a journalist.		
full of action	action-packed	充满动作元素的

This movie blew my mind with heaps of action-packed scenes.		
have a mixed feeling about...	twisting	纠结的
I felt twisting about the plot of this movie.		
boring	monotonous/tedious/humdrum	无聊的
The theme is so monotonous.		
proper	appropriate	合适的
On such an occasion, we need to dress up appropriately.		
improve	boost/foster/enhance/further	提高
Watching English movies could boost my understanding of western culture.		

People

hardworking	diligent/industrious/studious	努力的
I have never seen such a diligent guy like him.		
smart	brainy	聪明的
She is the brainiest girl in our class.		
attractive	appealing/tempting	吸引人的
I found Brad Pitt greatly appealing.		
hang out with	socialise/interact with	跟朋友出去玩
Dancing is a way of socialising with different people.		
do...without being told	self-starter	主动做事的人
Self-starters tend to achieve success more easily.		
cover a variety of grounds	well-rounded	全方面的
The essence of education is to provide well-rounded knowledge.		
confidence	self-belief	信心
I want to see a bit more self-belief from you.		
good friend	intimate companion	好朋友
As an intimate companion, she told me everything about her family.		

strong-minded	tenacious/tough	坚强的
I really admire his tenacity and toughness.		
work hard on	apply oneself to	致力于
Everybody can make a success as long as you apply yourself to it.		
practical	be down-to-earth	实际的，脚踏实地的
We need to be down-to-earth to start it over.		
encourage	inspire/motivate	鼓励、鼓舞
A leader should be able to inspire his subordinates(下属).		
average	mediocre	普通的，平凡的
We have mediocre appearances, yet it doesn't necessarily mean we have mediocre minds.		

Travel and Transportation

travelling place	destination	旅游目的地
Outbound travelling destinations are increasingly prevailing for Chinese visitors.		
different feeling	exotic	异域的
This restaurant is full of exotic sensations.		
travelling around the world	round-the-world tour	环球旅行
My lifelong dream is to take a round-the-world tour.		
trip	excursion	旅行
The purpose of excursion is not just to reach the destination.		
travel plan	itinerary	旅游路线
According to the itinerary, we would be there in three days.		
natural scenery	natural landscape	自然景观
Elders prefer places with natural landscape.		
traffic jam	traffic congestion	交通堵塞
The issue of traffic congestion tends to be more serious in my city.		
crowded	bumper to bumper	拥堵的

You can see the cars bumper to bumper every day during peak hours(高峰).		
car exhaust	gas emission	汽车尾气
Smart would produce less gas emissions than other vehicles.		
on time	punctual	准时的
Subway is the most punctual transport in my city.		
passenger	commuter	通勤的人
For commuters, traffic situation at peak hours is a nightmare.		
daily routine	daily timetable/schedule	日常安排
My daily timetable is pretty full.		

Shopping and Lifestyle

chase after fashion	fashion-conscious	赶时髦的
This magazine is attractive to those fashion-conscious youngsters.		
crazy about shopping	shopaholic	购物狂
Can you believe that Librans(天秤座的人) were born to be shopaholics?		
can't help buying something	compulsive shopper	强迫性购物者
As a compulsive shopper, I've decided to reduce my shopping frequency.		
use every penny wisely	bargain shopper	精打细算的购物者
This is a perfect place for bargain shoppers.		
limited pocket money	tight budget	手头紧
My budget has been tight recently.		
show off wealth	flaunt wealth	炫富
Luxury goods should be more than just flaunting wealth.		
shopping mall	commercial complex	商业综合体
During the weekend, I could spend my whole day in this commercial complex.		
expensive	pricy	贵的
Things in this shop are less pricy.		

convenient	handy/portable	便利的，便携的
You can take this handy gadget anywhere you go.		
Weibo/Renren	SNS(social network site)	社交网站
SNS is now a necessity for almost every youngster.		
QQ/MSN	IM(instant messenger)	即时通信工具
Do you have any sort of IM?		
delivery service	door-to-door service	上门服务
They provide door-to-door service.		
the lowest price	beat any price on the market	市场最低价格
They promise that they can beat any price on the market.		
quality goods	genuine/authentic goods	正品
This online shop is trustworthy(值得信赖的) because it sells genuine and authentic goods.		
price goes up/down	appreciate/depreciate	升值 / 贬值
Some people buy luxury goods with the belief that they might appreciate.		
internet	cyber	网络的
Cyber crime is becoming increasingly serious these days.		
cheating	fraudulent/deceitful	坑爹的
Shopping online might be fraudulent.		
delicious	tasty/flavourful/appetising/ mouth-watering/savoury	可口的，美味的
This place is a paradise with loads of tasty food.		
food	dish	菜肴
They serve special dishes in this restaurant.		
delicious food	cuisine	美食
I am a big fan of Italian/French/Japanese cuisine.		
healthy food	nutritious	营养的
Sushi is pretty nutritious with the combination of veggies and seafood.		

Fitness

health	fitness/wellness	健康
Swimming is good for my physical fitness and mental wellness.		
exercise	aerobics	有氧运动
We need to do some aerobics after a whole day's work.		
stay at home	stuck at home	宅在家
I used to be stuck at home all day long.		
relax	kickback/layback	放松
You can kick back by walking along the beach.		
refreshed	revitalised	重新提起精神的
After walking around in such a peaceful place, I feel revitalised.		
good at sports	athletic	有运动天赋的
Sam is athletic at track and field sports.		
endurance	stamina	耐力
Long-distance race training could foster my stamina.		

Housing and Places

long history	time-honoured	历史悠久的
My hometown is well-known for its time-honoured buildings.		
big place	spacious/roomy	宽敞的
The garden near my house is pretty spacious.		
near water	waterfront	滨水区的
It is my dream to live in a waterfront villa.		
quiet	serene/tranquil	安静的
At such a serene and tranquil place, I could find inner peace.		

cold hot	freezing/chilly stuffy	寒冷的 闷热的
The climate of my hometown is typical in northern China, which is stuffy during summer and freezing during winter.		
comfortable	comfy/cosy/homey	舒服的
I prefer watching movies at home, since it is comfy, cosy and homey.		
flower	blossom	花丛
This garden is enclosed by blossoms.		

Memories and Experiences

unforgettable	memorable/impressive	难忘的
The gig I went to last weekend was so memorable.		
impressive	a lasting impression in my mind	印象深刻
This movie left a lasting impression in my mind.		
a rare opportunity	once-in-a-lifetime chance	一生中难得的机会
This is a once-in-a-lifetime chance, I won't let it go.		
in my memory	in retrospect	在我的记忆中
In retrospect, I made the right decision at the very beginning.		
remember	recall	回想
We recalled all good memories we had in high school.		
starting point	incentive	出发点，动机
The incentive was that I wanted to extend my own limits.		
get married	tie the knot	结婚
Today is the big day for my sister to tie the knot.		
wedding dress	wedding gown	婚纱
This exquisite wedding gown is handmade.		

表示各种各样的“好”
Good/Beautiful/Nice/Great

形容不可思议的、很棒的、完美的			
incredible	unbelievable	astonishing	amazing
fabulous	excellent	fantastic	brilliant
classic	fascinating	epic	perfect
口头表达好、好极了			
awesome	terrific	wonderful	marvellous
bravo			
形容景色优美			
stunning	gorgeous	picturesque	scenic
形容建筑壮观			
splendid	magnificent	glorious	grand
形容名气大的、有声望的、一流的			
prestigious	reputable	celebrated	well-known
renowned	esteemed	honoured	notable
top-tier	top-ranking	superb	outstanding
形容优美的、精致的			
exquisite	tasteful	delicate	elegant
graceful	decent		
形容无与伦比的			
incomparable	unmatched	invaluable	phenomenal
exceptional	unbeatable	invincible	impeccable

第八章

剑桥8听力中的口语背诵经典

口语背诵经典

1. I've come across something really interesting.
我碰到了一件很有意思的事。

2. I haven't quite decided.
我还没有决定。

3. I am feeling quite keen now.
我现在特别感兴趣。

4. In regard to opening hours...
说到我们的营业时间……

5. As far as the amount of time you'll need...
关于你可能会需要的时间……

6. Some of the exhibits are fragile and we don't want them to be accidentally knocked.
我们的某些展品特别易碎，所以我们不希望有人不小心把它们弄坏了。

7. There are continuous screenings of short documentaries about dinosaurs.
这里会持续播放有关恐龙的纪录短片。

8. These games are a lot of fun.
这些游戏都特别好玩。

9. Please feel free to ask any questions.
请大家自由提问。

10. It is quite hard to follow your train of thought at times, so cut them down a bit.
有时候很难跟得上你的思路，所以再精简一些吧。

11. My father was a big fan of cowboy/the Wild West films.
爸爸特别喜欢看牛仔片 / 西部片。

12. I was subjected to seeing all the epics.
我也受到了这些经典电影的影响。

13. It's awesome both geographically and visually.
不论是从地貌上还是视觉上都堪称完美。

14. It is somewhere I've always wanted to visit.
这就是我一直想去游览的地方。

15. It's hardly surprising that tourists flock to see the area.
游客蜂拥而至也不足为奇。

16. Their culture is so rich—all those wonderful stories.
他们的文化太丰富了，特别是那些吸引人的故事和传说。

17. I think the best way to appreciate the area would be to hire horses instead and trek around on them.
我认为骑马是游览这个区域的最佳方式。

18. Our current use of carbon fuels is a good example of that.
我们目前使用的碳燃料就是一个很好的说明。

19. So, to summarize before we continue.
所以，在进入下一个部分前我们先做一个总结。

20. Studying this subject is important because without geographical knowledge, we would know very little about our surroundings.
学习这门科目很重要，因为如果不知道这些地理常识，我们就会对周围的环境知之甚少。

21. Maps can be folded and put in a pocket and can provide a great store of reference.
地图是可以折叠起来放在口袋里的，而且它可提供海量的参考信息。

22. Our insurance doesn't cover electrical problems.
我们的保险赔偿不包括电子故障问题。

23. We have a lovely set of china plates and dishes with matching cups and saucers.
我们有一套很好看的瓷器，里面包括盘子、碟子以及配套的茶杯和茶托。

24. We have lots of fascinating indoor and outdoor exhibits on our huge complex, spreading hundreds of hectares..
在这个几百公顷的综合区内，我们有很多很棒的室内和室外展品。

25. We are now situated in the reception block.
我们现在在接待处。

26. Do take time to browse around our shop.
请一定要花点时间逛逛我们的商店。

27. There is a wide selection of books on wildlife.
这里有各种各样有关野生动植物的书籍。

28. The quarantine service regulates all food brought into Australia.
检疫所会监控所有被带入澳大利亚的食物。

29. My current research involves trying to find a particular type of bee.
我目前的研究涉及寻找一种特定种类的蜜蜂。

30. That must have had a devastating effect on the natural flora.
那一定对自然植物造成了毁灭性的影响。

31. We managed to get them under control before that happened.
我们在那之前想方设法地控制了它们。

32. That sounds a bit unpleasant.
这听起来让人觉得有点不舒服。

33. I want to talk about the rationale behind what I decided to do.
我想分析一下我这么做的原因。

34. With the questionnaire, rather than limiting to one specific point, I wanted to include as much variety as possible.
有了调查问卷，我希望尽可能多地覆盖不同的方面，而不只是局限于某一点。

35. I will need to do more far-reaching research than I had anticipated.
我需要做比预想更多的深远的研究。

36. This first stage has proved very valuable.
第一阶段的成果证明了研究非常有价值。

37. There were odd cases that threw me.
我遇到了一些让我感到困惑的奇怪案例。

38. One of the people that I work with got a bit funny.
一个和我共事的人变得有点滑稽搞笑。

39. The most bizarre case was a telephone interview I did with a teacher.
最奇怪的一次是我电话采访一位老师。

40. It's a real eye-opener.
真让我大开眼界。

41. I'm interested in renting a house somewhere in the town.
我想在市里租一个房子。

42. I'm going to share the house with three friends.
我打算和三个朋友一起分租。

43. It'd be nice to be central.
最好是处在市中心。

44. It's very well furnished and equipped.
这个房子布置良好、家电齐全。

45. It's available for a minimum of a year.
租期是一年起。

46. There's a big demand for houses in that area.
这个地区的房源很紧张。

47. It's now in the process of being converted into a film museum.
它目前正在被改建成一个电影博物馆。

48. That's due to start next year.
预计明年开始。

49. It's famous throughout the world as one of the major venues for classical music.
这是世界闻名的古典音乐圣地之一。

50. The centre itself is a huge complex that caters for a great range of arts.
这个中心本身是一个综合体，里面可以举办各种各样的艺术表演和活动。

51. The choice of entertainment there is simply enormous.
可供选择的娱乐方式的确很多。

52. Ever since then it has proved to be a great success.
从那时起就证明了它是一个巨大成功。

53. It has some really fascinating paintings and sculptures by leading artistes from all over China.
它拥有一些由中国顶尖艺术家们创作的极具吸引力的绘画和雕塑作品。

54. He gave me lots of advice and guidance.
他给了我很多建议和指导。

55. Women are increasingly occupying positions in government and in other elected leadership positions in Latin America.
在拉丁美洲，越来越多的女性在政府或者其他经选举产生的领导岗位上担任职务。

56. You've had some practical experience in the field.
你已经在这个领域里取得了一定的实际经验。

57. I'll put that down as a definite.
我会把它列入"必做"选项。

58. It's a less glamorous activity than pure innovation.
相比于纯粹的创造，它就显得没那么出彩了。

59. A host of studies confirm this, covering a wide range of business settings: branch banks, retail stores, real estate agencies, factories, call centres…to name but a few.
大量研究都证实了这一点，研究覆盖了许多商业领域：分支银行、零售商店、地产中介、工厂、呼叫中心等等。

60. The modifications might compromise safety in some way.
这些修正从某种程度上来说可能会让安全性大打折扣。

61. You'd also get tips—our guests tend to be quite generous.
你也会收到小费，我们这的客人往往比较慷慨。

62. He will be telling us about the plan to improve the fast-growing suburb of Red Hill.
他会给我们讲述改进高速发展的红山郊区的计划。

63. They feel that it is only a matter of time before there is an accident as a lot of the children walk to the school.
他们认为出事只是时间问题，因为很多学生都是走路上学的。

64. That's all sorted out now.
现在都解决了。

65. We're rehearsing frantically.
我们正在疯狂地排练。

66. I've got behind with my work, but it's worth it.
我耽误了学习，但这是值得的。

67. I don't think the conductor **stretches us enough**.
我认为乐队指挥没有让我们得到足够发挥。

68. I'm finding it pretty **tough**.
我觉得这个挺难的。

69. I am hoping it'll help me to **build up my stamina**.
我希望这个能够锻炼我的耐力。

70. It'll probably be a **long haul**.
这将是一个长期的工作。

71. I don't think I'm **on the same wavelength as** my tutor.
我不认为我领会了导师的意图。

72. My tutor is very **demanding**.
我的导师对我要求很高。

73. I always **struggle with** revision.
我对复习这件事总是感到很纠结。

74. You also need a **timetable** to see how you can **fit everything in**.
你需要制定一个时间表来安排所有的事情。

75. There's more **incentive to tackle** them.
你会有更大的动力来处理它们。

76. With big topics you're **more likely** to **put off starting**.
如果题目太大，你往往会无从下手。

77. **One of the most significant characteristics** of different styles is the way that...
对于不同的风格，最重要的特征之一是……

78. In fact, fish **didn't start to appear** in paintings **until** the Yam period **along with** shells and other marine images.
事实上，直到 Yam 时期，鱼的形象才和贝壳以及其他海洋生物形象一起出现在画作中。

79. The Yam period **coincided with** the end of the last ice age.
Yam 时代正好出现在最近一个冰河时代末期。

80. Aborigines **see** the Rainbow Serpent **as a symbol of** creation.
澳洲土著居民把彩虹蛇看作是创造的象征。

67. I don't think the conductor stretches us enough.

[illegible]

68. I'm turning it around again.

[illegible]

69. I am hoping I'll be able to build up my stamina.

[illegible]

70. It will probably be a long trip.

[illegible]

71. I don't think I'm on the same wavelength as my tutor.

[illegible]

72. Chinese is very demanding.

[illegible]

73. I always struggle with my essay.

[illegible]

74. You have more information now, you can't fit everything in.

[illegible]

75. There's more I can have to tackle them.

[illegible]

76. [illegible] you're more likely to get frustrating.

[illegible]

77. One of the most significant characteristics of different species is the way that [illegible]

[illegible]

78. [illegible] didn't start [illegible] but developed into the [illegible] along with [illegible]

[illegible]

79. [illegible] period coincided with [illegible] the last ice age.

[illegible]

80. [illegible] see the [illegible] as a symbol of creation.

[illegible]

第九章

有关雅思口语，所有你可能会问的

准备篇

雅思口语都考些什么？口语三部分的考试目的和重点分别是什么？

✓ Part One：考官会就三个话题向考生提问，每个话题涉及四个小问题。

考试时间：4-5 分钟

考试目的：考查考生应用英文进行对话的基本能力。

常考话题：study; work; hometown; hobby; music; movie; sport; shopping; travel; transport

其他话题：animal; art; birds; change; clothes; collecting; computer; dancing; driving; email; flower; food; friend; gift; happiness; holiday; language; magazine; name; noise; number; outdoor; activity; reading; swimming; TV program; weather; weekend

✓ Part Two：考生要回答一道卡片题，进行 1-2 分钟的自我陈述。例如：

> Describe your favourite shop.
> You should say: what the shop specialises in
> how often you go shopping at such a place
> what kinds of shoppers like to shop here
> and explain further why you want to talk about it.

考试时间：纸上做笔记 1 分钟 + 独白 1-2 分钟

考试目的：考查考生独自应用英语进行叙述和议论的能力。

常考范围：

- Work and Study
- Media and Culture
- People and Wildlife
- Travel and Transportation
- Shopping and Lifestyle
- Fitness and Environment
- Housing and Places
- Memories and Experiences

注意：雅思口语考试的 Part One 和 Part Two 两个部分决定了考生能否达到 6 分的水平。

✓ Part Three：考官将基于 Part Two 的问题与考生进行对话或者讨论。这一部分的问答会比较正式和书面化，题目内容多涉及国家、社会情况等，而不像 Part One 的问题那样大部分是关于考生的个人情况。

考试时间：4-5 分钟 (5-8 个问题)

考试目的：Part Three 决定了考生能考到 6 分以上多少分，因为考生在回答这一部分的问题时需要运用更高级的语言技巧、结构、词汇和语法。另外，Part Three 对考生的生活经历和经验也是一个很大的挑战。

常考题型：

➢ Do you prefer…or…and why?	两个选一个
➢ Is… Important?	重要类
➢ What is the most popular…in your country?	流行类
➢ What are the differences between…and…?	区别类
➢ What are the advantages and disadvantages of…?	好坏处类
➢ How has…changed recently in your country?	改变类
➢ Why do some people like doing…?	观点类
➢ What are the qualities of…?	素质类（总分结构）
➢ Should…be free of charge?	免费类（一分为二）

我大学过了英语四六级，雅思会是个什么水平？

✓ 相同点

1. 两者所考的语法知识是相同的。
2. 四六级的词汇和词组能够用来讨论大部分的雅思口语话题。

✓ 不同点

1. 四六级重在笔试并且不强制考口语，通过多做练习和平时的积累可以取得理想的成绩，而雅思口语重在考查考生平时对英语的应用以及准确地表达自己的想法的能力。
2. 四六级的考查方式更加客观，而雅思口语的评判则更加主观。
3. 雅思口语和听力息息相关，是一种先输入再输出的考试。

所以，两者不存在分数对等转换的关系，通过四六级考试只能说明考生的英文基础和词汇达到了表达雅思口语话题的理论程度，并不代表考生在实际的雅思口语考试中一定能考出好成绩。

新托福口语考试和雅思口语考试的区别是什么？

- 托福口语考试为 20 分钟，雅思口语为 12-15 分钟。
- 托福口语考试中考生面对的是电脑，雅思口语考试中考生面对的是考官。
- 托福口语考试中考生要先听一段录音，然后再回答问题（部分需要结合阅读）；雅思口语考试分三个部分，除了第二部分外，其他都采取一问一答的形式。
- 托福口语考试内容偏重校园课堂或学术场景，雅思口语考试内容则偏向日常生活片段或元素。
- 托福口语考试中，回答内容比较重要；雅思口语考试中，回答内容不作为评分标准之一，重点在于表达方式，也就是说英语讲得越地道越好。

雅思口语考试中的卡片题是每次都换吗？

根据 Simon 过去几年的跟踪和总结（非官方），换题有以下的规律：

- 一年有三次换题的震荡期，分别是 12 月底 1 月初、4 月底 5 月初、8 月底 9 月初，每次大概会换掉 30% 的常考题目，其他月份的换题概率和频率相对较小。
- 除了这三个时期外，口语考试的范围都比较稳定，前一周所考的题目基本上有 80%-90% 会直接拿到下一周考。
- 全国乃至海外的每次考试的题目内容都是一致的，只不过每个考点的考试题目的频率会有所不同。

雅思口语考试在不同地点的考试题目、考试难度和评分标准是否会有差别？

不同地点的考试题目、考试难度以及评分标准都是统一的，但是口语考试毕竟是一个主观的考试，难免会存在一些判断上的偏差，因此考官给出的评分可能会受到考生整体水平的影响，但这个影响并不大。

平时应该如何练习英语语音语调？平时没有语言环境，我应该怎样练口语？看美剧、看电影会提高我的英语口语水平吗？

根据“孵化理论”，一个人的输入决定了他的输出，我们很难想象一个很少听原汁原味的英文但却能把英文说得非常地道的人，所以练习语音语调的源头在于听力。在此，Simon 给大家以下的建议：
从剑桥雅思的听力入手，其中 Section 1 是最好的口语练习材料，大家可以一句一句地跟读，直到自己所讲的和听到的一模一样为止。可分为 4 个步骤来达到最佳效果：

Step 1：正常答题，检查答案。
Step 2：听写训练 (dictation)，每听一句就把听到的内容写到纸上，当写不出来或者写错的时候，你可能就遇到了语音语调、速度、单词、句型、表达方式、口音等问题，亦或是你当时一不留神地没听到或者拼写错了。
Step 3：做类似同声传译的训练，听一句，暂停一下，把这句话的大概意思说出来，如果说不出来，那就说明还有某个要点没有理解透。
Step 4：跟读训练，模仿语音语调和说话的感觉，直到一模一样为止。模仿时，一定要注意轻读和重读的变化，该轻的要轻，重点词汇要重读出来。另外，是升调还是降调也要讲究。发声时要尽量使用丹田发音，以达到声音洪亮和圆润的效果。

推荐一个练习跟读的网站：www.breakingnewsenglish.com，每天三分钟练听力，练口语。
推荐一个真人发声的网站：www.cepstral.com/demos/，输入一句英文，让他 / 她读给你听。

要想让美剧发挥最大的作用，首先要选择生活化内容较多的来看，比如《老友记》、《绝望主妇》、《吸血鬼日记》等。Simon 建议大家尽可能提前把剧本下载下来，把其中的单词和表达方式弄懂，然后在观看时尽量不看字幕，并且要听一句按一下暂停，说出大概的意思，然后跟读。尽管可能需要花 3 倍的时间，但是效果却要好得多。

最后，Simon 始终认为，为儿童设计的英语有声童话故事是最好的语音练习材料，大家可以通过模仿简单的升降调、节奏、发音等来掌握最正宗的发音技巧。大家还等什么呢？来试试看吧！

如何克服哑巴英语？

哑巴英语的症结在于听得太少，所以要克服它就得从听力入手，先跟读模仿，然后再自己创造。另外，积累很重要，其中需要重点积累相关词汇、词组和句型。最后，利用生活中的一切机会使用英文。

雅思口语单词该怎么背？

口语单词要分类记忆。比如，在说到与电影有关的话题时，考生可能需要讲到剧本、导演、演员、演技、音乐、特效、对白、情节、寓意等方面的内容。这时，分类记忆的词汇就用得上了。

如何避免中式思维？什么叫做西式思维？

中式思维的特点：比较抽象；很少用连接词；往往先说原因，再给结论。
西式思维的特点：听完描述后能够有一个直观的感受和理解；逻辑关系要求很高，一般不会出现大的思维跳跃；论述问题时，先给出观点，再用一系列的理由去支持。
西式思维的要点：

- 当使用 convenient 和 comfortable 等抽象词的时候，你还需要给出更细节化的词汇，否则考官会问：How convenient it is? How comfortable it is?
- 任何描述都需要使用以下的连接词：firstly/and then/so/that's because/as a result/consequently/afterwards/eventfully

当描述一个事物或者地点时，西式思维的顺序是：
1. 先内后外，由里及表
2. 先观点，再支持
3. 先重要信息，再次要信息

如何在考试中体现出思路上的多层结构？我平时说话就没有逻辑，请问可以怎么练习？

1. 当考官问：What's the most popular sport in your country?
大部分学生会想到乒乓球，但是考官会认为：There are 1.3 billion people in China, is there only one sport that is popular in your country?

所以，大家要一分为二地分析：

- 对于年轻人来说，他们可能喜欢球类运动，比如说……
- 对于年纪大点的人来说，他们更喜欢轻松的运动，包括……

最后还可以辩证统一：

- ✓ 但某些运动是男女老少都喜欢的，比如说跑步、散步、爬山……

结论：回答任何问题前，都可以先想想，看能不能一分为二，再辩证统一。

2. 当考官问：What are the qualities of a leader?
罗列观点时，“3”的概念很重要，凡事想到三个观点，然后给出简单的支持理由。例如：

- Firstly, responsibility is really essential for leaders, since their decisions could influence people under their management.
- Besides, I also feel that leaders ought to be sociable, that's because they need to get along with all sorts of people.
- More importantly, leaders must be role models because without honesty and credibility, it would be hard for them to gain trust from others.

如何减少语法错误？

三个方法：

- 找到练习口语的 partner，互相记录语法错误的个数。
- 视觉刺激法，拿出一张白纸，上面写上大大的“-ed, did, was, were…”，然后盯着这些自述一个发生在过去的事情。
- 录下自己的答案，然后自己给自己找语法错误。

我讲些什么内容考官才能理解呢？

1. 避免讲述中国特色的答案，考生需要回归到日常生活中的衣食住行等层面，给出观点时要尽量为考官考虑，看他作为外国人能否理解你的意图。
2. 多联想国际社会和地球村等受人关注的话题，比如说：

环保 (environmental protection)；全球化 (globalisation)；文化交流 (cultural communication)；新媒体对人们的影响 (the influence of social network sites) 等。

我想背点模版去考试，这样有用吗？

在考官对考生进行面试之前，他会默认所有的考生都是用准备好的模版来答题的。考官深谙此道，而且考生从某本教材上准备来的段子可能早已被考官所熟知了，所以考生千万不要把一个段子背给考官听，一旦考官认定考生是在背答案，那么考官给出的分数基本上都在 5 分以下。

不过，考生可以将背诵好的词组和表达方式进行自由组合，然后再用来表达自己的观点和想法，比如说：

- As long as..., I would...(只要我……，我就会……)
- Not only do I enjoy..., but I am also a big fan of...(我不但喜欢……，还对……情有独钟)
- Only with a click of the mouse, doing...is as easy as it sounds like.(点击鼠标，轻松做……)

什么叫蹲题？

蹲题就是指考生在候考期间守在前一位考生考完后出来的门口等待题目。由于卡片题的重复性很高，所以考生蹲来的题目很可能就是考生自己等会会考到的内容。Simon 曾经有三个学生在同一个考场考试，结果这三个学生考到了一模一样的题目，所以蹲题也是一种比较靠谱的应对雅思口语考试的方式。

我能准备一个话题来解决所有的卡片题吗？

雅思口语没有捷径可言，也没有一个一劳永逸的解决方案。你永远不能指望一个话题能够覆盖所有的话题。每道题都有其侧重点，比如说与 book 有关的论述就必须和书息息相关。但是雅思卡片题确实具有很强的可合并性，比如说：

Describe a person you want to travel with.

Describe a place you want to travel in the future.

Describe a person who taught you something useful.

Describe a person who influenced you.

Describe a good student.

Describe one of your good friends who is a leader.

以上的题目都可以合并性作答。

我们的策略是：熟知 Simon 为大家总结的口语八大核心场景，然后准备各个场景中最核心的题目。也就是说在考试前准备 10 个左右的段子（必须是原创的）。如此，考生就可以气定神闲了。

考场篇

考官讲话有口音吗？

考官基本上都来自英语国家，当然也会有一些考官来自其他国家，例如泰国、日本、印度、俄罗斯等。但是考官的选拔标准非常严格，会确保考生不会因为考官的口音而影响双方的理解和沟通。以下是雅思官方招聘口语考官的标准要求：

The main requirements are:

- An undergraduate degree or equivalent
- A recognised qualification in Teaching English to Speakers of Other Languages (TESOL)
- At least 3 years full time (or the equivalent part time) relevant TESOL teaching experience gained after the qualification
- The required professional attributes and interpersonal skills

来源：www.britishcouncil.org(英国大使馆文化教育处)

听不懂考官的问题，我该怎么办？

考生可以请考官再重复一次问题，这样做并不会扣分。考生可以采用以下三种方式：

1. Would you mind rephrasing it?(你可以换个词吗？)
2. What do you mean by...?(请问……的意思是？)
3. 考生还可以把自己的理解讲给考官听：Do you mean that...?
   如果考官回答 Yes，那考生就可以 keep going。
   如果考官回答 No，那他就会换种方式来提问。

回答问题时突然卡壳怎么办？

如果思路突然中断了，考生应该马上想出一个生活中实实在在的例子来进行解说，以便于为自己争取更多的思考时间。比如：For example, my major is..., and my dream is to be a...in the future!/I still remember when I was little, I used to.../A good example might be...

面对考官的问题，我没有明确的思路，该怎么回答？

考官可能会问道：In your mind, what will Beijing's traffic situation be like in 20 years' time?

对于这类问题，考生可能连中文都没有考虑过怎么回答，更何况是英文，所以考生在雅思口语考试中需要：

1. 用一些套句来为自己争取思考的时间：Well, frankly speaking/Well, to be honest, this question is pretty tricky, simply because I've never thought of that before, yet in 20 years' time, I do believe that loads of things will be changed, and traffic is not an exception.
2. 坚持明天会更好的原则，即朝美好的方向联想：For example, the air quality will be less polluted, the vehicles should be more eco-friendly and the whole traffic system will be much smarter than what we have today.

总而言之，考生在回答问题时一定不能有过长的停顿。大家要牢记于心的是，考官并不在乎你说什么，只在乎你怎么说。只要能够自圆其说 (make sense)，那就是好答案。

我感觉自己说跑题了，该怎么办？

如果考官听完你的答案后眉头深锁，觉得不知所云，或者你已经意识到自己可能跑题了，请不要说：Sorry, can I start it over again?

你可以把思路重新再拉回来，例如，你可以通过以下的表达方式重新获得解释的机会：By this I mean…/What I am trying to say is…/To summarise, …/Anyway, the key point is that…

考试时有什么礼貌用语？

从头到尾，考生都需要表现出礼貌和积极的一面，直观上来讲，就是嘴上要带“小词”。

考试开始时，考官会问：Can I see your identification?

考生需要回答：Oh, definitely yes, here you are.

考试结束时，考官会说：All right, this is the end of today's test, thank you!

考生需要回答：Oh, thank you, and it's a pleasure talking to you./Oh, thanks for your time and have a good one.

不要试图去握手或者拥抱，一个真诚的微笑足矣。

如何让考官对我的回答感兴趣？

考生自己的故事，特别是考生充满了感情的回忆都能吸引考官的注意。比如说恋爱的经历（这个餐厅是我和我的男朋友相识的地方 / 这张照片是我们分手前拍的）；难忘的事情（这次旅行让我萌发了去国外上学的念头）；一直以来的梦想（我从小就想成为一名建筑师）；从小到大的内心情节（我喜欢看科幻片，因为从小我就幻想着有一天能见到外星人）；对事物不同寻常的见解（我最喜欢的花是向日葵，因为它总是朝向太阳，无论发生什么，都那么阳光、那么积极）；自己独特的经历 (18 岁时我爬上了喜马拉雅山 / 我代表了中国参加国际大赛 / 我是中国某项非物质文化遗产的继承人）等等。另外，考生如果有海外生活和学习的经历，也一定要记得跟考官一起分享，这些都能引起考官的兴趣。

总之，有本事让考官笑甚至是哭的考生，考官一定会让他在看到雅思成绩单时笑的！

考试时感到紧张，应该如何克服？

考前深呼吸、调整好心态。适当的紧张可以刺激肾上腺激素 (adrenalin)，从而让考生活力四射，但过度的紧张会让考生思路变窄、语无伦次。

考生应当从思想意识上想明白：我是花了钱来参加考试的，请考官给我打个分，没什么不好意思的。我不是为了考试而考试，而是希望能够把我的英文最好的一面呈现给考官看，"分享"才是我最主要的目的。

考生只有在放松的状态下才能够思如泉涌，大家一定要想清楚这个道理。考生在考试时应怀着"男的最帅，女的最美"的坚定信念，充满自信地应对挑战。

考试时，考官的表情很严肃，我应该怎么理解？考官一直对我笑，是说明我表现很好吗？

Simon 经常会碰到很严肃的考官，也经常会被问到刁钻的问题，例如：

How do you think of the one-child policy?

If you have a chance to go back in time, which period will you choose?

How could animals contribute to a country's economy?

但这也可能是考官为了给我更高的分数所设立的挑战。

如果考官一直对我微笑，那并不代表我一定能得高分，而更可能是一种鼓励我 keep talking 的方式。

所以，大家可不要被考官的表情所影响了，充满自信才是最重要的。

考试对我的着装有什么要求吗？

雅思口语考试也是一种正式场合的面试，所以请考生不要随意着装，但也没有必要正装出席，关键是要干净、大方、得体。

当然，考试时也可能出现这样的情况：因考生穿着运动装而引发考官提出许多关于 sport 的问题，或者因考生穿着时尚而引起考官提出一系列有关 fashion 和 design 的话题。

考官觉得给你 6 分也行，给你 6.5 分也行，他该如何判断呢？

考场上，考生也要懂得利用合适的机会给考官一定的暗示，比如：Well, I used to play basketball very often, yet since I began to prepare for the IELTS and put 100% effort on it, I seldom play the game. But as long as I get 6.5 or more this time, I could realise my dream and play basketball as much as possible!

但要注意的是，这个时机一定要合适且自然，考生要根据自己当时的情况给出一个合情合理的暗示。否则，不要也罢。对此，请考生谨慎对待，切忌弄巧成拙。

考后篇

口语成绩要多久才能出来？

一般是 10 个工作日，也就是说星期六考试的成绩会在一周后的星期四或者星期五出来，如果遇上节假日，则需等到两周后的星期一。

我想复议，靠谱吗？

复议是当考生对自己的分数存有疑问时向英国文化教育处提出重新批改的要求。复议的费用折算成人民币是 900 元，所需官方时间是一个月，但根据 Simon 以往的经验，复议的成绩会在三周后出来，并且会以 email 的形式寄送给申请的考生。复议是有风险的，因为大部分情况下，分数会保持不变，并且还存在分数降低的可能性。所以，除非是考生对自己的表现有强大的信心，或者对考官当场的表现存有异议，否则请考生不要轻易提出复议要求。当然，Simon 也有一个学生将 4.5 分复议成 6 分的成功案例。

我这次考了 5.5 分，请问我需要怎么努力才能考到 6 分？

只要注意以下非技术性因素，6 分其实指日可待：

- 弄清楚自己常犯的语法错误，一定不能给考官造成老犯低级错误的印象。
- 讲话的速度要慢下来，一定要把一句话中的重点以重读的形式呈现出来。
- 分析问题需要更加有条有理，凡事需想到“观点 + 支持”。
- 学习模仿 native speaker 说话的腔调和节奏。
- 在已有的词汇基础上，更加注意日常生活词汇的积累，特别是衣食住行方面的词汇。

总之：六分就是在尽量少犯错误的基础上，用考官不讨厌的语音语调跟考官来一次有效的沟通。

我已经考了三次，每次都是 5 分，都没有信心了，我该怎么办？

如果考了三次都是同样的分数，那就需要考虑以下几个问题了：

- 我讲的每一句话都严格符合“主系表”或者“主谓宾”的结构吗？
- 我的某些词的发音是不是从来就没有发对过？
- 我是否每次都因为讲话讲得太快，没有升降调，从而让考官认为我是在背诵准备好的段子呢？
- 我每次所讲的观点都解释清楚了吗？
- 我每次都讲到细节或者给出例子了吗？
- 我从每一次考试中吸取“正能量”或者“考试经验”了吗？
- 每次考完考试后，我是更迷茫了还是更加清晰自己的奋斗方向呢？

问完自己这些问题后，如果你的答案是“否定”的，那么是时候重新审视自己的思维方式和备考方法了，然后重新的回归到语言的本质上来，那就是“沟通”。英语口语不是自我感觉良好就行，而是要考官觉得你行你才行。

上次我没怎么复习，考了 6 分，这次认真努力了三个月，怎么才考了个 5.5 分？

作为主观性很强的口语考试，考试结果和成绩会因为考生的心态、题目的内容、面试的考官、临场的发挥等诸多因素的影响而上下浮动。对曾经拿到过 6 分的考生来说，技术上你已经处在 5.5 分和 6.5 分这个区间内，所有因素的影响都会让你的成绩降到下限或者升至上限，所以不必沮丧，调整好状态后，相信每一次考试都会有收获，而且会一次比一次考得好。

请问，考官会给什么样的考生 8 分？

8 分及以上的考生应该具备以下特点：

- ✓ 正确的语法、清晰的发音，能让考官清楚地理解其意图。
- ✓ 能够用到考官每天使用的词汇，比如 veggie, handy, awesome, appropriate, terrific, most importantly 这样的口头小词。
- ✓ 平时会看一些英文原版小说、杂志或者报纸；平时注重积累词汇及用法。
- ✓ 懂得把握机会和不同国家的人接触或者交流。
- ✓ 最重要的是明白自己不光是去考试，甚至可以就某个自己熟悉的领域与考官进行详细交流，比如说：

➤ What is group purchase(团购)?
Well, group purchase is a bunch of consumers signing up for the same item, by this, the discount can be available for all.

➤ What is hogwash oil(地沟油)?
Hogwash oil refers to the extraction(提取物) of oily floats from drains or leftovers from restaurants.

➤ What is Dota(魔兽争霸)?
Dota is the *Defence of the Ancients*, which is a kind of action role-playing game using real time strategy(实时的动作角色扮演游戏), with the purpose of destroying ancient opponents and structures.

➤ What is Weibo and Renren(微博和人人)?
Well, they are the most popular and common social network sites in China currently, you know, the equivalent(对等物) of Twitter and Facebook.

➤ What is *Killers of the Three Kingdoms*(三国杀)?
Well, it is a kind of board game with different roles from a Chinese literature classic called *Romance of the Three Kingdoms*(三国演义).

Simon 每日的英语学习

1. 书籍和杂志

大家可以根据自己的兴趣和爱好，从头到尾看完一本英文原版小说，比如《暮光之城》、《史蒂夫·乔布斯传》或者听其音频等。大家还可以选择阅读《经济学人报》，其每篇文章都配有牛津腔的音频，淘宝有售。

2. 电影——推荐看记录片

An Inconvenient Truth《不可忽视的真相》

Home《家园》

The Cove《海豚湾》

Inside Job《监守自盗》

Earth《地球》

3. 电视节目

Britain's Got Talent《英国达人秀》

X-Factor《X 因素》

The Apprentice《谁是接班人》

4. 新媒体

Simon 的 Apple App(应用程序) 推荐，输关键词查找：

- ✓ 雅思核心词汇
- ✓ 7 天听懂双语新闻
- ✓ 新浪公开课 / 网易公开课
- ✓ OMG 美语
- ✓ Aussie Radio(澳洲本土新闻)
- ✓ News Radio(包括了 Fox News Radio, BBC World Service, ABC News Radio 等等)